Christianity and Hegemony

This ground-breaking book about contemporary Christianity and politics deals, in particular, with evangelical churches in the Third World. Setting these in the context of a discussion of the role of evangelicals in American politics, it asks to what extent a right-wing political agenda underlies the recent upsurge of evangelical churches.

Jan P. Nederveen Pieterse is the author of *White on Black: Images of Africa and Blacks in Western Popular Culture* and *Empire and Emancipation: Power and Liberation on a World Scale,* for which he received the 1990 J.C. Ruigrok Award of the Netherlands Society of the Sciences. He is presently Senior Lecturer at the Institute of Social Studies in The Hague.

Christianity
and
Hegemony

*Religion and Politics on the Frontiers
of Social Change*

EDITED BY

Jan P. Nederveen Pieterse

BERG

New York / Oxford
Distributed exclusively in the U.S. and Canada
by St. Martin's Press, New York

Published in 1992 by
Berg Publishers, Inc.
Editorial offices:
165 Taber Avenue, Providence, RI 02906, U.S.A.
150 Cowley Road, Oxford OX4 1JJ, UK

British Library Cataloguing in Publication Data
Christianity and hegemony: Religion and politics
on the frontiers of social change.
I. Pieterse, Jan P. Nederveen
261.8
ISBN 0–85496–749–4

Library of Congress Cataloging-in-Publication Data
Christianity and hegemony : religion and politics on the frontiers of
social change / edited by Jan P. Nederveen Pieterse.
p. cm.
Includes bibliographical references and index.
ISBN 0–85496–749–4
1. Christianity and politics. 2. Evangelicalism. I. Nederveen
Pieterse, Jan.
BR115.P7C3815 1991
322'.1'09049—dc20   91–20336
                                                        CIP

Printed in Great Britain by
Billing & Sons Ltd, Worcester

Contents

Contents

ASIA

EUROPE

Contents

Preface

There is a growing literature on the upsurge of evangelical Christianity in the United States and its affinities with the New Right. This volume is concerned with the activities of such Christian organizations in Third World countries and in Europe.

The growth of evangelical churches in countries of the South takes place in the context of several large-scale dynamics – the penetration of the world market and the commodification of social relations, uneven development and urbanization, and, in some areas, industrialization. Evangelicalism also spreads in tandem with the cultural radius of United States hegemony, an effect that may be referred to as the "McDonaldization" of religion.

The activities of evangelical churches, although styled as apolitical, frequently carry political implications; in a number of cases they are even politically manipulated. The gray zone between intended and unintended political ramifications of the activities of Christian organizations is the focus of the articles in this volume. *Politics* in this context is meant in a broad sense, corresponding to Gramsci's understanding of hegemony and of the significance of popular religion and culture. The regions examined include southern Africa, the Philippines, the Middle East, Central America, and Europe.

Many discussions of Christianity and politics focus on Evangelicalism and on the United States both as the source and headquarters of most evangelical churches and as a hegemonic power. This leaves open the questions, however, of how the politics of the Catholic church and, more broadly, of how Europe as a whole fit into this overall picture of Christianity and hegemony. These lines of inquiry play a part in several of the articles in this book.

These themes were discussed at a research seminar on Christianity and politics convened by Dr. Kees van der Pijl at the Department of International Relations of the University of Amsterdam, which ran from late 1988 through spring 1990. It included Jeffrey Marishane of the Research Department of the African National Congress in Lusaka, Zambia, who was conducting research at the University of Amsterdam under a Dr. Govan Mbeki Fund fellowship and who concentrated on the role of evangelical organizations in southern Africa. Maria van Diepen of the Dr. Govan Mbeki Fund and Haile Selassie of the International Relations Department joined us as well. Ad van Wesel and Alexander Hulsman, graduates of the International Relations program, contributed their ongoing research. When I was invited to produce a book based on the seminar I sought to widen its scope and achieve a more balanced global representation by inviting other scholars to join the project. Lawrence Jones, an accomplished scholar in the field, joined the seminar on several occasions and contributed two articles based on his current research. I am also grateful for the long-distance cooperation of Sara Diamond and Paul Gifford, both authors of outstanding recent studies in the field. I am pleased that this collection includes the contribution of Jeffrey Marishane, which reflects, rather than scholarly research, the politically oriented research of an organization active on the ground.

While the main focus of this book is on contemporary evangelical organizations, we have tried to balance this by also devoting attention to the role of the Catholic church, which is unduly neglected in many accounts. In addition, we have tried to go beyond the usual preoccupation with the United States and U.S. foreign policy by considering developments in Europe as well. This combination of perspectives is apparent notably in the articles on the Philippines (Hulsman) and on Catholicism in postwar Europe (Van Wesel), while another contribution deals with evangelical missions in Poland (Jones). There is an extensive literature on Christianity and politics in Latin America, both on the role of the Catholic church and on the upsurge of the new Evangelicalism, which we do not seek to duplicate here. We have instead concentrated on other areas: Africa, Asia, and Europe. One article (Diamond) sets the stage by examining contemporary evangelical politics in the United States, especially with respect to Central America.

I gratefully acknowledge the permission of *NACLA Report on the Americas* to reprint Sara Diamond's article "Holy Warriors," which originally appeared in the September–October 1988 issue on "The Right After Reagan". "The History of a Metaphor: Christian Zionism and the Politics of Apocalypse" has also been published by the *Archives de Sciences Sociales des Religions* (Paris), No. 75, July/August 1991.

Without Kees van der Pijl this book would not exist, and I would like to cordially thank him. I am also indebted to Larry Jones, Maria van Diepen, and Haile Selassie for their insightful contributions, and I am grateful to Lisa Chason for her help in editing several articles.

JNP, AMSTERDAM

·1·

Christianity, Politics, and Gramscism of the Right: Introduction

JAN P. NEDERVEEN PIETERSE

In 1949, after four moderately successful weeks, Reverend Billy Graham's tent crusade in Los Angeles was winding down. William Randolph Hearst, the newspaper magnate, heard of Graham's impassioned attacks on communism and sent a famous telegram instruction to the editors of his newspapers and magazines: "Puff Graham." Graham was subsequently transfigured into a larger-than-life-size myth, with newspaper reports and ads proclaiming: "Visit the Canvas Cathedral with the Steeple of Light! All-Star Supporting Party – Held Over by Popular Demand – Sixth Great Sin-Smashing Week."

The support of Hearst, followed by financial donations from corporate establishments such as the Pew Memorial Trust (Sun Oil Corporation) and the Marriot Foundation (Marriot Corporation), turned the Billy Graham Evangelistic Association into a multi-million-dollar enterprise producing and distributing religious literature, films and records. What captivated the captains of industry were such pronouncements by Graham as "Paradise is a place with no union dues, no labor leaders, no snakes, no disease." As an observer noted, "Graham sturdily affirmed, for the nation's affluent and proprietorial, their own sense of the fitness of things."[1]

---

1. Marshall Frady quoted in C. Flake, *Redemptorama: Culture, Politics and the New Evangelism* (Garden City, N.Y., 1984), pp. 125–26. Cf. L. D. Streikor and G. S. Strober, *Religion and the Majority: Billy Graham, Middle America and the Politics of the 1970s* (New York, 1972), p. 30.

This episode in the annals of the new Evangelicalism illustrates one particular variety of the relations between Christianity and politics. The political conjuncture of this period is well known: the two major issues in these early years of the "American Century" were communism internationally and labor militancy domestically. Graham's crusade addressed both these issues. Senator Joe McCarthy did so as well, and McCarthyism flourished over the next few years. The parallels between Graham's evangelism and McCarthyism are unmistakable. If we examine the political process of this episode we find a preacher with a politically relevant message and a supporting network consisting of a media magnate and corporate leaders who find the message congenial to their interests and worldview, and who promote and sponsor it. While the preacher himself may or may not have a clear political agenda, his sponsors in this case certainly do.

This is one of the examplary situations of what may be termed "Gramscism of the Right": politically conservative or right-wing forces enlist religious messages and messengers (or cultural trends generally) on behalf of their political agenda. A wide variety of possible interrelationships between Christianity and politics can be imagined, ranging from the politically irrelevant or innocent religious message at one pole to an explicit political agenda at the other, and from politics manipulating religion to religion manipulating politics. This heterogeneous field is the terrain of the articles in this volume, which is concerned with the political ramifications of contemporary Christianity, whether intended or unintended.

Christianity and Hegemony

The contemporary politics of religion form part of a series which stretches far back in time. A brief look at past affinities of Christianity and empire, or more generally, hegemony, may help put contemporary processes in perspective.

Before there was Europe there was Christendom. In the formation of European states the politics of the church and local princes interacted closely. The pattern of Christianization *cum* early state formation dates back as far as the seventh century.[2] Conquests were made in the name of the cross, and papal sanction turned local princes into Christian kings; thus Latin Christianity expanded by means of a series of Christian kingdoms. This European mode of military-missionary expansion was projected outside Europe during the Crusades, which produced Europe's first overseas colony, the Kingdom of Jerusalem.

This pattern of joint state-church expansion was reproduced in the European expansion in Africa, America and Asia from the fifteenth and sixteenth centuries onwards. The *Conquista* of America was modeled after the *Reconquista* and was again undertaken in the name of the cross. Cross and sword were inseparable in the colonial systems of Spain and Portugal. English Puritans arriving on American shores planted a cross on April 29, 1607, to stake their claim that the land should be a Christian land. Puritanism, and Protestantism in general, played a key ideological role in North American continental expansion as a component of "Manifest Destiny."[3]

Evangelical missions also started in the late eighteenth century including in areas where no colonial state operated, such as the Pacific. Protestant missions were established in the early 1800s and Catholic missionary orders from the 1820s. The close collaboration between church and state continued in the context of colonial expansion. An example is David Livingstone, who undertook his first travels in Central Africa for the London Missionary Society but made his later journeys with the status of consul of the British government. The missions were regarded as powerful adjuncts to the colonial state, in paving the way for colonial expansion, in pacifying the indigenous population, and, once colonialism was established, in furthering education, health care, and general acculturation: "Where the seed of Christian teachings fell, the spirit of resistance was weakened."[4] In many areas missionary activities per se were only moderately successful. The church needed the colonial state for shelter and support and

---

2. J. P. Nederveen Pieterse, *Empire and Emancipation* (London, 1990), ch. 5.
3. See A. K. Weinberg, *Manifest Destiny* (Chicago, 1963).
4. A leading African quoted in W. Bühlmann, *Afrika eist: Afrikaans Christendom* (Hilversum, 1980), p. 30. (Original title: *Missionsprozess in Addis Abeba*, Frankfurt am Main, 1977.)

vice versa. Generally the character of domestic state-church relations was reflected in their relations in the colonies or dependencies. A general rule was *cuius regio eius religio*, i.e., subjects adopt the religion of the state.

In the course of the nineteenth century this overall pattern of colonial state-church symbiosis was complicated by a number of factors. Increasing interstate rivalry in imperial expansion began to be paralleled by interchurch rivalries, such as those between competing Protestant and Catholic missionary activities. In many areas Christianity was effective only in combination with "nativist" elements, in syncretic forms. Thus the rapid growth in the early twentieth century of the so-called Ethiopian and Zionist churches in Africa, that is, independent African churches, signaled the development of an alternative Christianity autonomous from or counter to colonialism and the colonial state.[5] Tensions also developed between the missions and colonial administrations.[6] The churches, after all, did have an agenda of their own and would not always serve as the handmaidens of colonialism.

Christianity thus appears historically as part of the politics, the civil institutions and the culture of empire. This affinity has been fundamental, and not accidental, in the rise and outward projection of Europe, which during much of its career has been equivalent with Christendom, that is Latin Christendom. At the same time this affinity has not been without friction. The relationship between Christianity and Western hegemony has been complicated by radical religious currents, the Reformation and other schisms and factional struggles within Christianity, and moreover by secularization.

While Puritanism was fundamental to American continental expansion, Evangelicalism began to serve as an ideological foundation of American globalism at an early stage. From the outset evangelical and Protestant missions played a significant part in the relations between the American republic and East Asia.[7] "Christianizing China" was among the early themes of

5. B. Sundkler, *Zulu Zion and Some Swazi Zionists* (London, 1976); J. Comaroff, *Body of Power, Spirit of Resistance* (Chicago and London, 1985).

6. K. E. Fields, "Christian Missionaries as Anti-Colonial Militants," *Theory and Society* 11 (1982).

7. "Along with commerce, a second persistent characteristic of the American–East Asian relationship has been evangelism." J.C. Thompson, Jr.,

American interest across the Pacific and has remained so virtually into the present; witness the legacy of missionary daughter and wife Pearl S. Buck and the present interest of the American National Religious Broadcasters in East Asia.[8]

In the 1950s, in the early days of the cold war, the Moral Re-armament movement (MRA) held mass meetings in gigantic stadiums aimed at steering youth away from communism and keeping them off the streets. Moral Re-armament had its beginnings at Hartford Seminary in the United States between 1916 and 1922. According to its founder, Rev. Frank Buchman, its objective was "a Christian revolution, whose concern is vital Christianity. Its aim is a new social order under the dictatorship of the spirit of God . . . . [A] world wide spiritual awakening is the only hope."

Sometimes referred to as Buchmanism, it took the name Oxford Group during a tour of South Africa in 1928 and Moral Re-armament in 1938. We can gauge its ideological amplitude from a statement by Frank Buchman in a 1936 interview: "I thank heaven for a man like Adolf Hitler, who built a front line of defense against the Antichrist of communism."[9] Buchman visited Himmler, and Rudolf Hess and Lord Hamilton were Buchman supporters. The MRA was active among delegates to the League of Nations in Geneva, organized "world assemblies" (e.g., in Birmingham in 1936, Utrecht in 1937, Interlaken in 1938, Caux in 1950) and was endorsed by Senator Truman, Admiral Byrd, General MacArthur, Henry Ford, Chiang Kai-shek, and, in 1946, the Vatican, for its anticommunism. MRA ran a newspaper, *New World News*, and produced a musical show, *You Can Defend America*.

What is striking about MRA is the militantly *political* character of the movement, from its origins (which coincided with the Red Scare in the United States) to its finest hour in Los Angeles's Hollywood Bowl. In the 1920s it was cast as a

---

P. W. Stanley and J.C. Perry, *Sentimental Imperialists: The American Experience in East Asia* (New York, 1982), p. 44. See also W.L. Neumann, *America Encounters Japan* (New York, 1963), ch. 2.

8. L. Jones, Report to the Catholic Institute for International Relations (London, February 1989. Unpublished mimeo).

9. W. H. Clark, *The Oxford Group: Its History and Significance* (New York, 1951), p. 77.

Christian answer to the Bolshevik revolution (a "Christian revolution") and in the 1950s as an American position in the cold war. The format of mass meetings in stadiums paralleled fascism and Nazism, and the rhetoric was targeted against communism. Christianity was merged with patriotism and nationalism on the one hand and with the concept of "the free world" on the other, and its stance and symbolism were militant to the point of being military ("Re-armament"). A 1951 propaganda tract praising MRA was replete with such lines as "the struggle to capture the heart of the masses is the basic ideological battle," which appears in a chapter entitled "Class War Superseded."[10] It quotes *The Times* report on the MRA World Assembly at Caux in 1950:

> Its purpose has been to outline and develop an alternative ideology to Marxist materialism sufficiently strong to unite the democratic world in answer to the communist challenge . . . . Powers at war today do not fight merely on the military front but on the ideological front as well.

In every respect this is the perspective and even the discourse of psychological operations.

This fusion of Christian and political discourses was by no means uncommon. Both in America and Europe from the 1920s onwards, Christianity and communism were widely perceived as ideological competitors.[11] It was common for American preachers in Los Angeles in the 1920s, such as Billy Sunday and Aimee Semple McPherson ("Sister Aimee"), to mix religious authority with social and political influence, to introduce ideological themes in preaching, and even to seek political office (such as Rev. Bob Schuler, who narrowly missed election to the U.S. Senate).

The career of Billy Graham was also launched in the cold war – atomic age mode. He came to prominence in the 1950s under Eisenhower, at a time when, as a conservative observer complained, "The U.S. has embraced a religion-in-general that is 'progressively evacuated of content.'" This "Christianity

---

10. P. Howard, *The World Rebuilt: The True Story of Frank Buchman and the Achievements of Moral Re-Armament* (New York, 1951), p. 69.

11. See J. Lewis, K. Polanyi and D.K. Kitchin, eds., *Christianity and the Social Revolution* (London, 1935).

amounts to little more than a vague spirit of friendliness, a willingness to support churches – providing these churches demand no real sacrifices and preach no exacting doctrines." Billy Graham brought the spirit of revival religion into the mainstream and put it center stage; for American conservatives, this was a welcome change from the "ethos of sociability."[12]

Elsewhere this change came across differently. Roland Barthes recorded his observations on one of Graham's early performances in France: "Billy Graham in the Vel' d'Hiv." "A pity," he noted, "that there was no Papua medicine man present to describe the ceremony – the Waiting, the Suggestion, the Initiation . . . the bible in the outstretched hand as a market salesman who is selling a universal can opener . . . the classical arsenal of show hypnotism . . . no difference at all between Billy Graham and Grand Robert."[13]

At the same time, in other parts of the globe, Christian churches had already been enlisted by agencies of the U.S. government as part of psychological counterinsurgency operations, such as in the Philippines in the 1950s (see Hulsman).

It may be helpful at this point to clarify some of the terms used and identify the Christian organizations under discussion. *Evangelicalism* is a movement originating in Protestantism which holds that humanity's destiny depends on spiritual salvation, which can only be attained by accepting Jesus Christ as one's savior. In the media the new Evangelicalism is often erroneously referred to as fundamentalism. Evangelicalism, however, is a broad tradition comprising several currents and, in any case, most of the organizations labeled fundamentalist are in fact Pentecostal.

Pentecostalism is a charismatic religion centered on the "gifts of the Holy Ghost," prayer and faith healing, speaking in tongues, and predicting the future. Pentecostalism originated in the emotional forms of worship of black slaves and poor whites who sang and prayed with their arms raised. *Fundamentalism*, on the other hand, is a strict form of Protestantism

12. Russel Kirk quoted in F. F. Siegel, *Troubled Journey: From Pearl Harbor to Ronald Reagan* (New York, 1984), p. 113.
13. R. Barthes, *Mythologies* (Paris, 1957 and London, 1972), pp. 125–29. The location is the Vélodrome d'Hiver, a Paris stadium.

centered on the Scripture. Its essential character is biblical literalism and it owes its definition to a "fundamental," as against a modernist, interpretation of the Scripture, arguing that it is to be taken "literally." Fundamentalism took shape in the late nineteenth and early twentieth centuries in the southern United States. In tone and style it is a Southern middle-class version of Puritanism.[14]

Most of the well-known names of American revival religion – Oral Roberts and Billy Graham since the 1940s and 1950s, and Pat Robertson, Jimmy Swaggart, and Jim Bakker among contemporaries – are Pentecostals. Only a few are fundamentalists, such as Jerry Falwell and Tim LaHaye. There used to be considerable differences in doctrine and organizational style between fundamentalists and Pentecostals, to the point of bitter animosity. These differences narrowed gradually in the context of the American postwar consensus and in particular since they came together in a theo-political alliance with the New Right in the mid–1970s; even so, the differences remain significant enough to bear in mind. The appropriate denominator for both types of organization is *evangelical*, in accordance with the tradition of Evangelicalism and with the way they collectively designate themselves in different countries as evangelical associations. The evangelicals are distinct from the mainline Protestant churches, most of which are assembled in the National Council of Churches and the World Council of Churches.

Another area of concern regarding the contemporary politics of Christianity is the Catholic Church and its lay orders, notably the Sovereign Military Order of Malta (the Knights of Malta), Opus Dei, and charismatic organizations such as Communione e Liberazione. Catholic, but not officially affiliated with the church, is Tradition, Family and Property (TFP), which is active in many areas of Latin America and which originated in Brazil. Syncretic organizations such as the Unification Church of Reverend Sun Myung Moon belong to a separate category; falling outside the boundaries of Christianity, they are only occasionally referred to in this volume.

The articles in this volume are mostly concerned with the

14. G. M. Marsden, *Fundamentalism and American Culture* (Oxford, 1980).

right-wing end of the spectrum of Christian organizations, whose ideologies range from militant anticommunism and espousing cold war positions to various forms of social and political conservatism. Frequently the organizations of the new religious Right present themselves as being expressly apolitical; they follow a dualist theology which advocates a separation between religion and politics, which in effect means acceptance of the status quo and noninvolvement in collective social action (see Gifford). Accordingly, they may be right-wing in different ways – by default or by intent.

Christianity, Power, and Capital

One of the leading perspectives on the historical role of Christianity concerns the relationship between religion and economic growth and the hypothesis of the Protestant ethic as the "spirit of modern capitalism," as discussed by Max Weber and R.H. Tawney.[15] When we reflect on the relationship of American Evangelicalism to the advance of the world market and neoliberalism, this perspective takes precedence.

Another approach is concerned with the problem of Christianity and empire. What has been the historical role of Christian churches in imperial expansion and colonialism? The antecedents of this question bring us back to the conversion of Constantine and the Christianization of the Roman Empire, to the Christianization of Europe and its significance for state formation, to the investiture struggle between the pope and the German emperor, to the Crusades, the *Reconquista,* the *Conquista,* and up to the present. The affinities of Christianity and empire, of course, predate those of Christianity and capitalism; that is, the relationship between Christianity and power or between Christianity and the state is an older configuration and an older question than the relation between Christianity and the market. The central focus in this volume is the general problem of Christianity and hegemony. This incorporates considerations of political economy, but not to the point of economism (or economic determinism).

15. M. Weber, *The Protestant Ethic and the Spirit of Capitalism* (1921; reprint, London, 1976); R. H. Tawney, *Religion and the Rise of Capitalism* (1926; reprint, New York, 1954).

Different forms of Christianity correlate with different modes of Western expansion – Roman Catholicism with the missionary colonialism of Spain and Portugal, and varieties of Protestantism with the expansion of northwestern European countries. This brings us to the present question: the correlation of Evangelicalism and U.S. hegemony. Does the simultaneous occurrence of the global expansion of evangelical Christianity and postwar United States hegemony reflect a particular mode or stage of Western expansion? Does it reflect specific characteristics of U.S. hegemony, political, economic, or cultural? Does it reflect the culmination or, rather, the waning of U.S. hegemony?

These perspectives and emphases interact when we consider the contemporary expansion of evangelical movements. Evangelicalism, or at least certain prominent forms of it, appears as a religion of international market society – promoting a free enterprise ethic of individualism and market-oriented attitudes. In addition, certain forms of Evangelicalism appear compatible with, sometimes even a part of, a politics of neocolonial penetration or control – a mode of propaganda and influence management related to "Western goals," a way of targeting areas and constituencies which otherwise could not be reached. In cultural terms, this is a form of religious "CocaColonization," Christian "McDonaldization." On certain occasions, evangelical churches have been involved in intelligence gathering and forms of political intervention in cooperation with the U.S. security apparatus.

The term *hegemony* is commonly used in the context of international relations. As such it refers to nonterritorial imperialism, specifically the situation when a state influences the foreign policy but not the domestic policy of another country.[16] We leave aside whether this strict definition of international hegemony is adequate to describe the postwar role of the United States. There is another usage of hegemony in an entirely different discourse which is relevant to our problem. Hegemony as used by Antonio Gramsci refers to rule based on moral prestige, cultural leadership, ideological persuasiveness, as against mere coercion. This may refer to the cultural leadership of a class vis-à-vis society, or of a

---

16. M. W. Doyle, *Empires* (Ithaca, N.Y., 1986).

leading institution vis-à-vis the populace.[17] In Gramsci's view, hegemony is the mainstay of rule in most Western countries. Here ideological consent rather than state coercion is the basis of rule and the state is but an outer ditch in a network of fortresses consisting of the private institutions of civil society, such as churches, schools and trade unions. In non-Western countries, however (Gramsci at the time referred to Tsarist Russia), civil society is weak and the public institutions of the state dominate the field. Gramsci, the "theoretician of the superstructures," has something to contribute in this context because of his concern with civil society, culture, and ideology, and his insights into the influence of the Catholic church in Italy and the role of popular religion.[18]

In analyzing the political role of Christianity globally, hegemony can serve as a key concept because what is at issue is cultural leadership.[19] Hegemony in international relations also finds expression in cultural hegemony, and local situations and conflicts can be seen to form part of a global Kulturkampf. The local efforts of Christian churches interlock in a global configuration. They are interwoven with the vicissitudes of Western hegemony and, in the case of American evangelical churches, with the ups and downs of U.S. Evangelicalism and the vicissitudes of U.S. hegemony on the world scene.

Frontiers of Hegemony

The rapid growth of evangelical churches in countries of the South, particularly in Latin America, has led to concern among established churches and among social organizations ranging from trade unions to political parties. According to one estimate, 32 percent of the world's population considers itself

17. The concept of cultural leadership may be compared to Lenin's notion of political leadership. N. Bobbio, "Gramsci and the Conception of Civil Society," in *Gramsci and Marxist Theory*, ed. Chantal Mouffe (London, 1979). (Originally published in Italian)

18. H. Mottu, "The Theological Critique of Religion and Popular Religion," *Radical Religion* 4, no. 1 (1978), pp. 4–15; H. Portelli, *Gramsci et la question réligieuse* (Paris, 1974).

19. A discussion which attempts to combine the two different concepts of hegemony, that of international relations and that of Gramsci, is R. W. Cox, "Gramsci, Hegemony and International Relations: An essay in Method", *Millenium: Journal of International Studies* 12, no. 2 (1983), pp. 162–75.

Christian and one-sixth of this is now evangelical. In 1900, 7 percent of the world's evangelicals lived in areas now referred to as the Third World. In 1970, according to an evangelical source, this had increased to 36 percent, in 1980 to 50 percent, and in 1985 to 66 percent. This growth has been greatest in Latin America, where evangelicals now number between thirty five and forty million.[20]

What accounts for the rapid growth of Evangelicalism and what are its implications? This raises the general question of "planning or growth," "manipulation or movement," in relation to popular trends. With regard to the "invention of tradition" (in particular the invention of nationalist traditions at the turn of the century), Eric Hobsbawm notes that "the most successful examples of manipulation are those which exploit practices which clearly meet a felt – not necessarily a clearly understood – need among particular bodies of people."[21] This principle also holds for the growth of mass Christian organizations: it must be accounted for in terms of dynamics from above and from below. Not only must the supply side be considered but the demand side as well. Hence this can be looked at in terms of structural dynamics as well as locally specific features and characteristics of social actors. First, there are the characteristics of the evangelical organizations and, second, the fact that, outside the United States, they insert themselves into a wide array of different situations.

The setting of contemporary religion is a global environment of rapid social change. The structural trends highlighted in studies of the sociology of religion are urbanization, industrialization, advancement of the world market, commodification of social relations, uprootedness, unemployment, poverty and marginalization.[22] These form the backdrop to the spread of Evangelicalism in Third World countries.

20. H. L. J. Keijzer, "COMIBAM, evangelische zending in Latijns Amerika," In-Formatie 19, no. 2 (April 1988). Cf. D. B. Barrett and J.W. Reapsome, *Seven Hundred Plans to Evangelize the World: The Rise of an Evangelization Movement* (New York, 1989).

21. E. Hobsbawn, "Mass-producing Traditions: Europe, 1870–1914," in *The Invention of Tradition*, eds. E. Hobsbawm and T. Ranger (Cambridge, 1983), p. 307.

22. E.g., J. A. Beckford and T. Luckmann, eds., *The Changing Face of Religion* (London, 1988); R. Robertson, ed., *Sociology of Religion* (Harmondsworth, U.K., 1969).

The political significance of right-wing Christian churches may be greatest at active *"frontiers of hegemony,"* that is, areas where social forces engage in ideological and political contest and competition, and border zones either politically or geographically. Generally, areas in political flux, contested zones, or countries during election times may witness heightened right-wing Christian activity. This includes situations of ongoing counterinsurgency, low-intensity conflict and pro-insurgency to destabilize postrevolutionary states. It includes situations where a repressive state apparatus attempts to win over "hearts and minds" among the rural population (Guatemala), where a state is competing with insurgents for ideological hegemony (the Philippines), where foreign powers back insurgencies against postrevolutionary states (the Contras in Nicaragua, destabilization in Angola and Mozambique), sensitive border areas (Costa Rica, southern Lebanon), or areas of intense political conflict (Northern Ireland).

Frontiers of hegemony also run through the Christian denominations themselves. Ideological currents within many Christian denominations span the political spectrum, from "liberation" theologies to conservative and anticommunist currents. The divisions within the Catholic church between the adherents of liberation theology and the conservative hierarchy are well-known. Beliefs held among the majority of the Southern Baptist Convention in the United States overlap with the views of conservative Pentecostals. There is, on the other hand, also a socially critical, leftist tendency among evangelicals and Protestants, in the circles of *Sojourner Truth* magazine and the groups assembled in the Peace Council of the World Council of Churches. Among Pentecostals there are likewise socially critical tendencies. In South Africa, Rev. Frank Chikane, a leading figure in the United Democratic Front and a well-known opponent of apartheid, is a Pentecostal minister. Thus, while some denominations tend to be identified with general political positions (the "liberal" World Council of Churches), there are significant second-order differences.

Evangelical groups frequently operate in areas where they compete with other Christian churches rather than in non-Christian cultural areas. Where they do operate in different cultural environments, as in Korea and Taiwan, at least the ground has been prepared and they are backed by a significant American presence. In recent years the attention of evangelicals has been drawn to different areas as well, such as in southern India's Tamil-Hindu region,[23] in Indonesia, and again in China.

In countries of the South, Christian churches operate in a terrain where the coercive power of state institutions often looms large while civil institutions are relatively weak. Often the churches are among the best-organized institutions of civil society and so their social and political influence can be considerable. We can think of a continuum of situations ranging from repression as the mainstay of rule to ideological consent, and hypothesize that the Christian Right operates differently or has a different impact at different points along this continuum. In countries where repression is the main basis of rule – South Africa, Guatemala, and Chile under General Pinochet come to mind – the religious Right may be concerned not only with evangelization among the poor and subjected, but also with morale and social cohesion within the privileged sector of society (whites in South Africa) or state organs (the armed forces in Guatemala and Chile). Here the legitimation of state repression becomes one of the functions of Christian churches, while we also encounter such phenomena as chaplains to torturers, and evangelical organizing within Third World armed forces.

In the armed forces of Chile under General Pinochet armed service was presented as a way to "honor God," and God was worshiped as a "supersoldier" and the "Lord of hosts" of the Old Testament. All churches, Catholic, evangelical and Protestant, participated in this militarization of Christianity and competed for influence in the armed services.[24] Spiritual assistance to death squads is not uncommon. Rev. Antonio Sandoval, a member of the extreme-right International Council of Christian Churches based in New Jersey, was a chaplain to the treasury police in Guatemala, who are notorious for their

23. L. Caplan, "Fundamentalism as Counter-culture: Protestants in Urban South India," in *Studies in Religious Fundamentalism*, ed. Lionel Caplan (Basingstoke, U.K., 1987).

24. H. L. Schuffeneger, "Ideologisch gebruik van religie in Chili," *Wereld en Zending*, 1986, no. 3, pp. 252–58. (Original title: "La funcion de la religion en el gobierno militar, en el modelo político autoritario y en las Fuerzas Armadas y de Orden de Chile," unpublished before 1985.)

death squad activities.[25] Ministers of General Ríos Montt's Verbo church in Guatemala, where Ríos Montt's junta was in power in 1982 and 1983, have been accused of participating in espionage and torture. In 1982 a pastor of the Verbo church, when asked about the army murdering the indigenous peasants, responded:

> The Army doesn't massacre the Indians. It massacres demons, and the Indians are demon-possessed; they are communists. We hold Brother Efraín Ríos Montt like King David of the Old Testament. He is the King of the New Testament.[26]

A so-called apolitical religion can easily give way to the demonization of political opponents where the underlying world view is so strongly polarized.

Societies in which civil institutions are not as strong and well-entrenched as in Western countries, and regions and eras characterized by ideological cleavage and political instability frequently constitute the field of operations for right-wing Christian organizations. The strength and manner of their impact is affected by several factors and we can begin to distinguish the following dynamics:

Is God an American? The leading evangelical churches are headquartered in the United States, are financed from the United States, use American broadcasting technologies and American mobilization methods, and reflect American culture.[27]

Theology. In terms of theology and culture the evangelical organizations tend to parallel world market influences and "American" worldviews. Theologies advocated by evangelicals, such as the "Prosperity Gospel," which emphasize success and individual achievement, the spiritual blessings of entrepreneurial activity, and the sanctity of private property, together represent an ethic of success in a world market

25. L. Jones, Report to the Catholic Institute, 34. Cf. M. McClintock, *The American Connection*, vol. 2, *State Terror and Popular Resistance in Guatemala* (London, 1985), pp. 235–39; L. Frank and P. Wheaton, *Indian Guatemala: The Path to Liberation* (Washington, 1984).

26. Quoted in S. Diamond, *Spiritual Warfare: The Politics of the Christian Right* (Boston, 1989), p. 166.

27. Cf. Soren Hvalkof and Peter Aaby, eds. *Is God an American? An Anthropological Perspective on the Missionary Work of the Summer Institute of Linguistics.* (London, 1981).

environment which is dominated – if no longer economically, at least culturally – by the United States.

The theology of the virtues of the market articulated, among others, by Michael Novak, a Catholic theologian associated with the American Enterprise Institute and the Institute on Religion and Democracy (IRD), is a free enterprise theology, a theological articulation of neoliberalism, the Gospel according to the American Enterprise Institute.[28]

Nevertheless, the theological tendencies among evangelicals are not entirely uniform or consistent. There are also tendencies which run counter to the world market regime.[29] Armageddon theology is *not* conducive to either capital accumulation or popular commitment ("bugout theology does not produce armies, only refugees"). Reportedly it has lost its first place in evangelical circles to "dominion" or "kingdom" theology. This particular version of "endtimes" teaching encourages social activism, arguing that "by getting involved in politics, evangelicals can build God's kingdom here on earth" (see Diamond).

Mobilization methods. Generally, an active outreach is characteristic of the evangelical movements, in the form of door-to-door evangelization (Jehovah's Witnesses), street-corner preaching, street theater and musical performances, and mass meetings. The use of broadcasting technologies, which have been developed furthest in the United States, is another element in the impact of the evangelicals.[30] Radio and television broadcasting in local languages and the use of mass meetings in stadiums, tents or the open air all add to the strength of the movements' outreach. Modern marketing methods for appealing to the public are utilized to target audiences with a particular version of the Gospel.

Their allegedly apolitical version of the Gospel contrasts with the liberation reading of the Gospel preached in Latin

28. M. Novak, *The Spirit of Democratic Capitalism* (New York, 1982). Cf. F. J. Hinkelammert, "The Politics of the Total Market, Its Theology and Our Response," *North-South Dialogue* 1, no. 1 (Fall 1985).

29. Cf. R. Craig, "Resistance to Capitalism within the American Protestant Tradition," *Radical Religion* 4 no. 1 (1978).

30. See S. M. Hoover, *Mass Media Religion: The Social Sources of the Electronic Church* (London, 1988).

America, the Philippines and elsewhere by base communities. The "apolitical" Gospel finds expression in a tendency toward withdrawal from collective action, known in Latin America as the *huelga social*, or social strike.[31] On the other hand, a radicalization of Pentecostalism has also taken place, for instance in Venezuela, where the Pentecostal church has chosen the "option for the poor."[32]

Modes of organization. It generally is preferable to speak of evangelical organizations or churches rather than of evangelical movements, in view of the degree of their institutionalization and their hierarchical, top-down structure. We will not be dealing here with the "new religious movements," the cults and sects, which, it has been argued, should be analyzed according to the same principles as the new social movements.[33]

Some of the organizational methods of evangelical organizations are reminiscent of, and sometimes derived from, American business techniques. These include networking with local government and opinion leaders and the recruitment of local leaders and notables (e.g., a well-known white sports champion in the leadership of the Rhema church in South Africa). Other forms of organization were developed in the 1960s and 1970s in the United States, on colleges and in suburbs, such as prayer groups (or "cells") and the hierarchical command structures of "shepherding,"[34] sometimes imitating the organizational methods of progressive political groups. Quite striking is the frequent cooperation and coordination among different evangelical organizations in mass campaigns (e.g., Namibia during the 1989 elections).[35]

31. R. Aalbersberg, "Een boodschap aan de armen? Opkomst van nieuwe sekten in Latijns-Amerika," *ICCO-Nieuwsbrief* 5 no. 1 (April 1987).

32. R. Aalbersberg, *Een boodschap aan de armen? De opkomst van sekten in Latijns-Amerika* (Zeist, 1988), p. 23.

33. J. A. Beckford, "Are New Religious Movements New Social Movements," (Seminar paper read at Institute of Social Studies, Social Movements, The Hague, 1990); Beckford and Luckman, eds., *The Changing Face of Religion*; T. Robbins, *Cults, Converts and Charisma: The Sociology of New Religious Movements* (London, 1988).

34. S. Diamond, *Spiritual Warfare*, pp. 127 ff.

35. "The biggest joint evangelism operation in the history of southern Africa will soon be launched by the newly formed Evangelical Fellowship of Namibia (Efswan) in SWA/ Namibia." B. de Villiers, "Mass Joint Evangelism Operation Planned," *Windhoek Advertiser*, 23 February 1989.

Financial support. Lavish private funding from the United States supports the broadcasting, the campaigns, the renting of stadiums. These funds of "dollar Protestantism" exceed the resources of the established churches. In addition, the evangelicals spend their funds on evangelization only, whereas the mainline churches also support development projects (see Gifford). The main source of funds is religious broadcasting in the United States. In the wake of the scandals involving Jim Bakker, Jimmy Swaggart and others, these funds have dropped considerably.[36] Another source of funding – although probably not nearly as significant – is the network of right-wing institutes and think tanks with which many evangelical organizations are connected.[37]

Holism. The religion of the evangelicals, notably the Pentecostals, tends to be a total religion which does not end with the ceremony and at the church door but concerns itself with every aspect of life. It provides an all-embracing social environment where prayer and healing relate to everything from spiritual solace to business and everyday problems, such as praying for a parking space or for the success of business ventures.

"Traditional" morality. Traditional views of the family, gender roles and parental authority may be an important source of support to people in *favelas* who are uprooted from the countryside. The neo-Puritan ethic of abstinence from alcohol and drugs, and disdain for luxury, may also be of vital importance to survival in conditions of poverty.

But how "traditional" are these views? *Not* traditional is the emphasis on individualism and on individual achievement and success, as against community solidarity, in the preaching of many evangelical churches. Besides this, what is or appears to be a traditional social morality in the United States – profamily, antiabortion and so forth – may be modernist in Third World countries. The American family model is the nuclear family, a model consistent with industrial society; this runs counter to the extended family characteristic of

36. L. Jones, Report to the Catholic Institute
37. D. Huntington and R. Kaplan, "Whose Gold is behind the Altar? Corporate Ties to Evangelicals," in *World Capitalist Crisis and the Rise of the Right*, ed. M. Dixon et al. (San Francisco, 1982); R.C. Armstrong, "Reagan's Uneasy Alliance", *NACLA* 15, no. 4 (July–August 1981), pp. 8–24.

agrarian societies, but it may parallel, on the other hand, the social ramifications of urbanization.

Development. The neo-Puritan ethics of many evangelicals represent a "this-worldly ascetism." In combination with the ethos of individual achievement and entrepreneurialism, this resembles the profile of an "accumulation religion," along the lines of the Protestant ethic, that is, a religion conducive to savings and investment. In sub-Saharan Africa, employers are reported to prefer members of the independent African churches as employees, rather than nonchurchgoers, because of their abstinence from alcohol and their disregard for traditional taboos and time-consuming social rituals. On the other hand, there are disadvantages as well:

> The excessive disciplines of prolonged fasting, the effects of all-night rituals and exhausting ecstatic experiences do not produce people fit for work. The prophet's warnings against quite normal actions on journeys, such as "never travel on Tuesdays," interfere with rational economic activity. Belief in having enlisted the "power of the Spirit" on one's behalf may lead to unrealistic attitudes to one's own capacities and plans. Encapsulation within the comprehensive activities of an apolitical religious movement deprives credit unions, trades unions, and political structures of the support they need. New forms of conspicuous consumption can arise in otherwise ascetically minded churches – in cathedralesque buildings, laces and frills, silks and satins in the prayer gowns, elaborate printing, and rich vestments and high-status life-style for the leader, even if this is vicariously enjoyed with pride by his simple-living members.[38]

Yet the overall effect of membership in the independent churches is deemed to be on the credit side of development. No doubt this is a significant dimension of Evangelicalism and perhaps a significant explanation for its success. In this aspect evangelical movements *can* be a form of empowerment in an environment perceived to be controlled by market forces.

38. H. W. Turner, "African Independent Churches and Economic Development," *World Development* 8, no. 7/8 (July-August 1980), pp. 523–33. The concept of "accumulation religion" and the implicit equation of development with accumulation are critically examined in the lead article of this special issue on religious values and development. See also C. K. Wilber and K. P. Jameson, "Religious Values and Social Limits to Development," pp. 467–80.

Overtly political forms of popular religion, such as those advocated by liberation theology, then represent another, political form of empowerment, in line with community action, trade unions, and peasant leagues, as strategies in an environment perceived to be controlled by political forces.[39] Evangelicalism thus exemplifies a development ethos which corresponds to the kind of development pursued and advocated by global hegemonic forces.

To what extent can this be generalized across evangelical churches in countries of the South? The example given above refers to independent African churches rather than to American-export Evangelicalism. Characteristic of American Evangelicalism is an ethos of *consumption* rather than *production*. According to television preacher Jimmy Swaggart, "If you ask the Lord for a camper, don't forget to mention the color."[40] This kind of mentality is congenial to late capitalism at the stage of high mass consumption, and obviously not merely irrelevant but counterproductive for countries at a preindustrial level of development. The effect of empowerment may occur *only* if, and to the extent that, the religion is indigenized. The lottery ethics of many American television preachers (several of whom are televised on Third World screens) are the reverse of empowerment. They broadcast forms of self-deception which are as conducive to development as a cargo cult, as effective as a salesman's magic talk in an Avon cosmetics pyramid system, as enticing and as productive as a chain letter. The developmental potential of Evangelicalism in the South must be assessed on a case-by-case basis, considering theology, ethics, mode of organization and degree of indigenization.

Class. Evangelical churches address different classes in different countries and at different times, so generalizations are precarious. Nevertheless, evangelicals often appeal especially to the poor, whereas the established churches, Catholic and Protestant, often cater to the middle class. Frequently the social basis of evangelical organizations is multiclass, includ-

---

39. Cf. T. C. Bruneau, "The Catholic Church and Development in Latin America: The Role of the Basic Christian Communities," *World Development* 8, no. 7/8 (July–August 1980), pp. 535–44.

40. Quoted in G. F. Mehrtens, *Alles het einde: Beloften van een massacultuur* (Amsterdam, 1989).

ing upwardly mobile entrepreneurs, students and professionals.

Nationalism. Generally in the Western world the Right and the New Right have identified themselves with patriotism and tried to present themselves as champions of national identity. This has been the dominant pattern since the later nineteenth century. In Reagan-era America and Thatcher-era Britain patriotic posturing was, along with neoliberalism, a powerful current. The evangelical Right, in particular the organizations with an overt political agenda, has followed the example of claiming to represent the Main Street mainstream. Ministers with a pronounced political profile, such as Pat Robertson, a candidate in the 1988 U.S. presidential elections, claim to represent not merely "American values" but "American destiny." His book, *America's Dates with Destiny*, exemplifies this attitude.[41]

When exported to other shores American Evangelicalism seems to undergo two changes: first, Americanism is toned down for a more universal "Christian" appeal, and, second, politics may be given a low profile. Politically sensitive themes and controversial theologies tend to be soft-pedaled in the missionary setting, at any rate in the early stages.

A general perspective on the growth of the evangelical churches is to view them as a cultural tendency accompanying the extension of the world market. This would be the obvious Marxist or neo-Marxist interpretation of the evangelical tide, but it does not say anything about the specifically *evangelical* and, largely, *American* character of this stage of the saga of Christianity and capitalism. This brings us back to the question of United States hegemony. The present episode of the extension and deepening of the world market is taking place under specific conditions of U.S. hegemony and neoliberalism.

U.S. hegemony. The present wave of Evangelicalism corresponds with a particular stage of United States hegemony – post-Vietnam and neoliberal. This situation differs from prior episodes of American globalism in several ways. First, it is associated, manifestly so during the Reagan years, with a trend toward the "privatization" of American foreign policy (see Diamond). Second, the emphasis has not been on military

41. P. Robertson, *America's Dates with Destiny* (Nashville, 1984).

solutions of regional conflicts but on more complex holding operations, and the dominant mode of intervention, at least during the 1980s, was no longer counterinsurgency as in the 1960s, but low-intensity conflict.[42] In the recent Gulf crisis yet other directions were taken.

In this regard, the emphasis in evangelical discourse tends to be more on free enterprise, or the "magic of the market-place" (Reagan's familiar phrase), or on democracy, than on (American) nationalism. In this respect it is a more outward-looking stage of evangelicalism than in the 1950s. This raises the question as to what extent the upsurge of evangelical activities in Third World countries represents not so much an increase in American influence as a growing weakness of U.S. hegemony. The latter can be taken as the inability, or the reduced ability as compared to before 1967 or 1973, of the U.S. state to impose its will internationally, whether militar-ily or economically. Thus, on the one hand, the upsurge of evangelicalism may represent a more advanced and sophisti-cated mode of neocolonial intervention (transnational Gramscism of the Right), while on the other, it may represent the ideological outpourings of a waning hegemonic power, reduced to peddling popular religions in its latter days.

Gramscism of the Right

Let us shift attention to the underlying analytical theme of Gramscism of the Right and try to assess the extent to which this is a useful perspective in relation to contemporary Chris-tianity. The term "Gramscism of the Right" has come up in recent years in relation to the Nouvelle Droite in France. Ever since the late 1960s, when GRECE (Groupe de recherche et d'étude pour la civilisation européenne), the principal organization of the Nouvelle Droite, was founded, it was explicitly premised on a Gramscian point of view. This was taken to mean that the cultural sphere had to be won before political power could be gained; it was a departure from *direct* political action, the line of development that was to lead to Jean-Marie le Pen and the National Front.

42. See S. Miles, "The Real War: Low-Intensity Conflict in Central Amer-ica," *NACLA* 20 (April-May 1986).

GRECE is a "cercle de pensée" which has been seeking to develop a right-wing ideology that would serve as a counter-weight to left-wing cultural influence. Aligned with this circle are *Le Figaro* and *Figaro* magazine (which belong to the media conglomerate of Robert Hersant), numerous other magazines and journals, historical revisionists such as Robert Faurisson, members of several right-of-center political parties, and the Club de l'Horloge, an association of civil servants and politicians. The Nouvelle Droite itself has had but limited impact, for its ideological points of view have been too extreme to gain many adherents; paganism, anti-Christianity and anti-Americanism are not particularly popular positions. But, on the other hand, it has contributed to the creation of a climate of opinion in France in which right-wing ideologies have regained the intellectual respectability they had lost since the war. The Right has also developed to perfection the tactic of adopting their opponents' arguments. Thus, for GRECE spokesman Alain de Benoist, the "right to self-determination" has become "the duty of each people to remain itself." For Louis Pauwels of *Figaro* magazine, antiracism, identity, and difference – key words in the left-wing lexicon – have been harnessed to a conservative plea for maintaining "European identity." Benoist has referred to the Nouvelle Droite position as "intelligent racism" or "differential antiracism."[43]

Nouvelle Droite organizations form part of the transnational New Right archipelago. In 1981 the Club de l'Horloge organized the Paris conference of the Mont Pélerin Society. Established in 1947 in Switzerland as a circle of Von Hayek economists, in the 1980s this had grown to include some four hundred neoliberal economists. In 1983 the Institut Economique de Paris (IEP) was founded to advocate free market economics as part of the neoliberal international. Together with, for instance, the Institute of Economic Affairs in London, which advised the Thatcher government, and the Institut Européen in Brussels, the IEP forms part of the Mont Pélerin Society network. It is in this wider context that certain potentially significant tendencies have been developing.

43. R. Rollat, *Les hommes de l'extrème droite* (Paris, 1985); Anne Frank Foundation, *The Extreme Right in Europe and the United States* (Amsterdam, 1985), pp. 53–56; D. Kouijzer, "De culturele revolutie van Nieuw Rechts," *Intermediair* 23, no. 24 (12 June 1987).

The ideological direction taken by the Club de l'Horloge in the 1980s is to merge the neoliberal eulogy of market forces to social-conservative and right-wing Catholic concerns with social order and morality. Thus, according to Raoul Audouin of the Club de l'Horloge, the "liberal and spiritualist credo" may be summed up in the "social tripod" of market, law and morality.[44] He refers in this context to Thomas Aquinas's concept of "tranquillity of order."

What is striking about this "liberal spiritualism" is the fusion of two modes of politics and two traditions which were archenemies through most of the nineteenth century: liberalism with its Enlightenment heritage, rationalism and secularism, and Catholicism with its Roman and medieval heritage, corporatism and antisecularism. Through the nineteenth century the major political cleavage ran between the church and the liberals, particularly in the Catholic countries of Latin Europe and Latin America.[45] "Bien étonnés de se trouver ensemble," or is this but the ideological reflection of a political convergence which has already long been taking shape? It does appear to form part of a larger trend:

> We are thus witnessing the emergence of a new hegemonic project, that of liberal-conservative discourse, which seeks to articulate the neoliberal defence of the free market economy with the profoundly antiegalitarian cultural and social traditionalism of conservatism.[46]

What stands out in this context is the principle of the Right following a Gramscian strategy. It may not necessarily be a successful formula; indeed the extreme-right positions of GRECE have not been. It does, however, draw attention to the general phenomenon of Gramscism of the Right: the pursuit of cultural influence as a right-wing political strategy.

44. R. Audouin, "Comment peut-on être libéral et spiritualiste?" *La Presse Française*, 20 November 1981.

45. But compare the liberal Catholic tendency which developed in several European countries in the nineteenth century and which has been considered the precursor of modernism or the tradition of Christian democracy. Antonio Gramsci, *Prison Notebooks*, eds. Q. Hoare and G. Nowell Smith (New York, 1971), p. 61.

46. E. Laclau and C. Mouffe, *Hegemony and Socialist Strategy* (London, 1985), p. 175.

Can this be a fruitful point of departure for looking into some of the manifestations of Christianity and politics?

To put this in perspective, we need to take a closer look at Gramscism and at Catholic hegemonic politics, and step for a moment back into the world of fin-de-siècle Europe. In what has been termed Gramsci's "double perspective," institutions such as the state and the church "occupy two spaces at one time; they can have meaning *both* in terms of political society *and* civil society."[47] This involves a fish-eye view of politics, that is, politics not simply as it manifests itself in the public realm of state affairs but also the politics of the classroom, of voluntary organizations, of directions and trends in civil society and popular culture.

These dynamics operate on the Left as well as on the Right. Cultural strategies are important to a ruling class because of the need for consent, and to a subaltern class because, without cultural influence and allies outside of its social confines, it cannot attain power. The Kulturkampf of the late nineteenth century held lessons for all concerned – for the Right, the church and the working class. The various parties put these lessons into practice. The Right promoted nationalism and imperialism to outmaneuver the class struggle. The church competed with the worker movement over the allegiance of its mass base. The church, taking heed, zigzagged, first rejecting and then imitating several of the cultural and social forms of the working-class movement – from trade unions, elections, and political parties, to Friday evening singing clubs and youth associations. The Left took lessons in turn, lessons that were theorized by Gramsci.

What makes this perspective relevant is that it developed, in part, out of an analysis of the politics of religion, of the Catholic church at the turn of the century. Issues of particular importance to Gramsci were the southern question and the urban-country alliance. With respect to both issues the Italian Communist party was outmaneuvered at the time by the church. In the momentous period of 1920 and the factory occupations in Turin, it was not possible for the urban workers to find allies in the countryside. Yet for the church-backed Partito Popolare Italiano (PPI) it was possible to enter

47. A. S. Sassoon, *Gramsci's Politics* (New York, 1980), p. 112.

the town from their base among the peasantry of northern and central Italy and to expand their constituency among the southern peasantry.

This forms part of a broader trend which surfaced with the 1891 encyclical *Rerum Novarum*, which formulated the outlines of "Social Catholicism." "The first major Christian Social modern mass party" was founded in the same period, the 1890s, by the Austrian demagogue Karl Lueger. Genuine Catholic mass parties and movements existed at the time only in Germany, the Netherlands, and Belgium.[48] In Italy the Milan Program of 1894, the "Program of Catholics faced with Socialism," ended by "looking forward to the "Christian democracy of the twentieth century," in which all classes would work together in social harmony."[49] The lay organizations implementing the program were engaged in youth work, education, the press, local elections, rural banks, cooperatives and charities; it was a *reconquista* of Italian society, and it resulted in the creation of a Catholic subculture. The growth of Catholic institutions such as trade unions was not sustained through the 1900s. "Modernism" was condemned by Pope Pius X in 1907 and momentum was regained only after 1918, notably through the PPI. In later years, the Catholic lay organization Opus Dei has been particularly active in the media and universities and concerned with influencing public opinion.[50] (These developments are discussed in Van Wesel.)

"Gramscism of the Right" is the Right adopting theses of Gramsci's which were based on an analysis of what the Right did in reaction to the Left. "Gramscism of the Right" is the Right applying left-wing lessons drawn from the Right drawing lessons from the Left. The Kulturkampf of the late nineteenth century was in many ways a game of mirrors in which various social forces began to adopt and develop similar techniques of political mobilization, several of which had first been used on a mass scale by the working-class movement.[51] These methods included forms of cultural cohesion

48. E. J. Hobsbawm, *The Age of Empire, 1875–1914* (London, 1987), pp. 90–91.

49. M. Clark, *Modern Italy, 1871–1982* (London, 1984), p. 106.

50. M. Walsh, *The Secret World of Opus Dei* (London, 1990).

51. A study of these relations between the Catholic church and the worker movement in a local area, a town in the south of the Netherlands, is J. Perry,

and the use of symbolism to reinforce a common culture and politics. When first applied by the working class, these cultural forms were mostly spontaneous, growing out of common conditions of work and residence; when coopted and paraphrased by right-wing social forces, elements of deliberation and methodical mobilization from above crept in.

To what extent is Gramscism of the Right a relevant concept in relation to the postwar politics of Christianity? When we are confronted with crass political manipulation of religion, does a concept such as Gramscism of the Right make sense?

One notorious instance of the political manipulation of religion in the postwar period is the "Banzer Plan," named for Bolivia's military dictator Hugo Banzer, and hatched in the Bolivian Interior Ministry in 1975. The plan consisted of a campaign to isolate and incriminate the progressive clergy within the Catholic church. Developed in collaboration with the CIA, the plan was later implemented by ten governments belonging to the Latin American Anti-Communist Confederation, including Chile, Brazil, and Honduras. In the words of Penny Lernoux,

> The three main thrusts of the campaign were to sharpen internal divisions within the Church, to smear and harass progressive Bolivian Church leaders, and to arrest or expel foreign priests and nuns, who make up 85 percent of the Bolivian clergy. According to the plan, "The Church as an institution should not be attacked, much less the bishops as a body, but only a part of the Church, the vanguard." Nationalism should be encouraged among Bolivian priests, nuns, and laymen to "isolate foreign missionaries and damage their prestige. . . ." Propaganda should emphasize "the idea that they [foreign missionaries] have been sent to Bolivia for the exclusive purpose of directing the Church towards communism."[52]

We hear an echo of the Banzer Plan in the "Santa Fe Document," issued in 1980 by the Council for Inter-American

---

Roomsche kinine tegen roode koorts: Arbeidersbeweging en katholieke kerk in Maastricht 1880–1920 (Amsterdam, 1983). It details the successful assimilation by the church of the same weapons which the worker movement had used to its own advantage.

52. P. Lernoux, *Cry of the People*, 2nd ed. (Harmondsworth, U.K. 1982), p. 143.

Security and regarded as one of the early statements of what became the Reagan Doctrine. This policy proposal argued that

> U.S. foreign policy must begin to counter (not react against) liberation theology as it is utilized in Latin America by the "liberation theology" clergy. The role of the church in Latin America is vital to the concept of political freedom. Unfortunately, Marxist-Leninist forces have utilized the church as a political weapon against private property and productive capitalism by infiltrating the religious community with ideas that are less Christian than communist.[53]

In the United States, Christian Right groups have traditionally been concerned with political power, and their statements and projects tend to be phrased in a vocabulary of power and influence; in recent years they have been concerned with outmaneuvering "secular humanists" and the "liberal Left." They have not been overly innocent when it comes to collaborating with government agencies. It has not always been clear whether it is their evangelical inspiration that propels them, or their conservative political agenda. To the extent that the latter predominates, it is appropriate to speak of the Gramscism of the American Right. This strategy produced the coalition of the New Right and the National Evangelical Association, which was effective in electing Ronald Reagan to the U.S. presidency in 1980.

During the Reagan administration it was not merely the cultural influence of Christian groups that was enlisted on behalf of U.S. executive policies but their political and financial assistance as well. After General Ríos Montt came to power in Guatemala through a military coup in 1982, the State Department gave a briefing to evangelical organizations on the necessity of "private" assistance to Ríos Montt, at a time when Congress prohibited U.S. governmental support of the Guatemalan regime. Pat Robertson of the Christian Broadcasting Network (CBN) unrolled his "Operation Blessing," which contributed over a billion dollars in aid and sent missionaries to help set up "model villages," which were the Guatemalan

---

53. Quoted in P. Gifford, *The Religious Right in Southern Africa* (Harare, 1988), p. 27.

equivalent of "strategic hamlets" in Vietnam.[54] The operation was assisted by the U.S. Navy in "Project Handclasp," in which navy vessels carried CBN cargo to ports in Central and South America, West Africa and East Asia.

The support of Christian churches for General Ríos Montt was a dress rehearsal for the evangelical assistance to the Contras in Nicaragua, during the period that Congress had barred the U.S. government from assisting the rebel forces (see Diamond). CBN sent "Bibles and chaplains" as well as military airlifts in cooperation with the Catholic organizations Americares and the Knights of Malta. Lt. Col. Oliver North, the coordinator of the Contra-support network, himself belongs to the charismatic-Pentecostal movement. He attends (or attended) a charismatic Episcopal church, the Church of the Apostles in Fairfax, Va., takes part in monthly Bible study and the church's men's fellowship. He also belonged to the Officers' Christian Fellowship, a charismatic–Pentecostal organization in the American military. Several evangelical organizations were involved in North's network. Phil Derstine of Gospel Outreach mentioned close contacts with North and frequent debriefings by the CIA. North supplied Gospel Outreach and Christian Retreat, another evangelical organization, with helicopters. Evangelical missionaries stayed in Contra command bunkers and helped the contras with "motivational training" and produced video tapes for the training of the forces.[55]

The logic of the manipulators, well aware of the strategic implications of different varieties of religion in Latin America, thus appears to overlap with the logic of the believers who, in addition to pulling strings, may feel themselves part of a larger momentum, possibly an Armageddon scenario (see Nederveen Pieterse and Jones's second article). "Gramscism of the Right" seems too intellectual and yet too mundane a term for this kind of shoulder-rubbing between cynicism and belief.

54. S. Diamond, *Spiritual Warfare*, p. 166. "Las sectas fundamentalistas y la contrainsurgencia en Guatemala," *CeriGua* (Delegacion Iztapalapa, Mexicō D.F. and Managua, Nicaragua), March 1987.
55. Jones, Report to the Catholic Institute; Diamond, *Spiritual Warfare*. Cf. J. Marshall, P. D. Scott and J. Hunter, *The Iran-Contra Connection* (Boston, 1987).

Finally, what can one say about the general prospects for the spread of Evangelicalism and evangelical politics in the 1990s? One question is the extent to which the upsurge in evangelical activity in Third World theaters represents not so much the triumphal march of a type of Christianity more in tune with contemporary global dynamics, but, rather, the export of a religion whose home market has been saturated and is shrinking. American televangelism is too deeply entrenched and institutionalized to simply crumble and fade in the wake of the scandals involving leading preachers, but, on the other hand, indications are that its political momentum has halted, its political clout shrunk, its cultural radius dimmed, and that its funds are diminishing. Eight years of the Reagan administration has not brought his conservative backers nor his evangelical supporters many manifest political benefits, at any rate as regards their socially conservative positions on abortion, family issues, and prayer in schools, which have all been defeated. Politically and culturally deflated in the United States, the evangelicals may try to keep their momentum by focusing on overseas missions.

How durable will be the impact of evangelical missions overseas? What remains after the dust has settled on the campaign trails, the rallies, the mass meetings? When no lasting tangible benefits, either materially or politically, emerge from evangelical campaigning, will the impact here be drastic but short-lived, as, perhaps, in recent years in the United States itself? It is, of course, impossible to generalize across so wide a terrain. One conceivable impact may be a contribution to "conservative modernization" in countries of the South: modernization because it brings people from a local into a global cultural environment, in terms of methods and technologies of organization, styles of discourse, and attitudes, and because under certain conditions it can induce a development ethos of a kind; conservative because of the ideological predilections that prevail in the evangelical tide.

Furthermore, how will the Christian Right deal with the waning of the cold war? Through most of its twentieth-century political career, from Buchmanism to Pat Robertson, Evangelicalism has identified with the "free world" and thrived on the ideological opposition of the two great blocs. What new enemy can it generate now? So far two tendencies are in evidence. One is a marked upsurge in evangelical missions to Eastern Europe, which are now legal (see Jones). Evangelical organizations are flocking into Eastern Europe in the same way corporations are (as are West European political parties, including Christian Democratic parties).[56] As these missions become standard and routine, some organizations, such as Christen in Not in West Germany, that once undertook illegal missions and smuggled Bibles into the Eastern block are now shifting their operations from the European continent southward, to the Islamic world, and are doing so without much fanfare.

---

56. A. Riding, "Christian Parties Court East Bloc," *International Herald Tribune*, 15 May 1990.

· 2 ·

Holy Warriors

SARA DIAMOND

The Right After Reagan

As she escorted reporters to her booth at the 1988 National Religious Broadcasters convention, Beverly LaHaye crowed, "Let me tell you what we're doing in Costa Rica." A decade ago, the Concerned Women for America exhibit might have featured a life-size display model of an aborted fetus. This time Mrs. LaHaye's table was piled high with recruitment literature for CWA's upcoming pilgrimages to Nicaraguan refugee camps. A television featured videotapes of Mrs. LaHaye's recent meetings with *La Prensa* editor Violeta Chamorro and other opposition leaders in Managua.

One of the lasting legacies of the Reagan era is the involvement of Concerned Women for America and scores of like-minded organizations in U.S. foreign policy. Even if congressionally approved military funding for Central America were to dry up tomorrow, the "private" networks now in place, would take it upon themselves to carry forth Reagan's crusade against change.

Because of their ability to manipulate theology and ideology, missionary organizations can utilize humanitarian aid very effectively in the psychological operations characteristic of low-intensity warfare. Hiding behind the facade of good intentions, Christian Right activists, in tandem with secular rightists and often with direct support from the U.S. government, have targeted the collective psyche of Third World and North American communities. In Nicaragua, they run anti-Sandinista schools and study groups to fight "satanic" liberation theology. In El Salvador, they blanket the airwaves with progovernment diatribes, build medical clinics and minister to army troops about the ordained right to kill communists.

Meanwhile, in the United States, the Christian Right uses broadcast media and "parachurch" organizations to rally ideological support for interventionism. It maintains an ongoing campaign to counter progressive church activism. And, as a steadfast minority block within the Republican party, it pulls the nation's politics continually rightward.

Though George Bush is probably less enamored of the religious Right than Ronald Reagan, its political influence will not be toppled simply because Reagan leaves office, a television network goes bankrupt, a preacher is disgraced, or a political candidate fails in his bid for office. Despite the growing secularization of society, the marriage of evangelical religion and right-wing politics remains a potent mix, one which – after eight years of official blessing – deeply infects the foreign policy of the United States.

Throughout the 1980s, viewers of Pat Robertson's *700 Club* witnessed frequent cameo appearances by Contra leaders Adolfo Calero, Steadman Fagoth, Enrique Bermudez, and their U.S. advocates Gen. John Singlaub, NSC consultants Constantine Menges and Michael Ledeen, and Assistant Secretary of State Elliott Abrams. After each appearance, the preacher-emcee urged his audience to lobby Congress in favor of aid to the Contras.

In May 1985, following a telethon on behalf of private Contra benefactor the Knights of Malta, Robertson traveled to Guatemala to deliver nearly $2 million worth of supplies to chief-of-state Gen. Oscar Humberto Mejía Víctores. He then flew on to Honduras where he was saluted by a unit of Contra fighters he helped feed and clothe. All of the proceedings were duly filmed and aired for the home audience.

Though not always as crassly political as the *700 Club*, televangelism has been the single most important ingredient in the rise of the Christian Right. At the end of 1987 – *after* the scandal of television preacher Jim Bakker's sexual improprieties and financial mismanagement – religious broadcasting still grossed two billion dollars a year. At that time, Christian broadcasters controlled more than one thousand full-time radio stations and more than two hundred full-time television stations, about 10 percent of radio and 14 percent of all television stations in the United States.[1]

Except for the corporate network owners, evangelical Christians are the only political constituency to enjoy such unrestrained access to television and radio airwaves, a literal license to bombard the U.S. public with their theo-political message. While statistics on audience size vary, millions of American viewers do watch the television preachers regularly. Even assuming that the religious broadcasters preach to the already converted, they hold enormous power to mobilize the faithful.

Just as control of the secular media has become increasingly monopolized by several dozen corporations, the executive committee of the National Religious Broadcasters Association and the leaders of the major religious cable networks are in a position to determine what kind of broadcast message sinks or swims. Pat Robertson's Christian Broadcasting Network is the largest, followed by Trinity Broadcasting Network and the Inspirational Network (formerly PTL). Dozens of independently produced daily and weekly programs are syndicated on these three big networks.

Although the spring 1988 demise of Jimmy Swaggart's television empire dealt a serious blow to the prestige of religious broadcasting in the eyes of secular society, neither the Swaggart nor the PTL scandal seems to have hurt the industry as a whole. Trinity Broadcasting, the second largest of the religious networks (which owns and operates 130 stations in the United States), continues to expand and, in fact, recently became the first religious network to broadcast in the South African bantustans. By October 1988, TBN had opened new stations in the United States, completed construction on a station in El Salvador, received permission to broadcast in Honduras, and begun plans for stations in Bolivia and Brazil.[2]

For all its media power, the Christian Right represents a

---

1. A. Dubro, "All that Heaven Allows," *Venture*, November 1987, pp. 83–90; National Religious Broadcasters figures as of February 1988. In July 1988, the Federal Communications Commission reported a total of 10,348 radio stations and 1,381 television stations in the United States. These figures exclude the many local television stations that broadcast only one or two religious programs daily and several on Sundays. The rough proportions also do not account for relative signal areas, which vary greatly for Christian radio stations.
2. TBN newsletter, October 1988.

disproportionately small slice of North American Christianity. Prior to the 1960s, the mainline denominations were fairly well represented on the screen, as government regulations required that churches and other public groups be provided with a weekly allotment of free air time.

The rules of the game changed dramatically in 1960 when the Federal Communications Commission decided that no public interest was served by distinguishing between "sustaining time programs" – those using air time offered free by the networks – and "commercially sponsored programs," in evaluating a station's commitment to the public interest.[3] Local network affiliate managers began to include the air time sold to syndicated evangelical programmers in their weekly "public service" allotment.

At about the same time, the FCC also determined that religious programming should not be restricted by rules limiting the amount of commercial time for each broadcast hour. While non-religious shows would continue to be held to a specified proportion of air time for commercials, paid-time religious programs were allowed to become essentially program-long fundraisers.

The ability to buy air time, then, became the primary factor behind the spread of a particular brand of Christianity. The mainline denominations, with their staid Sunday morning inspirationals and public affairs talk shows, simply could not or would not compete with the more zealous fundamentalist broadcasters who seemed not the least bit squeamish about passing the proverbial collection plate on the air.

The lack of government regulation allows religious broadcasters to sidestep normal prohibitions on political lobbying by non-commercial, tax-exempt organizations. In 1987, a congressional committee chaired by Rep. J.J. Pickle, Democrat of Texas, went through the motions of investigating the major television ministries, following widespread concern over the PTL network's dubious fund-raising ethics. The committee spent much of the hearing day reassuring representatives of the National Religious Broadcasters that Congress had no intention of interfering with their tax-exempt status.

3. P. Horsfield, *Religious Television: The American Experience* (New York, 1984), p. 13.

The committee was undisturbed by testimony that on eighty-five of Pat Robertson's programs alone, a total of 122.5 minutes of air time were spent lobbying for aid to the Contras. The more than $400,000 this cost the Christian Broadcasting Network (not counting the expense of flying film crews to Central America) was paid out of tax-deductible donations, in an apparent violation of CBN's tax-exempt status.[4]

A pair of 1984 studies, conducted by the Gallup Organization and the University of Pennsylvania's Annenberg School of Communications, concluded that, contrary to popular belief, religious television viewing does not decrease church attendance nor donations to churches, but rather inspires activism. The study also found that Pat Robertson's Christian Broadcasting Network – with its programming focus on news and public affairs instead of religious instruction – tended to attract more educated urban young adults than any of the other television ministries.[5]

While religious broadcasting was still in its infancy, politically minded evangelicals were already capitalizing on the link between TV preaching and activism to launch a movement. First came a number of influential "parachurch" organizations. In 1951, Campus Crusade for Christ formed student "cell groups" on the UCLA campus. It then concentrated on drawing young people from the 1960s counterculture into the born-again "Jesus People" movement. In 1967, it formed a countercultural "front" organization on the University of California's Berkeley campus and launched a "Revolution Now" campaign to siphon off anti-Vietnam war protesters.[6] Today, it is one of the most important missionary organizations in Latin America.

Full Gospel Businessmen's Fellowship International was conceived in 1952 by founder Demos Shakarian as a means to bring middle-class businessmen to Christ. It played a major

---

4. U. S. House of Representatives, Subcommittee on Oversight of the Committee on Ways and Means, *Federal Tax Rules Applicable to Tax-Exempt Organizations Involving Television Ministries* (Serial 100–43), 6 October 1987, p. 360–368.

5. B. Spring, "A Study Finds Little Evidence that Religious TV Hurts Local Churches," *Christianity Today*, 18 May 1984.

6. See B. Bright, *Come Help Change the World* (San Bernardino, Calif., 1985), and R. Quebedeaux, *I Found It: The Story of Bill Bright and Campus Crusade*, (San Francisco, 1979).

role in the burgeoning "charismatic renewal movement," unifying classical Pentecostals and denominational Christians who were discovering the "spirit baptism." By the early 1960s, clusters of straight-laced denominational Protestants found themselves speaking in tongues and challenging the mainstream view that supernatural "gifts of the spirit" were meant only for Christ's early disciples. In the aftermath of the second Vatican Council, with its emphasis on empowering laity, young Catholics active in the Cursillo movement (started in Spain under Franco) began experiencing the "charisms" and forged links with their Protestant Pentecostal brethren.[7]

In the late 1960s and early 1970s, part of the charismatic movement adopted what is called "shepherding" or "discipleship" to offer Christians the close bonds of a "spiritual family" in exchange for full-time commitment and "submission" to elders. An estimated one million U.S. Christians belong to shepherding churches. As their leaders intended, shepherding dramatically increased rates of evangelism.

The most extreme groups require members to obtain approval from their leadership before buying a car, starting a new job or going out on a date. Coerced confessions of sin, all-night "prayer cell" meetings and large financial commitments are commonplace in shepherding churches. At the top of the pyramidical chains of command are a group of Protestant and Catholic "apostles" who have worked together for nearly a decade; for a time they met secretly and called themselves "the Council."[8]

One of the missionary groups sponsored by U.S. shepherds is the Texas-based Paralife Ministries, which conducts "civic action" projects in El Salvador – including mobile health and dental clinics, construction of schools, seminars for evangelical pastors and Sunday preaching at Salvadoran military bases. In one session, Paralife's "Brother" John Steer explained to the troops that "killing for the joy of it was wrong, but killing because it was necessary to fight against an anti-Christ system, communism, was not only right but a duty of every Christian."[9]

7. See A. McNicoll, *Catholic Cults* (Toronto, 1982); and V. Synan, *The Twentieth Century Pentecostal Explosion* (Altamonte Springs, Fla., 1987).
8. S. Diamond, *Spiritual Warfare*, (Boston, 1989).
9. As quoted in Paralife Ministries newsletter, "Living Words," September–October 1986, p. 8. Paralife leader Cubie Ward works with the

The conviction that the ends justify the means is a component of "dominion" or "kingdom" theology, which shepherding leaders have been preaching since the early 1980s. In this
version of eschatology, or "endtimes" teaching, through social
activism the Body of Christ gradually takes over secular institutions and ushers in Christ's millennial reign on earth. That
is, by getting involved in politics, evangelicals can build God's
kingdom here on earth.

On the surface, dominion theology rhetoric sounds like the
pronouncements of liberation theologians. In the same way,
the authoritarian "cell groups" used by Christian Right shepherds mirror the democratically constructed "base communities" and Bible study groups spawned in Latin America by
Vatican II.

However, the political lessons drawn by dominionists and
liberationists are totally at odds. In fact, dominion theolo-
gists see themselves as an on-the-ground combat force against
liberation theology. "The war ideologically is being fought
between the Protestant liberationists and us," says Dominion
publisher Gary North, whose materials are now being incorporated into the training program for Youth with a Mission
missionaries.[10] Shepherding churches got involved in politics
precisely to counter the grass-roots success of liberation theology.

In shepherding circles, dominion has gradually displaced
Armageddon theology – the notion that immediately prior to
Christ's return believers will be "caught up in the air" and
spared seven years of "tribulation" climaxing in the Battle of
Armageddon. Leaders of the Christian Right undoubtedly
recognized Armageddon theology's limited potential to
mobilize activists for the long haul. After the sense of ur-
gency fades, it produces, at best, a contented fatalism. As one
"dominionist" puts it, "bugout theology does not produce

---

shepherding umbrella organization Coalition on Revival. Paralife is assisted
by the Church on the Rock in Rockwall, Texas, whose senior pastor Larry Lea
doubles as Dean of the Oral Roberts School of Theology. See M. O'Brien,
"The Christian Underground," *Covert Action Information Bulletin*, no. 27 (Spring
1987), p. 35.

10. G. North, *Backward Christian Soldiers: An Action Manual for Christian
Reconstruction*, (Tyler, Texas, 1984), p. 107.

armies, only refugees."[11] Besides, if anything might arouse public outcry over the political clout of the Christian Right, it would be the realization that millions of born-again Christians might be eagerly awaiting their fellow citizens' bloody demise.

While the Charismatic wing of the evangelical movement experimented with authoritarian group dynamics and developed a rigid, dichotomous worldview, political commitment also intensified among the more moderate evangelicals affiliated with Billy Graham. Beginning in the early 1960s, Graham encouraged his colleagues at *Christianity Today* magazine to criticize the policies of the World Council of Churches, the largest Protestant umbrella organization. The WCC, Graham argued, was downplaying global evangelism in favor of assisting progressive political movements around the world, when "the task is to relate the changeless gospel to a changing world."[12]

Beginning in 1966, Graham sponsored a series of evangelical conferences to address this concern, culminating in the 1974 International Conference on World Evangelism in Lausanne, Switzerland. There, four thousand evangelical leaders from 150 countries – including one thousand from the Third World – concluded that political action was consistent with the Biblical mandate to evangelize the world. With a growing proportion of the church residing in underdeveloped nations, they noted, to be at all effective evangelists have to address in some way the real human needs of their potential converts.

In the Lausanne Covenant, a fifteen point doctrinal treatise, the conference participants adopted a social mandate that read:

> Although reconciliation with man is not reconciliation with God, nor is social action evangelism, nor is political liberation salvation, nevertheless we affirm that evangelism and sociopolitical involvement are both part of our Christian unity.[13]

11. Author's interview with Gary North, 2 March 1988.
12. Quoted in J. Pollock, *Billy Graham: Evangelist to the World*, (San Francisco, 1979), pp. 200–201.
13. "The Lausanne Covenant," and "The View from Lausanne," *Christianity Today*, 16 August 1974, p. 23; "The Gospel and Society," *Christianity Today*, 13 September 1974.

Christianity Today editor Harold Lindsell then threw down the gauntlet, promoting the Lausanne movement as an ideological alternative to the progressive direction taken by the World Council of Churches:

> It boldly challenges the increasing theological deviations of the WCC . . . theological compromise, syncretistic concessions, universalistic presuppositions, a radically changed view of the mission of the church, and a commitment to revolution to break down political structures and to bring in socialism by the overthrow of capitalism. . . . The conciliar movement and the Marxists both sound the note of a forthcoming man-made utopia. The eschatology of Lausanne left no room for such farfetched and unrealistic dreams. Rather, there was the warning of the coming of false christs and false prophets before the advent of the Antichrist.[14]

Since 1974, countless evangelical organizations have adopted the Lausanne Covenant as their own statement of faith. Thousands of Christians faithful to Lausanne met in Manila in the summer of 1989.

The Lausanne emphasis on culturally relevant evangelism inspired the creation of the U.S. Center for World Missions in Pasadena, California, in 1975. USCWM founder Ralph Winter teaches anthropology and linguistics at what he calls his "Missions Pentagon." Divided into regional "institutes," the Center's three hundred researchers are engaged in sophisticated studies of as yet unevangelized "people groups." Winter's most prized contribution to world evangelism is the Global Mapping Project, a computer data bank that compiles field data gathered by dozens of U.S. missions agencies, including the Wycliffe Bible Translators and World Vision. At the touch of a button, missionary strategists can retrieve color-coded up-to-the-minute statistics on the language, culture, political attitudes, and natural resources of ethnic groups from Papua New Guinea to the Amazon jungles.[15]

14. H. Lindsell, "Lausanne '74: An Appraisal," *Christianity Today*, 13 September 1974.
15. "Unreached peoples: a movement – a strategy," The U.S. Center for World Missions booklet, 1988. Contrary to popular stereotypes generated by the preacher scandals of 1987 and 1988, evangelical missionary strategists display a remarkable degree of interorganizational cooperation, often with

This social science approach to evangelism has coincided with the growth of the Protestant missionary force. Between 1975 and 1985, that force expanded by 26 percent, growing from 31,186 to 39,309 full-time missionaries in the field. A more dramatic rise was seen in the number of "short-term" missionaries, which grew from 5,764 to 27,933 during the same ten-year period.[16] In 1985, World Vision's Missions Advanced Research and Communications Center (MARC) reported 764 U.S. and Canadian missions agencies supporting 67,200 overseas representatives and spending in excess of $1 billion in a single year.[17]

Beyond mere growth, there has been a shift in the theo-political orientation of those in the field. Until World War II, Protestant missionary activity was dominated by denominations belonging to the National Council of Churches (NCC), such as the United Methodists and the Presbyterian Church, U.S.A. By the late 1960s, less than half the total missionary force was represented by these "mainline" churches.[18] According to missionary strategist C. Peter Wagner, the NCC's Division of Overseas Ministries had 8,279 missionaries in the field in 1969. Ten years later, that figure had dropped 40% to 4,817.[19] By 1988, Wycliffe Bible Translators was sponsoring 5,500 linguists and missionaries in the field; as of 1985, Youth With a Mission (closely aligned with the shepherding movement) had 1,741 foreign missionaries.[20] This trend toward dominance by conservative evangelical missionaries is certainly due in no small part to the ideological fervor and commitment induced by the shepherding movement's tight organizational structures.

---

overlapping high-level personnel. World Vision president emeritus Ted Engstrom, for example, uses his WV office to direct Campus Crusade's "Global 2000" project. Dale Kietzman, who spent decades as Wycliffe Bible translator coordinator for anthropology and community development, now heads the U.S. Council for World Missions' short-term missionary project.

16. "Overseas Missions: What Lies Ahead?" *Christianity Today*, 5 February 1988.

17. S. Wilson and J. Siewert, eds., *Mission Handbook: North American Protestant Ministries Overseas*, 13th ed. (Monrovia, Calif., 1985), p. 11.

18. "Protestantism's Foreign Legion," *Time*, 16 February 1987, p. 62.

19. C. P. Wagner, "The Greatest Church Growth is Beyond our Shores," *Christianity Today*, 18 May 1984, p. 25.

20. Interview with Wycliffe, 27 July 1988; also Wilson and Siewart, *Missions Handbook*, p. 313.

The sheer number of individual missionaries and missionary projects offers a feast for U.S. government agencies. In 1975, Christianity Today estimated that

> between 10 and 25 percent of America's thirty five thousand Protestant and seven thousand Catholic foreign missionaries have given information to intelligence authorities... The average would be higher among missionaries serving in rural areas – where reliable information is hard to come by – and in places where there is social and political unrest; lower among missionaries in urban areas, where information is readily obtainable.[21]

Overseas Crusades, until recently headed by Argentine evangelist Luis Palau, reported that at one time virtually all of its personnel were regularly debriefed by the CIA.[22]

In 1976, amid general public outcry over CIA abuses, the agency released a carefully worded statement at a joint National Association of Evangelicals – National Religious Broadcasters meeting: that the CIA would no longer initiate contacts but "would listen if a missionary or clergyman volunteers information."[23]

After Billy Graham and his associates propagated the Lausanne Covenant, Christian Right politics in the United States went big time. The dramatic entrance of conservative Christians into the political arena during the 1970s became a crucial factor in the rise of the New Right.[24] According to Carolyn

---

21. "Conversing with the CIA," *Christianity Today*, 10 October 1975.

22. Ibid.

23. "New CIA Policy," *Christianity Today*, 12 March 1976. The policy is contained in a declassified CIA memo, dated 12 February 1976, which reads: "CIA recognizes that members of these groups may wish to provide information to the CIA on matters of foreign intelligence of interest to the U.S. government. The CIA will continue to welcome information volunteered by such individuals.

"It is agency policy not to divulge the names of cooperating Americans. In this regard CIA will not make public, now or in the future, the names of any cooperating journalists or churchmen." Declassified CIA cable, No. 1217002, dated 12 February 1976; released 28 September 1978; (Woodbridge, Conn., 1984).

24. Author's interview, 3 February 1988, with Carolyn Sundseth, head of Americans for Robertson, and President Reagan's former Associate Director for the Office of Public Liaison at the White House. Sundseth worked as Joseph Coors's chief administrative assistant and helped Coors and Weyrich establish these right-wing organizations. She later assisted Weyrich and his colleagues Richard Viguerie and Howard Phillips in persuading Jerry Falwell to set up the Moral Majority.

Sundseth, former assistant to beer magnate Joseph Coors, it was with the intention of organizing the political yearnings of evangelicals, that Coors and his junior associate Paul Weyrich founded the Heritage Foundation in 1973 and the Committee for the Survival of a Free Congress a year later. In 1974, Bill Bright of Campus Crusade and several of his wealthy business associates started Third Century Publications and began issuing manuals for evangelical political activism.[25] That same year, New Right direct mail expert Richard Viguerie launched *Conservative Digest* magazine to bridge the gap between the "populist" Right in the southern states (including George Wallace's constituency) and the northeastern conservatives who dominated the Republican party.

By 1980, a panoply of Christian Right groups – most prominently the Moral Majority, the Religious Roundtable and Christian Voice – took credit for defeating liberal congressional incumbents, including Senators George McGovern, Democrat of South Dakota, John Culver, Democrat of Iowa, and Birch Bayh, Democrat of Indiana (who lost his seat to Dan Quayle), and for sending Ronald Reagan to the White House. The number of conservative Christians who registered to vote for the first time in 1980 has been estimated at two million, a sizeable proportion of the 26 percent of the electorate who voted for Reagan.[26] Pollster Louis Harris estimated that white fundamentalist voters accounted for two-thirds of Reagan's ten-point margin over Jimmy Carter.[27]

It was their preoccupation with abortion and school prayer that brought fundamentalist and charismatic Christian voters

---

Coors provided seed money, but over the years an even larger contributor has been Richard Mellon Scaife. See J.S. Saloma III, *Ominous Politics* (New York, 1984), pp. 24–32. On Scaife, see K. Rothmeyer, "Citizen Scaife," *Columbia Journalism Review*, July–August 1981. Rothmeyer notes Scaife's business ties with Forum World Features, a CIA media proprietary, and later his joint ventures with Michigan newspaper publisher John McGoff, who received millions of dollars of South African "Information Project" money to purchase U.S. media outlets during the 1970s.

25. For example, J. Wallis and W. Michaelson, "The Plan to Save America," *Sojourners*, April 1976.

26. J. K. Guth, "The New Christian Right," in *The New Christian Right: Mobilization and Legitimation*, R.C. Liebman and R. Wuthnow, eds., (New York, 1983), p. 37.

27. K. Phillips, *Post-Conservative America*, (New York, 1982), p. 191.

to the polls, but leaders of the moral crusade quickly joined experienced activists on foreign and military policy issues. In 1981, Moral Majority's Tim LaHaye became the first president of the Council for National Policy, a secretive organization modeled on the "liberal" Council on Foreign Relations. CNP brought together an impressive array of television preachers, corporate executives and government and military leaders. According to one founder, Central America topped their agenda.[28] In fact, CNP would soon become responsible for coordinating private aid to the Contras.

A little more than a year after Reagan's inauguration, the Christian Right saw its first major victory when a military coup in Guatemala brought a "brother in the Lord" to power. Press accounts of Gen. Efraín Ríos Montt's membership in the Verbo church portrayed U.S. evangelical support for his regime as a fluke involving only that isolated Pentecostal "sect." In fact, Ríos Montt drew material support and good press from small shepherding sects like Verbo, from the large, well-heeled broadcast networks, and even from the usually centrist *Christianity Today* magazine.

In many ways, the Ríos Montt tenure marked a turning point for Christian Right activists, who midway through President Reagan's first term realized that some of Reagan's promises – ending abortion, instituting school prayer, etc. – would not be fulfilled. Organizationally, the private aid campaign to Ríos Montt was a dry run for later involvement in funneling aid to the Nicaraguan Contras. However vicarious, the experience of a born-again Christian shepherding an entire nation reinforced the notion that they could seize the reins of power and install – by force if necessary – their version of the kingdom of God on earth. The massive human rights violations which characterized the general's rule failed to diminish his stature among conservative evangelicals, who to this day consider him a hero.

While Christian activists were getting hands-on experience in Guatemala, another form of low-intensity warfare was being

---

28. Author's interview, July 1987, with Alton Ochsner, who claims he was the major organizer of the Council for National Policy. It was Ocshner who recruited Louisiana state legislator Louis "Woody" Jenkins into the Contra cause and helped him start Friends of the Americas.

waged against liberation theology here at home. The first sign was the 1981 formation of the Institute for Religion and Democracy, which had its roots in the "Good News" movement, a right-wing sector of the United Methodist church. IRD was the brainchild of a coterie of intellectuals linked to the Reagan Administration, mostly "neo-conservatives" from Social Democrats U.S.A. and the Coalition for a Democratic Majority (right-wing Democrats who split from the party in the wake of the McGovern candidacy in 1972). IRD picked up in the United States where Billy Graham and the Lausanne movement left off, fueling long-standing charges that the World Council of Churches was aiding and abetting "terrorism" through its indirect support of Third World liberation movements. In 1982, IRD provided *Reader's Digest* with material for a hit piece on the WCC and the U.S.-based National Council of Churches. CBS's "60 Minutes" then broadcast the smear in prime time. This set off an organizing drive by conservatives within the mainstream Protestant churches to challenge the NCC's progressive posture on U.S. foreign policy. Some would argue that the recent relocation of the Presbyterian Church's national office from the NCC building in New York to Louisville, Ky., was one of the consequences.

After its much publicized media attacks on the NCC, the IRD adopted the role of "religious" critic of Nicaragua's alleged persecution of the faithful. Yet by 1988, the IRD was all but invisible to those not on its short mailing list. Through its newsletter, it continues to play watchdog on "religious persecution" in the Soviet Union and Cuba, and has focused on the need to prevent "violent revolution" in South Africa, financing "democratic" church and development organizations in that country.

A far more subtle and insidious attack against the liberal church is in the making and its targets seem blissfully unaware of it all. For years, the National Association of Evangelicals has been concerned that the loudest Christian voices on arms control and peace issues are on the Left. Now they have come up with a detailed long-term strategy to counter that by instituting programs of "Peace, Freedom and Security Studies" (PFSS) in churches, evangelical colleges and seminaries.[29] Should PFSS be successful in propagating a right-

wing worldview on national security issues, the IRD's spo-
radic propaganda blitzes against the National Council of
Churches may well be replaced by a greater threat to progressive church politics: a network of educated, committed church
ideologues prepared to mobilize their constituencies in favor
of U.S. militarism and political subversion abroad.

The PFSS project was dreamed up by veteran right-wing
activist Robert Pickus, an early proponent of the IRD[30] who
has spent most of his life working to undermine the peace
movement, first during the Vietnam war and later through
his World Without War Council. The National Association of
Evangelicals (NAE) is in the process of recruiting a PFSS contact
at each of the scores of evangelical colleges in the United
States to, as Pickus says, "find people who want to make part
of their portfolio the understanding of these problems," to
recruit evangelical professors and university students, and to
arrange fellowships for the promotion of their careers.

One result of the NAE project is likely to be a continuing
realignment of evangelicals toward the Republican party.[31]
Since the late 1970s, whether to work within the Republican
party has been a major question for Christian Right leaders.
Despite disappointment over Ronald Reagan's social policy
and distrust of establishment cabinet members like George
Shultz and Frank Carlucci, the President's persona appealed

---

29. *Christianity Today*, 15 May 1987. Until the NAE entered the debate on
nuclear weapons, the major evangelical groups addressing the issue were
Evangelicals for Social Action and Sojourners, both progressive outfits.

30. Author's interview with Pickus, 22 August 1988. Former OSS officer
Robert Pickus has served as a consultant to the State Department and to the
USIA. The World Without War Council receives the largest chunk of its
funding from the U.S. Institute of Peace, a government-linked organization
similar to the National Endowment for Democracy, for a project to "profile"
the movements against intervention in Central America and against apartheid. In the 1960s, Pickus was the mentor of David Jessup who went on to
found the IRD. He later trained the IRD's current director Kent Hill. Pickus
and his protégé George Weigel were among a small group who promoted the
formation of the National Endowment for Democracy.

31. In 1976, the majority of evangelicals voted for Southern Democrat
Jimmy Carter (himself a Baptist). Philips, *Post-Conservative America*, p. 91.
When Carter ran for reelection in 1980, 17% fewer white Protestants voted
for him, and traditional Democratic Southern and border states swung to the
Republicans for the second time in history (the first was Nixon's 1972 vic-
tory). *Christianity Today*, 12 December 1980, p. 53.

to the Christian Right and kept it publicly loyal to the GOP. Christian Right activists are less than enthusiastic about George Bush and worry that he will not even give lip service to their social agenda. They did, however, formally close ranks to campaign against Michael Dukakis.

Though Pat Robertson did not come close to winning his party's presidential nomination, his forces gained valuable campaign skills and penetrated state and local Republican parties, re-registering thousands of Democratic evangelicals to vote for their candidate in Republican primaries.[32] The head of the Robertson campaign in Nevada became the state party chair and, at the GOP convention in New Orleans, Robertson supporters dominated the national delegations of Alaska, Georgia, Hawaii and Washington.[33] Robertson claimed that 13 percent of all the delegates, though committed to vote for Bush, were Robertson workers in their home states.[34] Even before the convention was over, Robertson established a political action committee to bankroll voter registration and education efforts, groom right-wing candidates for local, state and federal races, and lay the groundwork for his own future presidential campaigns.

A survey of Republican party voters conducted in 1987 showed that almost 30 percent of Robertson's donors had become politically active only within the previous ten years, contrasted with 7 to 12 percent of contributors to other GOP contenders. The same survey found that Robertson backers were as concerned about fiscal and foreign policy issues as the more traditional Republicans.[35]

The Republican establishment, though skeptical and more than a little nervous about letting a crop of zealous Christian crusaders join the ranks, has had no choice but to embrace them. Despite their unpolished demeanor, Christian Right activists offer the GOP something it has lacked this century: a grass-roots constituency through which the party can expand its base beyond the wealthy and replace the Democrats as the majority party.

32. *Washington Post*, 12 February 1988.
33. *Christian Science Monitor*, 15 August 1988.
34. *Wall Street Journal*, 16 August 1988.
35. J. C. Green and J.L. Guth, "The Christian Right in the Republican Party: The Case of Pat Robertson's Supporters," *The Journal of Politics* 50 (1988), p. 159.

The introduction of Christian Right activists to the concept and logistics of counterinsurgency warfare – first on behalf of Guatemalan dictator Ríos Montt and later as part of the private Contra aid network – established a very dangerous precedent. Out of the reach of congressional control, missionary organizations can pursue foreign adventures that the government is prevented from engaging in directly, and they can use their media power to build support for such activities. Private foreign policy practiced by right-wing evangelicals, with veiled encouragement from the national security establishment, is likely to be repeated as the Bush administration confronts liberation movements (and congressional restrictions) in southern Africa, the Philippines and, most imminently, El Salvador. Should the Bush administration decide to pull out all the stops to "save" El Salvador, the Christian Right's broadcasters, ideologues and hands-on counterinsurgency operatives may prove to be irresistible assets.

In spite of the Christian Right's considerable strengths – its phenomenal media access, missionary infrastructure, and value to the Republican party – victory at home and abroad remains a far-off vision. It is not likely that these zealots will actually "take dominion" over an increasingly secular North American society. Even with the encouragement of the White House, evangelicals have failed to legislate the supremacy of the traditional nuclear family. But how much damage will they do in pursuit of the "kingdom"? How many "freedom fighters" will they arm? How many converts will be persuaded to accept the status quo and wait for their just rewards in the hereafter?

This will depend, first of all, on the extent that evangelical leaders are able to consolidate the commitment of activists aroused by the leadership of Ronald Reagan. But in the long run, the success of the religious Right will be determined by the response of progressive forces to the ideological warfare being waged against them.

The Contras' Chaplains

Rev. Phil Derstine of Gospel Crusade, Inc., in Bradenton, Fa., kept the U.S. government informed of his activities in support of the Contras. "Often as soon as we get out of Nicaragua, there's somebody at the door with a tape recorder in Honduras trying to get intelligence. You've got the CIA. You've got the State Department and who knows who all trying to get information," he told me in early 1987.

But the congressional committees investigating the Iran-Contra scandal apparently were not among those "trying to get information." Religious operations like Derstine's were left completely untouched, even though he told reporters that Oliver North had "set up" the logistics for him to bring tons of supplies to the contras, and that he "could have" received money from North's infamous safe at the National Security Council. Derstine confirmed that North had made similar arrangements for other U.S. Christian Right groups, but said that North kept that information compartmentalized.

A number of factors made the Christian Right's decentralized Central America projects ideal for low-intensity warfare. Incorporated as religious entities, they are exempt from financial disclosure requirements. Should one small operation be exposed for wrongdoing and/or direct links with the U.S. government, another is ready to take its place. The sheer number of U.S.-based "ministries" makes it difficult to monitor their activity.

Among the Christian contra aid groups left intact – and therefore potentially useful in the future – is the Christian Emergency Relief Teams (CERT), based in southern California. CERT claims to have supplied sixty thousand pounds of tools, medicine and seeds and to have constructed a 2,700-foot jungle warehouse with an adjoining 3,000-foot airstrip.[36] CERT teams accompanied Contra combatants during battles with Nicaraguan troops. "We are protected by the freedom fighters. They are our guides. They will not allow us in areas that are not safe," a CERT spokesperson told me. Among other supplies, CERT gave Contra fighters specially designed hot-weather boots, donated by High Tech Boots, a company owned by Youth with a Mission missionaries. CERT's self-promotional packet included a congratulatory May 1986 mailgram from President Reagan and a photocopy of a 4

36. CERT fundraising letter, 16 September 1985.

February 1986 White House schedule for a National Religious Broadcasters briefing, featuring presentations from CERT's David Courson and Oliver North. Even after the Contras signed a ceasefire agreement in March 1988, CERT circulated a "thank you" note from Adolfo Calero and continued delivery runs to contra camps in Honduras. In September 1988, CERT announced that FDN leader Joseph Douglas had joined the California office staff.

El Salvador has been a favorite target of the Christian Right. One of the largest projects there is Paralife Ministries headed by Dr. Cubie Ward of Texas. Ward has boasted of his close relationship with the Salvadoran military and President José Napoleon Duarte, claiming that Duarte was having dinner with him on the December 1980 night when four U.S. churchwomen were murdered by a death squad.[37]

Paralife has constructed medical clinics in San Salvador, Colima, and other parts of the country with financial assistance from the Tear Fund in England and from U.S. AID, channeled through the Missionary Assistance Program (MAP) of Georgia. Most of Paralife's church sponsorship comes from Larry Lea's thirteen thousand-member Church on the Rock in Rockwall, Tex., which is closely affiliated with Oral Roberts University. Church on the Rock's Dr. Joyce Shotwell organized Paralife's ten-day medical brigades to El Salvador. Paralife staff also provided "ministry" to Salvadoran soldiers at the El Paraiso army base.

Christian Anti-Communism Crusade's Latin America director James Colbert worked with the Duarte government to blanket San Salvador with anticommunist messages on state-owned radio stations. Colbert said the Salvadoran government provided CACC with helicopters to deliver thousands of pieces of literature in FMLN-held territories.[38] The Salvadoran government also worked with Assemblies of God minister John Bueno to provide New Testaments to Salvadoran school children. Bueno's Centro Evangelístico sponsored a network of grade schools attended by thirty thousand students.[39]

---

37. Paralife organizational outline, distributed in 1986.
38. Author's interview with James Colbert, 7 July 1988.
39. Information provided by Life Publishers of Miami, Fla.

Denver-based Harvesting in Spanish (HIS) sponsored a Christian school for one thousand children near La Libertad. HIS purchased seventy-five acres of ocean-front land for what it describes as a model village that will include an orphanage, medical and dental clinic, drug and alcohol rehabilitation center, and occupational training center. HIS has organized teams of short-term missionaries to do construction work. While in the country, they also travel to military bases to minister to Salvadoran troops.[40]

World Relief has also been active in El Salvador, an arm of the National Association of Evangelicals. World Relief maintains numerous projects in Central America, largely funded by U.S. AID. In effect, the U.S. taxpayer has been subsidizing World Relief's evangelical agenda: overhead costs have been paid by the government, freeing privately solicited income for evangelism. A World Relief project report on the resettlement of Salvadoran refugees since 1985 explained the process:

> Funds for the project come from U.S. AID and cannot be used for Christian activities. So World Relief works with a local association of evangelical churches to provide spiritual as well as physical ministries. With private funding World Relief will hire a coordinator to involve village churches in the project.[41]

In Costa Rica, Beverly LaHaye's Concerned Women for America sponsored a refugee camp project called "Amor de la Libertad," [sic] started in 1986 by Rev. Jim Woodall.[42] Woodall was the Costa Rica director for Trans World Missions, which has been active in the region since the early 1960s. Trans World Missions President John Olson produced virulent pro-Contra radio broadcasts syndicated throughout the United States. He also headed his own refugee camp project near San Carlos, Costa Rica, and maintained an anti-Sandinista center in Managua. His field director, Luis Mejía, coordinated medical missions in the Nicaraguan countryside.[43]

40. Interview with HIS's Teresa Chichester, 15 June 1988.
41. World Relief Spring-Summer 1988 project report.
42. L. Witham, "Spontaneous Donation Began Nicaraguan Relief," *Washington Times*, 8 April 1988.
43. Interview with John Olson, 7 June 1988.

It is not known to what extent the religious opposition in Nicaragua received CIA funding, nor how much of it instead relied on "private" donations from the Christian Right. What is clear is that the Christian Right took advantage of the government's respect for religious freedom to sow subversion. One of the U.S. ideological warriors who has been active in Nicaragua is Rev. Geoff Donnan of Caribbean Christian Ministries. In 1987, Donnan began organizing anti-Sandinista clergy using Nicaragua's existing private Christian schools as bases of operation.

"What we hope to do is assist teachers to work within the guidelines of the government so that they're legal, but at the same time promoting a biblical world and life view of Christianity," he explained in early 1987.[44] But a little over a year later, Donnan was more blunt:

> Our plan is simple. We intend to use the current relaxed circumstances to beef up the evangelical church in biblical world and life view teachings which will give them the ability to discern between satanic "liberation theology" and the true liberating Gospel.[45]

Within weeks of the Sapoá truce agreements, Donnan travelled to Nicaragua, opened a center in Managua, and hired an Atlantic Coast Creole, Rev. Ernan Savery, as local director. Donnan spoke with a number of Nicaraguan Christians about his plan to publish a "Christian" history of Nicaragua to be used as a textbook in anti-Sandinista schools. Donnan said he would finance the production and distribution but the text would be written by Humberto Bell, whose book, *Nicaragua: Christians Under Fire*, was financed by the CIA, according to ex-Contra Edgar Chamorro.

In Nicaragua, Donnan made contact with the Consejo Nacional de Pastores Evangélicos Nicaragüenses, a coalition of several hundred Nicaraguan evangelical leaders. CNPEN's

44. Interview with Geoff Donnan, 2 February 1987. Donnan works under the formal sponsorship of Dr. Paul Lindstrom, long-time John Birch Society organizer, leader in the "home schooling" movement, and director of the Christian Liberty Academy Satellite Schools (CLASS) in Illinois. Home schooling, a major organizing issue for the Christian Right, opposes the supposed "secular humanist" bias of public education.
45. April 1988 Caribbean Christian Ministries newsletter, p. 3.

membership is theologically and politically diverse, though generally far more critical of the government than the other leading evangelical umbrella group, CEPAD.[46]

In 1986, the *Washington Post* reported that CNPEN was the primary vehicle through which the United States coordinated antigovernment Protestants in Nicaragua. According to the *Post*, the embassy in Managua included on its staff a political officer who "cultivates and organizes Protestant religious resistance to the Nicaraguan government and keeps track of the activity of church figures who favor the government."[47]

Until January 1986, that embassy official was Jessica Le Croix, who was then replaced by T.J. Rose. Anti-Sandinista ministers who said they received assistance from the embassy included Rev. Boanerges Mendoza, Rev. Ignacio Hernández, and Rev. Rolando Mena. In 1985, when a burned out transmitter tube knocked the evangelical radio station off the air, Le Croix reportedly offered her support in finding a replacement if the broadcasters would denounce the government for closing the station.[48]

Regardless of the diversity of the CNPEN pastors themselves, U.S. Christian Right groups have considered CNPEN as the primary means through which to "pressure" Nicaraguan society, now that the shooting war is largely over. One of these groups is the Pentecostal Chapel Hill Harvester Church in Atlanta, Georgia, pastored by Bishop Earl Paullk. The church is part of the shepherding movement.

"We don't want to make a lot of publicity about what we're doing or how we do it," said Chapel Hill's international director and CNPEN coordinator Pedro Torres, who is Puerto Rican.[49] However, he admitted to providing CNPEN President Felix Rosales with money, videotape players, video teaching

---

46. CNPEN was first brought to the attention of the U.S. evangelical community in 1985 when the Institute for Religion and Democracy published an interview with a journalist named Kate Rafferty of "Open Doors News Service." Rafferty and IRD called on U.S. evangelicals to support CNPEN over CEPAD. The IRD "briefing paper" was reprinted in the State Department's December 1986 report, *Human Rights in Nicaragua under the Sandinistas: From Revolution to Repression.*

47. James A. Gittings, "U.S. Link to Nicaragua Churches Seen," *Washington Post,* 30 August 1986.

48. Ibid.

49. Interview with Pedro Torres, 8 June 1988.

tapes, and books in Spanish. In June 1988, Chapel Hill sponsored a four-week training institute for selected Third World leaders. In addition to teaching some of the seminars, shepherding movement leader Dennis Peacocke paid the travel expenses for two CNPEN pastors. Peacocke and his associate Michael Bresnan have made frequent trips to Central America and have recruited CNPEN pastors to be trained in Costa Rica.

Missionary outfits working through CNPEN have hoped to gradually siphon off public support for the government's fledgling social services infrastructure by offering a private alternative, thereby undermining the Sandinistas' legitimacy. In the rest of Central America, Christian Right "civic action" projects have been working closely with governments to achieve precisely the opposite objective.

Not all right-wing missionaries have given up on the Sandinistas. Members of the Full Gospel Businessmen's Fellowship International and World Vision have begun a campaign to proselytize Nicaraguan leaders, including Daniel Ortega and Tomás Borge. When Jimmy Swaggart took his roadshow to Nicaragua in February 1988 – shortly before his infamous public confession of sexual sin – some evangelical leaders thought their careful work had finally paid off. But no, speculation to the contrary, Daniel Ortega had not been "born again."

AFRICA

·3·

The Religious Right and Low-Intensity Conflict in Southern Africa

JEFFREY MARISHANE

The conscious and intelligent manipulation of the organized habits and opinions of the masses is an important element in democratic society. Those who manipulate this unseen mechanism of society constitute an invisible government which is the true ruling power of our country.... It is the intelligent minorities which need to make use of propaganda continuously and systematically.

— Edward Bernays, 1928

Precedents

The ideas which Bernays expressed[1] demonstrate a distinct pattern of thinking and approach to the role of information and public relations on one side of the class divide in a capitalist society, in particular during a crisis period. Since this style of thinking will be encountered in one form or another throughout our work, it is worth noting early.

Though seldom so clearly articulated, the idea that the popular masses are a blind mob whose actions would lead nowhere unless guided by a select group of heroic leaders is still strongly ingrained in the political thinking of the U.S.

---

1. Cited in J. Mathebula, "Vigilantes: The Myth of Black-on-Black Violence," *Sechaba* (Lusaka), January 1988, p. 24. Bernays was a former consultant to the U.S. Delegation to the Versailles Peace Treaty Conference, and was a former executive of United Fruit Company.

upper class. This idea, which betrays an inherent and deeply held attitude of scepticism of and scorn for the role of the masses, views any action towards social development as determined by the role of leaders rather than an act of social progress in which the popular masses play an active and conscious role. How clearly articulated this idea is depends on a number of factors, among which one can single out the level of economic and scientific development of that particular society.

In recent American history, this idea held particular sway in the Kennedy administration, which had surrounded itself with a group of intellectuals from the Northeastern establishment elite. These intellectuals, who served as advisors, consultants and even heads of federal agencies, viewed world political events from the position of conspirators, as an artful game of successful coups and countercoups in which the popular masses were skillfully manipulated by charismatic if not magical leaders, whom they would blindly follow, regardless of whether these leaders represented their interests or not. Taken to its ultimate end, such a philosophy would even lead to the murder of foreign leaders, such as the assassination of Patrice Lumumba on CIA orders on 17 January 1961, simply because he had accepted Soviet help after the United States itself had turned him down, and because he reportedly practiced traditional forms of worship and smoked marijuana.[2]

It followed from these beliefs that such political intellectuals, who like so many Americans practiced anticommunism as their true religion, would interpret all popular revolutions, in particular those in which some communist presence could be established, as plots masterminded by the Kremlin. If, unfortunately for them, a communist presence in such popular revolutions could not easily be established, they would then go to extreme lengths to find or even invent what they derogatorily referred to as "the hand of Moscow." To them, then, what better solution was there to fighting conspiracy

2. For more details on the circumstances surrounding Patrice Lumumba's assassination see J. Ranelagh, *The Agency: The Rise and Decline of the CIA* (New York, 1986), pp. 336–45; W. Blum, *The CIA: A Forgotten History* (London, 1986), pp. 174–81, 292–99; T. Powers, *The Man Who Kept the Secrets: Richard Helms and the CIA* (New York, 1979), pp. 165–200.

than to organize a counterconspiracy, to combating insurgency than counterinsurgency, to the "export of revolution" than exporting a counterrevolution spearheaded by a murderous elite military force which, more often than not, included mercenaries and was guided by a small group of "special operations" planners from the Defense Intelligence Agency (DIA) or the CIA? Since the Kennedy administration, this philosophical outlook was most strongly embraced by the Reagan administration, with its development of the "low-intensity conflict" doctrine and military strategy.

In going about their work of ideological subversion among the oppressed majority and certain sectors of the privileged white minority in South Africa – and indeed among the entire region's population – American religious right-wing groups and their local offshoots and partners have consciously adopted and then proceeded to implement the CIA maxim that

> the U.S. should make increasing use of nonnationals who, with an effort at indoctrination and training, should be encouraged to develop a second loyalty, more or less comparable to that of the American staff. As we shift our attention to Latin America, Asia and Africa, the conduct of U.S. nationals is likely to be increasingly circumscribed. The primary change recommended would be to build up a system of unofficial cover; to see how far we can go with non-U.S. nationals, especially in the field. . . . Such career agents should be encouraged with . . . training and . . . a prospect of long-term employment to develop a second loyalty . . . . The central task is that of identifying potential indigenous allies – both individuals and organizations – making contact with them, and establishing the fact of a community of interest.[3]

Though this CIA decision has a large bearing on our topic, it is important to avoid adopting too simplistic an approach by attempting to draw a straight line between it and the penetration of American religious Right groups in southern Africa during the last few years. Long before the CIA, British colonial authorities had come to recognize the significant role that religion plays in African politics, and African society

---

3. R. Bissel, former CIA Deputy Director for Covert Operations (Clandestine Services), cited by V. Marchetti and J. D. Marks, *The CIA and the Cult of Intelligence* (New York, 1980), pp. 337–38.

in general, and consequently proceeded to manipulate it in their favor during the independence struggle in Nyasaland, just to mention one case. As a former British police intelligence officer once explained:

> Religion in Central Africa was an alternative to politics. It provided an alternative structure of ambition. In Malawi, we monitored the different religious sects as they emerged and kept an eye on the external organizations willing to support breakaway sects; especially the American ones.... We kept a tight watching brief on them. They also controlled the leading university and were involved with many tribes, so they were a useful place to pick up information.[4]

For their part, the apartheid ideologues had also long before learned to harness the power of religion to pursue their political objectives and justify their harsh oppressive laws against the majority of the South African people. This simple fact can clearly be seen when one reads the South African Constitution, whose authors undoubtedly considered it to be a divine document. Articles 1 and 2, for example, state that

> in obedience to God Almighty and His Holy Word, the Afrikaans people [sic] acknowledge their national destination as embodied in their Voortrekker past, for the Christian development of South Africa, and for that reason accept the Republican Constitution.

The constitution additionally reveals its true nature as a document inspired by fascist ideals, rather than by any divine will, by investing the head of state with powers over and above not just all the enfranchised citizens, but also their elected representatives as assembled in parliament. "The State President," it states, "is further directly and only responsible to God and over against the people for his deeds in fulfilment of his duties.... He is altogether independent of any vote in Parliament.... The State President decides on all laws, which can only become valid by his personal signature."[5]

---

4. Cited in J. Bloch and P. Fitzgerald, *British Intelligence and Covert Action*, (Dingle, Ireland, 1983), p. 76.
5. Articles 1 and 2 of the South African constitution, in Bunting, *The Rise of the South African Reich* (London, 1986), pp. 107–8.

By the time South Africa became a republic in 1961, a local brand of anticommunism, heavily steeped in Nazi ideas and parading under the cloak of religion, was already in existence. At the core of this reactionary phenomenon was the so-called Inter-Church Anti-Communist Action Committee led by Dr. Jacobus D. (Koot) Vorster, former moderator of the white Dutch Reformed Church (DRC) and brother to the late South African Prime Minister, John B. Vorster. As has been recounted on many other occasions, John Vorster was a former Nazi sympathizer and a leading member of the Ossewa Brandwag (Ox-wagon Sentinel), an avowedly pro-Nazi paramilitary body which opposed South Africa's participation in World War II as a partner of the Allied powers. He was jailed for his pro-Nazi activities, including military sabotage of South Africa's war effort, between September 1942 and January 1944, and thereafter was put under house arrest. While South African troops, including black soldiers, were heroically dying in the war against Nazi Germany and fascist Italy, John Vorster, then an Ossewa Brandwag general for the Port Elizabeth district, made the following statement in 1942:

> We stand for Christian Nationalism which is an ally of National Socialism. You can call this antidemocratic principle dictatorship if you wish. In Italy it is called Fascism, in Germany German National Socialism, and in South Africa Christian Nationalism.[6]

The undiluted Nazi spirit found in the political thinking of the ruling Nationalist party does not stop here. According to its own political philosophy, even the most basic rights of the individual, including those recognized in most Western countries, are to be subjected to the interests of the state and thereby the party which rules it under the slightest pretext. Dr. Cornelius P. (Connie) Mulder, then Minister of the Interior and Information, left no doubt about this when, in the aftermath of the 1976 Soweto youth revolts, and obviously presuming South Africa to be a free state – which it never was under any criteria – he stated:

6. Cited in ibid., p. 98.

In the event of the freedom of the state being threatened and the Government having a choice between the freedom of the state or the individual, we will choose the freedom of the state and will abandon the freedom of the people.[7]

Two years before, Dr. Andries P. Treurnicht, then a prominent member of the Nationalist party and contending to succeed John Vorster, and now leader of the ultra-right Conservative party and still an influential theologian of the white DRC, was trying to find a rationale for the evil apartheid system on Biblical grounds when he wrote, "I know of no other policy as moral, as responsible to the Scriptures as the policy of separate development."[8]

In April 1964 the Inter-Church Anti-Communist Committee sponsored a conference designed to stem the tide of liberal influence then slowly finding its way into the white Dutch Reformed Church and Afrikaner intellectual circles. Convened with heavy-handed anticommunist rhetoric in Pretoria, its organizing committee included Dr. Piet Koornhof, a former secretary of the Afrikaner secret society, the Broederbond, a leading proponent of the apartheid regime's Bantustan policy for many years, and currently South African ambassador to Washington; Ivor Benson, former chief press censor for Ian Smith's renegade Rhodesian regime, and once a senior staff member of the South African Broadcasting Corporation (SABC) and chair of the South African chapter of the World Anti-Communist League (WACL);[9] S.E.D. Brown, past editor of the *South African Observer*, an ultra-right weekly publication; and several Afrikaner racist professors and religious leaders. The conference, which was also attended by several "experts" on communism, called on the apartheid regime to introduce more stringent measures of press censorship, and passed a resolution for the establishment of a permanent National Council to Combat Communism, ostensibly from a Christian perspec-

7. *The Argus* (Cape Town), 6 November 1976.
8. Dr A. P. Treurnicht, *Credo van 'n Afrikaner* (Cape Town, 1975), p. 2, cited in C. Villa-Vicencio, "South Africa's Theologized Nationalism," *The Ecumenical Review* 29, no. 4 (October 1977), p. 381.
9. See Bunting, *South African Reich*, p. 75; D. Knight, *Beyond the Pale: The Christian Political Fringe* (Lancashire, 1982), p. 40; S. Anderson and J. L. Anderson, *Inside the League* (New York, 1986), p. 83.

tive. Dr. J.D. (Koot) Vorster was voted as chairman of this council, and under this mantle he proceeded to organize an International Symposium on Communism in Pretoria in September 1966.

Attending the symposium as special foreign guests were Prof. Stefan Possony, director of Stanford University's Hoover Institute of Peace, War and Revolution and a long-standing member of the defunct American Council for World Freedom (ACWF) and its successor, the U.S. Council for World Freedom (USCWF) which is currently chaired by Maj. Gen. (ret.) John K. Singlaub; Maj. (ret.) Edgar Bundy, a former U.S. Air Force intelligence officer and now head of the Church League of America as well as a Religious Roundtable member; and Suzanne Labin, who is a notorious French right-wing author and head of the WACL's French chapter.

As might be expected, this chapter maintains close ties with the Rev. Sun Myung Moon's CAUSA organization, which in turn is an important sponsor of Jean-Marie Le Pen's National Front.[10] In 1986, the head of CAUSA in France was part of the French delegation to the WACL's annual conference in Luxembourg. Suzanne Labin is also closely associated with the CIA-linked Tradition, Family and Property (TFP), and was "honored" with an invitation by that Catholic sect to St. Michael's Auditorium in São Paulo in 1974. In 1982, the English edition of her pro-Pinochet book, *Chile: The Crime of Resistance*, was published by the U.K.-based Foreign Affairs Publishing Research Institute (FARI) run by Geoffrey Stewart-Smith, a former British Army officer, Conservative M.P., and WACL member until 1974. By February 1983 it had become public knowledge that since the mid-1970s FARI had been both directly and indirectly funded by the apartheid regime.[11] Part of this information was inadvertently revealed by the disgraced Dr. Eschel Rhoodie, the former director of South Africa's now-defunct Department of Information, in 1978, during the height of the "Muldergate" scandal, when in a

10. A report in the British publication *Searchlight* (October 1986) states that "according to Le Pen's estranged wife, CAUSA is an important financier of the National Front."

11. Report by D. Pallister and I. Black in The Guardian (London), 11 February 1983; see also J. Jennings, *Enemy Within: the Freedom Association, the Conservative Party and the Far Right* (London, 1986), p. 9.

recorded interview with a South African journalist, he said:

> The Foreign Policy Institute was the one that was set up by Mr. Geoffrey Stewart-Smith to distribute anticommunist material in Britain and the United States and Europe, and also from time to time to publish such works and material that we felt was necessary for the promotion of South Africa's image in the world, or that would serve to highlight the strategic importance of South Africa.[12]

Among such publications was Bernard Smith's book, *The Fraudulent Gospel*, whose American edition was published by the Church League of America in 1977. In this book, whose revised edition, despite soaring costs in publishing, was strangely enough still selling for two dollars at the end of 1979, Smith bitterly and falsely accuses the World Council of Churches (WCC) of having abandoned the need for evangelism, and complains that its "member churches have too readily surrendered their authority and independence to the WCC."[13] Under the pretext of rejecting terrorism, Smith is also prepared to condone, if not openly support, the state-sponsored terror from which many Third World peoples suffer at the hands of fascist or racist dictatorship regimes, with the explanation that "there are occasions when the Christian is justified in using violence, but never in using terrorism."[14]

In early 1979, when Geoffrey Stewart-Smith was under tremendous pressure to reveal the true source of his body's funding, he would only admit that FARI "was in contact with many similar institutes in other countries" and add that "many of the institutes we deal with are government financed, and you can draw what conclusions you like from that. We do not object to it."[15]

However, one source of FARI's funding was finally exposed when *The Guardian* published a confidential letter, dated 3 October 1980, and addressed to Geoffrey Stewart-Smith at his Whitehall office. The letter was from Johan Adler, a very senior diplomat at the South African embassy in London, and

---

12. Cited in Jennings, *Enemy Within.*
13. B. Smith, *The Fraudulent Gospel: Politics and the World Council of Churches* (London, 1977), p. 6.
14. Ibid., p. 10.
15. *Sunday Telegraph* (London), 25 March 1979.

read in part: "I have been instructed by Pretoria to inform you that the amount allocated to you for 1981 has been cut from R 175,000 [£ 96,000] to R 125,000 [£ 68,000]."[16]

FARI's association with such forces went much further than its links with the apartheid regime. For example, two of its Governing Council members, namely Robert Moss and Brian Crozier, are well known for their key roles in CIA projects. Moss, a former reporter for *The Economist* newsmagazine, was heavily involved in the CIA propaganda campaign which led to the overthrow of Chilean president Salvador Allende in 1973, while Crozier was the director of the London-based Forum World Features news agency between February 1966 and 1974. From its founding until it closed down, Forum World Features was funded by the Paris-based and inaptly named Congress for Cultural Freedom (CCF), which in 1967 was exposed as a CIA front organization. Talking about the many publications under the financial aegis of the CCF during that period, Ray Cline, a former CIA deputy director, once openly stated that they "would not have been able to survive financially without CIA funds."[17] Incidentally, these publications also included *Africa Report*, the New York-based bi-monthly newsmagazine published by the African-American Institute (AAI).

Until its demise in the mid-1970s, the ACWF had been the WACL's U.S. chapter, with Professor Possony playing the major role in persuading its leadership to join the international terrorist network federation. The Unification Church's link to the ACWF was provided by its U.S. president and director of the Tong-il Armaments Industries Co., Neil Salonen, who, along with the Christian Anti-Communism Crusade's Fred Schwarz, Accuracy in Media's Reed Irving, and others, was an ACWF board member. After its demise, the ACWF was replaced by the USCWF, founded on 22 November 1981 with a seed grant of nearly $20,000 from Taiwan, as the WACL's U.S. chapter.

Unlike most of the religious Right groups, the Church League of America, set up in 1937 by Henry P. Crowell, then chairman of the Quaker Oats Co. and founder of the Crowell

---

16. Cited in Jennings, *Enemy Within*.
17. Cited in W. Blum, *The CIA*, 114, 240; see also Jennings, *Enemy Within*, p. 8.

Foundation Trust, and by G.W. Robnett and F.L. Loesch, does not engage itself in evangelical work. Instead, its value to the New Right and religious right-wing causes lies in its purportedly being the largest private intelligence body gathering information on progressive and left-wing organizations and individuals in the United States. Sponsored, among others, by the Conservative Caucus's Howard Phillips; Gen Robert E. Wood, former chairman of Sears, Roebuck and Co.; Savell Avery, chairman of Montgomery Ward and Co. and also of the U.S. Gypsum Corp.; William Randolph Hearst; and the Coors family, it prefers to do its work in almost complete seclusion and offers its services to selected customers on a "need-to-know" basis. In some of its fund-raising brochures, it boasts that

> the Church League of America is the largest private research organization and information center on the operations of the Communist party and the New Left movement in the entire United States.[18] Its research files are priceless and irreplaceable. To them have come representatives of security agencies from the entire free world, staff members of U.S. government committees ... missionaries, policemen, FBI men, business men.[19]

The 1966 International Symposium on Communism held in Pretoria was opened by Dr. J.D. Vorster, who declared in his speech that the greatest enemy they had to confront were the "anti-anticommunists" and "liberals," whom he regarded as the "fifth column" paving the way for a communist take-over of South Africa. His diatribe was supported by none other than Maj. Gen. H.J. van den Bergh, the notorious and disgraced former head of the South African Bureau of State Security (BOSS), who in turn stated:

> We have experienced a considerable amount of political activity by certain student organizations, newspaper reporters, churchmen and other intellectuals. We can assume that at least some of this

18. Fund appeal, Church League of America, 8 January 1977, cited in D. Huntington and R. Kaplan, "Whose Gold is behind the Altar? Corporate Ties to Evangelicals," *Contemporary Marxism*, no. 4, (Winter 1981–82), p. 75.

19. "A Day in the Life of the Church League of America," *Contemporary Marxism*, no. 4 (Winter 1982–82).

can be attributed to subtle influencing and persuasion by secret members of the Communist party.[20]

When he said these words, Major General van den Bergh undoubtedly had in mind the upsurge of an unprecedented mood of "left-wing" dissidence in certain white Afrikaans-speaking circles. This development was illustrated most clearly by the formation of the Christian Institute of Southern Africa in 1963 and the emergence of the "Sestiger" literary movement among Afrikaner writers. The first body included Rev. Dr. C.F. Beyers Naudé, the prominent white Dutch Reformed Church minister who had turned his back on the teachings of his church and the Broederbond, while Prof. André P. Brink, the renowned writer, was a leading Afrikaner member of the second group. To Van den Bergh and most South African supremacists, the fact that the Christian Institute had emerged as a truly multiracial and interfaith body working in close collaboration not only with Catholics but also with the African independent churches, and had even managed to attract the support of Afrikaans speakers of the caliber of Rev. Dr. Beyers Naudé, meant that any white Afrikaans speaker who followed this example would henceforth be denounced as anything from a turncoat to a deserter, if not a traitor, and would be ostracized from the Afrikaner community.

A few months after the Pretoria symposium, Dr. J.D. Vorster paid a visit to the United States and attended an equally anticommunist conference sponsored by the Church League of America. In his address to the conference, he is reported to have made the unfounded and nonsensical statement that the late President John F. Kennedy and South African prime minister Hendrik Verwoerd were both killed by communists. Dr. J.D. Vorster continued his diatribe by blaming the United Nations, "apostate liberalism, misguided humanists, yellow and weak-livered souls, black-hearted traitors and morally rotten creatures"[21] for South Africa's problems and the world's ills. During the next year or so, the Inter-Church Anti-Communist Action Committee continued to organize a series

20. Cited in Bunting, *South African Reich*, p. 77.
21. *Sunday Times* (Johannesburg), 19 March 1967; also cited in Bunting, *South African Reich*, p. 76.

of conferences, seminars and other activities designed to draw white Afrikaans-speaking churchgoers throughout South Africa together under the banner of anticommunism and hatred against their black fellow South Africans. However, the activities of the committee during that period seem to have come to almost nothing, as the group itself withered away into thin air.

While the white South African Dutch Reformed Church was encouraging anti-communist elements with the help of the Church League of America, the U.S. Army, on the other hand, was grooming a group of young white South African military officers to become "low-intensity conflict" warriors. Among them was Gen. Magnus Malan, the current South African Minister of Defense. In 1962 Gen. Malan, freshly graduated from a South African Defence Force (SADF) military staff course, was among those selected to undergo a two-year course at the U.S. Army's Command and General Staff College at Fort Leavenworth, Kansas. Upon graduating from Fort Leavenworth, he was attached for a short while to the 35th Armored Division in Colorado. The Fort Leavenworth college is the leading U.S. military institute for the training of army officers and the formulation of military doctrine. It is therefore hardly surprising that during General Malan's tenure in high military office, the National Security Doctrine (NSD) started to become the norm in South African military thinking. As a result, the SADF organizational structure, though originally based on the British model, gradually came to resemble that of the U.S. Army, with its own counterpart to the U.S. National Security Council (NSC), namely, the State Security Council (SSC), founded in 1978 and complemented by the National Security Management System (NSMS) since 1979. BOSS, now known as the National Intelligence Service (NIS), is also modeled on the CIA, thanks to the role which the U.S. intelligence agency's chief for counterintelligence played in its formation in 1969 and the training which General van den Bergh and some of his associates received from the U.S. during the first days of its existence.[22] Appar-

---

22. See "The SADF: a survey" in *Financial Mail* (Johannesburg), supplement, 10 July 1987; J. K. Mathebula, "Vigilantes: An Arm of State Terrorism," *Sechaba* (Lusaka), 1987, p. 27.

ently influenced by all the above factors, Piet W. Botha, then South African minister of defense, said in 1973:

> I do not wish to spread the alarm, but I must state unambiguously that for a long time already, we have been engaged in a war of low intensity and that this situation will probably continue for some considerable time to come.[23]

Described by Col. John Waghelstein, the commander of the U.S. special operations forces in El Salvador between 1981 and 1982, as "total war at the grassroots level," in which the counterinsurgency forces "use all the weapons of war, including political, economic and psychological warfare, with the military aspect being a distant fourth in many cases,"[24] "low-intensity conflict" was perhaps most succinctly defined by Maj. Gen. John Singlaub in 1980 when he explained:

> The term "unconventional warfare" includes, in addition to terrorism, subversion and guerrilla warfare, such covert and non-military activities as sabotage, economic warfare, support to resistance groups, black and gray psychological operations, disinformation activities and political warfare.[25]

However, to call this brutal form of warfare "low-intensity conflict" is misleading. This was deliberately designed to be misleading since its advocates had come to acknowledge that, as Lt. Gen. Samuel Wilson, former director of the DIA, put it, "there is little likelihood of a strategic nuclear confrontation with the Soviets."[26] Implicit in this acknowledgment is the belief that in order to save Europe and North America from the danger of a nuclear catastrophe, the theater of military confrontation must be shifted to the Third World, whose inhabitants are not only non-Caucasian in terms of their racial origin but, with the exception of a very tiny elite, mostly

23. P.W. Botha, *Defence White Paper* (Pretoria, 1973), p. 2.
24. Col. J. Waghelstein, *Military Review* (Fort Leavenworth, Kansas), May 1985; also cited in S. Miles, "The Real War: Low-Intensity Conflict in Central America," *NACLA Report on the Americas* 20, April–May 1986, p. 19; and Mathebula, "Vigilantes: An Arm of State Terrorism," p. 28.
25. Cited in J. Marishane, "World Vision International: What Is It up to in South Africa?," unpublished mimeograph, January 1989.
26. Cited in S. Miles, "The Real War," p. 19.

poor people. Thus seen in strictly military terms, this latest development in warfare strategy can be "low-intensity conflict" from the perspective of those who plan and implement it, but it is as high-intensity as it is deadly brutal for those who are at the receiving end. Any method used in the execution of this brutal kind of warfare, including assassinations, mutilations, torture, and rape, are allowed under the most unheard-of, hypocritical justifications.

Among such justifications is that, for its proponents, low-intensity conflict is an economically viable enterprise in terms of both human and material costs because it is others who do most of the dying in defense of American interests. As Arnaud de Borchgrave, the New Right ideologue, explains "It is low-intensity warfare in which U.S. troops are not involved. It also involves a small amount of money. . . . It is low-risk warfare with a tremendously high political payoff."[27] If these "others" are perchance not Third World citizens or nations, they would very likely be mostly U.S. citizens of Afro-American or Latin extraction. For instance, it is a little known but nevertheless indisputable fact that during the Vietnam war, many of the "special" operations units trained at Fort Bragg could not master English and that the U.S. Army would send a disproportionate number of Afro-Americans and Latino soldiers to fight the Vietnamese. According to statistics issued by the U.S. Department of Defense in relation to the Vietnam war:

> Blacks were more likely to be (1) drafted (30 percent [of draftees] out of 19 percent [of the general population]); (2) sent to Vietnam; (3) serve in high-risk combat; and consequently, (4) kill, be killed or wounded in battle.[28]

When Grenada, the small Caribbean island of only 133 square miles and with a population of 110,000, was invaded by the United States in October 1983 under the pretext of

27. Arnaud de Borchgrave, cited in "The Reagan Doctrine and Counterrevolution," *NACLA Report on the Americas* 20, July–August 1986; see also *Barricada Internacional* (English edition), 11 September 1986.
28. Cited by J. Mathebula in "Vigilantes: The Myth of Black-on-Black Violence," p. 21.

saving American lives and restoring democracy, blacks, both U.S. citizens and Caribbean nationals, played the major role. The same applied to the occupation of both Beirut and Honduras by U.S. forces.

In the case of Honduras, most of the Texas National Guard troops involved in the Reagan Administration's military maneuvers were Latino-American or, to be more specific, Mexican-American youths. This clearly discernible pattern in U.S. military strategy has understandably raised serious concern in some quarters that one day the U.S. may dispatch Afro-American troops for deployment somewhere in southern Africa to fight their fellow blacks in defense of the interests of the U.S. ruling circles. The building and renovation of the Kamina military air force base in southern Zaire to provide back-up support to UNITA; the refurbishing of the spy satellite communications system operated by the National Security Agency (NSA) in both Swaziland and Hartbeesfontein in South Africa; opening of a Voice of America broadcasting station in Botswana; and heightened CIA activity in general in southern Africa, all seem to indicate a strong move in this direction.

The SADF seems to have lost no time in adopting and implementing this method of counterinsurgency warfare in its low-intensity conflict strategy. For instance, though blacks were only 5 percent of the SADF's troop strength during the late 1970s and early 1980s, they nevertheless represented 20 percent of all the soldiers fighting in the "operational areas." In November 1985 Gen. Magnus Malan, speaking at a Nationalist party meeting held at the military base town of Hoedspruit, revealed that the proportion of black soldiers deployed in Namibia had increased so that they comprised 66.16 percent of all the SADF troops fighting against SWAPO.[29] Earlier on, in February 1981, Maj. Errol Mann, commanding officer of the Caprivi Batallion, made a remark to a SADF press briefing session, according to which "the best way to fight blacks is with other blacks. . . . They are very good in the bush."[30] According to General Malan's bizarre logic, the

29. Cited in J. Mathebula, "Apartheid South Africa Destabilizes Zimbabwe," Sechaba (Lusaka), May 1986; also in Business Day, 15 November 1985.
30. Cited in Mathebula, "Vigilantes: The Myth of Black-on-Black Violence."

use of black soldiers as cannon fodder in the Pretoria regime's first line of defense under the commanding eye of white officers and elite military units is clear proof that the SADF is representative of all South African population groups.

The rapid recruitment of over six thousand black youths, most of them from the ranks of right-wing vigilante groups, the rural poor, and the urban unemployed who are given a fast three-week training course as "special" constables, seems to follow such logic. During this short training course, the future special constables are drilled in the use of the most brutal forms of police repression. This is in addition to the systematic use of black policemen in an auxilliary capacity in the 48,000-strong South African police force, 50 percent of whose members are black (about 40 percent African, 10 percent colored and Indian). To many concerned people, the relative ease with which the Pretoria regime manages to exploit black people in this way would indeed seem odd. It is only when one bears in mind, however, the effects of the unequal development of capitalism in South Africa and the region as a whole, such as the contradiction of the standard of living and lifestyle between urban and rural, the high unemployment rate, influx control measures, etc., that one gets a firm grasp of the real situation.

Another "low-intensity conflict" justification which merits no less attention is the purported defense of the much-talked-about "traditional values" as propagated by former U.S. president Reagan and former British prime minister Thatcher. In an attempt to justify U.S. support of racist and dictatorial regimes all over the world under the pretext of promoting such traditional values, Jeane Kirkpatrick, the former U.S. ambassador to the United Nations, once clearly stated:

> Traditional autocrats leave in place existing allocations of wealth, power, status, and other resources which in most traditional societies favor an affluent few and maintain masses in poverty. But they worship traditional gods and observe traditional taboos. They do not disturb the habitual patterns of family and personal relations. Because the miseries of traditional life are familiar, they are bearable to ordinary people who, growing up in the society, learn to cope.[31]

31. J. Kirkpatrick, "Dictatorships and Double Standards," *Commentary*,

It thus becomes very clear that low-intensity conflict is a reactionary form of warfare, not only because it is designed to protect the ill-earned wealth of the rich against the demands of the poor throughout the world, but also because it is imbued with a deep spirit of racist hatred against blacks in particular and all Third World peoples in general. One observer captured the true essence of this particular form of warfare when he wrote:

> LIC is "total strategy" for the Third World. It weds military programs to humanitarian programs to economic and psychological projects. It is how to wage war invisibly, or wage war and not call it war; how to kill large numbers of people without having to pay the political cost of having your own forces shipped back in zippered body bags. And above all, the LIC strategy weaves all these activities together in the same quilt and titles it "defending freedom."[32]

While the Pentagon was still busy debating the merits and demerits of low-intensity conflict as a new counterinsurgency strategy, South African military planners seemed to have fast absorbed the lessons of the U.S. defeat in Vietnam. These were supplemented by the experience gained in the Rhodesian guerrilla battlefields since Pretoria joined the war in support of the Ian Smith regime in late 1967. With that understanding, South African military intelligence and security police would enjoy the dubious credit of helping the Rhodesian Central Intelligence Organisation (CIO) form the Mozambican National Resistance (MNR) as the first "proinsurgency" in the history of counterinsurgency in 1976.

By 1977 the SADF came up with a proposal made by Piet W. Botha, who, after drawing upon German, French, U.S. and Latin American military literature on counterinsurgency strategy, partly explained the SADF's own "total strategy" against "total onslaught" in the following manner:

November 1979, p. 44; see also J. N. Pallmeyer, *War against the Poor: Low-Intensity Conflict and Christian Faith* (New York, 1989), p. 22.

32. P. Nexbitt, "Terminators, Crusaders and Gladiators: Western Support for Renamo and UNITA," paper presented to the ECASAAMA Conference, Bonn, December 1988.

The process of ensuring and maintaining the sovereignty of a state in a conflict situation has, through the evolution of warfare, shifted from a purely military to an integrated national action. The resolution of a conflict in the times in which we now live demands interdependent and coordinated action in all fields - military, psychological, economic, political, sociological, technological, diplomatic, ideological, cultural, etc. We are today involved in a war whether we like it or not. It is therefore essential that a total national strategy was formulated at the highest level.[33]

Nevertheless, the apartheid regime still holds the contribution of U.S. military doctrine, especially the NSD, in high esteem. During a press conference held in September 1983, the South African State Security Council (SSC) even tried to make an open comparison of its structure and role with the U.S. National Security Council (NSC). For his part, Steven Metz, who graduated from the same U.S. military academy as Gen. Magnus Malan, gladly and repeatedly praised the apartheid regime's "total strategy" against "total onslaught" as "the highest development of low-intensity warfare strategy currently in existence."[34] This is said regardless of the untold damage and human suffering caused the peoples of southern Africa by the apartheid regime's direct military actions and destabilizing activities through such surrogate forces as UNITA and the MNR. By the time the Reagan administration took office in January 1981, the apartheid regime already had in place its own surrogate military forces in the form of the MNR, which it had completely taken over in mid-1980, and UNITA. Most significantly, within a year of Reagan's inauguration, the South African government instituted the Eloff Commission of Inquiry into the affairs of the South African Council of Churches (SACC).

33. P. W. Botha, Defence White Paper, cited in Mathebula, "Vigilantes: The Myth of Black-on-Black Violence," p. 14; A. Pahad, "JMCs: Centres for Control and Repression," p. 26.
34. S. Metz, "Pretoria's 'Total Strategy' and Low-Intensity Warfare in Southern Africa," *Comparative Strategy* 6, no. 4 (1987), pp. 437, 438, 458, 460.

The Eloff Commission 1981–1984

Appointed in late 1981, the Eloff Commission was named after its chairman, Justice C.F. Eloff. He is a close relative of Dr. G. Eloff, the racist scientist[35] who studied the physical features and other traits of Afrikaners. His conclusion that miscegenation between whites and blacks yielded negative results, that whites had higher spiritual values, particularly in regard to character and intelligence, and so on, made him the closest South African parallel to the Nazi Dr. Joseph Mengele. Dr. G. Eloff, a former lecturer at the University of the Witwatersrand, was a fellow inmate of John B. Vorster at Koffiefontein internment camp, and not long after his release was made head of the conservative University of the Free State's Department of Genetics. It is with such history in mind that Rev. Dr. Allan Boesak, moderator of the "colored" Nederduits Gereformeerde Kerk (NGK, also known as Dutch Reformed Church, or DRC) and President of the World Alliance of Reformed Churches (WARC) castigated members of the apartheid regime in July 1985 as the "spiritual children of Adolf Hitler."[36]

Though, as previously indicated, it may not be wise to draw a straight line between President Reagan's first term in the White House and the appointment of the Eloff Commission (hereafter referred to as EC), it is undoubtedly true that the mood within U.S. foreign policy circles since then seems to have seriously encouraged the apartheid regime to launch its first major assault against the SACC and to adopt measures which have had the effect of stimulating or favoring the emergence and growth of right-wing religious groups in South Africa and the region as a whole. One direct effect of the changed mood is that since the Pentagon and State Department began pressuring the Carter administration to abandon its policy emphasizing human rights and to broaden the CIA's scope of activities, one can detect an unprecedented expansion of

35. *Die Antropogenetika van die Afrikaner* was written during Dr. G. Eloff's period of internment (see below) and scheduled for publication by the South Africa Akademie vir Wetenskap en Kuns (Suid Afrikaanse Academy for Science and Art), but by 1967 it had not yet been published. For more details see Bunting, *South African Reich*, pp. 98–99.

36. *The Star* (Johannesburg), 23 July 1985.

U.S. military intelligence covert operations on a systematic and sustained basis throughout the region. For instance, between that time and Reagan's first anniversary in office, there was a record number of fifty such cases.[37] Since then, these have become an almost daily occurrence.

It was precisely during the period prior to Ronald Reagan's election that South Africa began to witness the first stirrings of American right-wing religious groups on any noticeable scale. This development was taking place parallel to or even hand-in-hand with the emergence of right-wing vigilante and death-squad activity, as seen in the violent break-up of student school boycotts by Inkatha bands in KwaMashu in May 1980, followed by the mysterious assassination of the progressive lawyer, Griffiths Mxenge, in 1981; the murder of five students at the University of Zululand in 1982; the assassination of community leader, Harrison Msizi Dube, in 1983; the brutal suppression of the Mdantsane bus strike and boycotts by the Ciskei Bantustan authorities' vigilante thugs between June and October of the same year; and, finally, Victoria Mxenge's cruel murder in 1985. This was the atmosphere in which Ronald Reagan declared the apartheid regime a long-time ally in March 1981, followed by public enunciation of "constructive engagement" as official U.S. policy toward South Africa in May of the same year, later defended by Chester Crocker, who stated that "the Reagan administration has no intention of destabilizing South Africa in order to curry favor elsewhere." The Reagan Administration did not stop at attempts to repeal the Clark Amendment Act and to modify U.N. Resolution 435 on Namibia, and went much further than that.

Appointed ostensibly with the aim of looking into the financial records of the SACC, the EC took as its starting point the separation of state and church in South Africa as expressed by P.W. Botha, then prime minister, during a meeting with the church body in 1980. During the meeting, Botha stated:

---

37. The estimates are made by the author and largely based on K. Danaher, *In Whose Interest? A Guide to U.S.–South African Relations* (Washington, 1984), pp. 140–161; Dr J. Mader, "CIA Machinations in Africa: Not as Easy as in the Past," *Panorama DDR*, 1 September 1984, pp. 2–6.

I see the state and the church as two independent or autonomous bodies *both of which are appointed by God*, each with its own commission, task and field. For this reason the state does not want to meddle in the affairs of the church and does not expect the church to meddle in the affairs of the state. We, however, are a Christian state and desirous of ruling according to Christian principles and for this reason the state is attentive to the voice of the church since both are concerned with the welfare of the people entrusted to their care.[38]

Thus, the premise on which the EC based its inquiry is both controversial and misleading, since it makes the dangerous assumption that because over 70 percent of South Africa's population professes to be Christian, the country is a Christian state and must therefore guide itself according to Christian moral precepts. In practice, what this kind of reasoning implies is that those 30 percent of South Africa's population who still follow their traditional African religion, Hinduism, Islam, or Judaism, are not considered to be of the same importance as Christians in the eyes of the apartheid regime. In fact, one can go further and say that they are despised and looked down upon, as the white DRC attack against Islam as the "devil's religion" in 1986 shows. Indeed, this clearly reflects the prevalent myth which exists among most supporters of the apartheid regime that the Afrikaner holds a special relationship with God.

Most dangerous to the common unity, loyalty and patriotism for which so many South Africans of different political, cultural and religious backgrounds have shed their blood is the submission made to the EC by the South African Police, which, after prepotently urging that the churches should put the focus of their ministry on "personal salvation and conversion," threatened the cultural norms of large sectors of the South African population in stating:

It [the SACC] does not involve itself in its primary area, and does not undertake, for instance, large-scale campaigns for money in

---

38. From the account given in the Eloff Commission Report (see note 40), it is not clear whether the meeting took place in 1980 or 1981. Emphasis added.

overseas countries for converting non-Christians in the Republic of South Africa to Christianity.[39]

The premise on which the EC based its inquiry is even more misleading because most South African Christians happen to be black and, along with those in the same Dutch Reformed family of churches, do not in any way share the apartheid regime's nor the DRC's intolerance of other religious faiths. Within South Africa's black community, especially among the indigenous Africans and so-called coloreds, it is not uncommon to find people intermingling and even marrying across denominational lines, as well as members of the same family belonging to different religious faiths or denominations. This has never been an issue for discussion or conflict. From a socio-historical point of view, this tolerance among black South African Christians can largely be attributed to the positive influence which the indigenous African culture has exercised on Christianity. This "informal ecumenism" is largely ignored but in reality is more widespread and deeply rooted than is officially acknowledged. In fact, this is the foundation on which the present South African ecumenical movement is based.

It is with due regard to all the above factors that the premise on which the EC based its inquiry and its terms of reference, one of which was to look into "any other matter pertaining to the SACC, its present and past office-bearers or officers and other persons connected [with it] . . . *in the public interest*," flies in the face of the moral precepts of our society. Consequently, with only the exception that the SACC was not declared an "affected organization," the conclusions and recommendations of the EC represented a clear attempt by the apartheid regime to favor or encourage the emergence and growth of right-wing religious groups in South Africa and subsequently their spread throughout the region.

The EC not only took a swipe at the SACC but also a strong

---

39. *S.A. Raad van Kerke: 'n evaluasie deur S.A. Polisie vir voorlegging aan die Kommissie van Ondersoek na die SARK* [S.A. Council of Churches: an evaluation by the S.A. Police for submission to the Commission of Inquiry on the SACC], pp. 10, 109, cited in C. Villa-Vicenco, "Theology in the Service of the State: the Steyn and Eloff Commissions," *Resistance and Hope: South African Essays in Honour of Beyers Naude* (Cape Town, 1985), pp. 112–25.

position against black liberation theology. This is clear from its stated position on the SACC, which says:

> From an organisation whose main activity originally was the coordination of efforts to spread the Gospel, and *whose principal interests lay in spiritual matters, the SACC developed into one largely concerned with political, social and economic issues*, and having specific objectives in those fields.... In the process ... the SACC increasingly identified or aligned itself with the struggle termed the "liberatory struggle," waged on many fronts by several organisations having the common aim of achieving radical socio-political and economic changes in South Africa.[40]

While it stated that "it is not for it to [be] judge of these [spiritual] matters," the EC nevertheless went on to warn that

> the potential of black liberation theology is to evoke extreme opposition to all things white, to create an intense confrontationist climate, and to instil in the minds of its adherents a spirit of revolt. The deep religious undertones of black consciousness with its message of liberation [sic] may drive its adherents into a desperate struggle in which many value systems are rejected and in which peaceful co-existence may be seriously imperilled.

Finally, the EC reached the conclusion that it finds it "inappropriate" for the SACC or any church "(a) to formulate or to endorse political or economic policies for adoption in South Africa and (b) to take part in or to initiate actions designed to implement political objectives." The position which the EC advocates in this particular case would most obviously seem to reveal the double standards and hypocrisy inherent in the apartheid regime's approach to the relation between politics and religion. It is on record that as long as the white DRC continued to support and bless the apartheid regime's policies on scriptural grounds, the present ruling Nationalist Party never complained about religion mixing with politics. On the contrary, it did everything in its power to assist those who were involved in this. But once others saw through this and began challenging its policies as a heresy

40. For more details on the Eloff Commission see *Sechaba* (Lusaka), May and June 1984; *South African Outlook*, August 1984; or Government Printer, "The Eloff Commission Report 1981–1984," R.P. 74/1983 (Pretoria, 1983).

and blasphemy, it accused them of mixing religion with politics and initiated a campaign of lies, vilification and, most recently, open terror against them.

At this juncture, it is important to point out that the separation which the EC makes between "spiritual matters" and "worldly" ones is largely artificial and even irrelevant to most black South Africans, including those who profess to be Christian. In fact, the concept, known as "dualism" in theological circles, is foreign to the Judeo-Christian tradition and therefore is to be found nowhere in the Bible. Essentially, it is an ancient Greek philosophical concept adopted and inserted into Christian belief by Western theologians and scholars at a particular period of history in order to give legitimacy to a specific socio-economic system and justify the exploitation of ordinary working people.[41]

Translated into the political realm, those who advocate this concept end up adopting a bipolar approach towards the major problems of our present world, be they political, economic, social or even those related to health such as epidemics. This bipolar approach divides the world into such categories as good and evil, God and Satan, Christian and heathen, regardless of whether one has his or her own religious faith and practice or not. In such a world, the United States and therefore the capitalist system of production is associated with good, God, Christianity and one's own nation, while the notion of sin, evil, Satan is associated with the Soviet Union and communism and anyone else who does not share the same values as those held by the advocates of dualism and the bipolar approach. In order to mislead the majority of Christian believers into their worldview, those who have a vested economic and political interest in perpetuating the economic exploitation and political oppression of the working people of our societies would insist on employing a false dichotomy, viz. Christianity versus communism, in their discussion of anything related to the issue of politics and religion. But it never occurs to the advocates of dualism and

41. For more details on the concept of "dualism" see D. Cosmas, *Christians or Capitalists? Christianity and Politics in South Africa* (London, 1978), pp. 42–43; *Evangelical Witness in South Africa: Evangelicals Critique Their Own Theology and Practice* (Johannesburg, 1986), pp. 9–10.

bipolarity that Christianity is a religious faith and therefore cannot fairly be counterposed to communism or socialism, which is a political system for organizing social and economic relations of production. It would seem that the advocates of dualism and the bipolar approach are guided by the fear that if they were to strike the proper equation and compare capitalism and socialism, the achievements of the latter system, especially in such important fields as health, education, and social welfare (let alone industrial output) in such a historically short space of time, would put their system at an ideological and moral disadvantage.

Since the end of the Second World War, in particular during the cold war period, many people in the United States came to adopt a bipolar approach towards the major problems of our world. In fact, most of them, under the heavy influence of Sen. Joseph McCarthy's campaign against communists and other American radicals, embraced anticommunism as their country's new religion and guiding principle in their relations with other countries and peoples. It was in this atmosphere of anticommunist hysteria that the U.S. Army managed quietly to recruit a record number of nine hundred Nazi scientists and doctors into its fold.

The best example of dualism translated into the political realm in our period is the Reagan Doctrine. According to this doctrine, the United States is the new Israel, God's chosen nation, and its actions, no matter whether they constitute an act of aggression or not, are presumably sanctioned by divine will and therefore should not be condemned. Accordingly, America's God is a God of war, unleashing His wrath against evil forces. The Reagan Doctrine, deeply steeped in the ideas of fundamentalist evangelism, also imparts a new image to both the world capitalist system as represented by the business corporation and the church, as well as their roles in society. The corporation becomes sanctified, develops its own gospel of big business and even starts looking upon its executive personnel as modern missionaries bringing good news to the poor through misleading advertisements in the press or on the radio. These days, some corporations even include a priest or theologian on their board of directors as a means of improving their "ethical performance." Michael Novak, a board member of the Institute on Religion and Democracy (IRD), director of the American Enterprise Institute (AEI) and the Reagan administration's former representative to the U.N. Commission for Human Rights, made an outrageous comparison between the text of Isaiah 53:2–3 and the modern business corporation, which he defended as "a much despised incarnation of God's presence in this world."[42] Thus, when the world capitalist system is rejected or the business corporation is criticized or even admonished, Jesus Christ is crucified in the process. This cannot be otherwise, since, as the rest of the Christian community understands it, the Isaiah text refers to the crucifixion of Christ.

On the other hand, the church ceases to be a religious institution and is transformed into the counterpart of the business corporation – the "corporate" church. The theological foundation of this "corporate" church is based on the gospel of prosperity, which is deeply rooted in fundamentalist evangelism and has been most strongly advocated by Kenneth Hagin, founder of the Rhema Bible Church in Tulsa, Oklahoma; his disciple, Ray McCauley; Gordon Lindsay, founder of Christ for Nations in Dallas, Texas; Reinhard Bonnke of the Christ For All Nations (CFAN); Kenneth and Gloria Copeland from the Oral Roberts Evangelistic Association (OREA); Jim Bakker; Elijah Maswanganyi; and Benson Idahosa. According to this gospel, the most wealthy members of a capitalist society are rich because of God's blessing. Poverty, illness, poor health, and other misfortunes are sure signs of sin and lack of true commitment to Christianity. Taken to its logical conclusion, the image of a millionaire evangelist living in a mansion, owning a chauffeur-driven limousine, dressed in an elegant suit and shiny expensive shoes to give a sermon to an equally well-dressed congregation, is presumably a living example of God's blessing on those who follow His ways. This is regardless of how their wealth was acquired.

Though not all religious Right preachers openly subscribe to the gospel of prosperity, a factor which even led Jimmy Swaggart to criticize repeatedly Jim Bakker and his wife Tammy for preaching this false belief, the opulent lifestyle of almost

---

42. Michael Novak, "A Theology of Corporation," in *The spirit of democratic capitalism* (New York, 1982), p. 52.

all of them seems to be in line with it. In Africa, the gospel of prosperity has been preached perhaps most widely by the Rev. Benson Idahosa, head of the Church of God Mission International, in Nigeria. In imitation of his American mentors, he has built a thirty thousand-seat cathedrome, a junior secondary school called Word of Faith Day School, and a well-equipped, modern television studio; he owns a luxurious 200-model Mercedes Benz, lives in a mansion adorned with palatial furniture and paintings, and is one of the most expensively clad men in his country. The Reverend Idahosa, who is a regular visitor to southern Africa and considers himself to have "been privileged to meet with American president Ronald Reagan four times," has expressed his belief in declaring: "My God is not a poor God. God did not say you should worship Him in rags. My God is a living and kind God."[43]

It is no wonder that with such prophets supporting it, the Reagan administration was characterized by more cases of public office corruption than any other in recent U.S. history and that the "corporate" churches' millionaire evangelists have themselves been plagued by one sexual and financial fraud scandal after another. Rather than dismissing their setbacks as merely moral scandals, it would be wise to take the phenomenon of right-wing religious groups very seriously, for despite the downfall of one or two of their leading evangelists, they have plans, strategy, financial resources, and personnel enough for worldwide expansion.

The 451-page EC report, submitted to the South African Parliament in February 1984, elicited varying reactions in South African society. Dr. Pierre Rossouw, chief executive of the white DRC, praised the commission's work as having been "thorough and without prejudice."[44]

Chief Gatsha Buthelezi, president of Inkatha and head of the KwaZulu Bantustan, expressed his satisfaction that the EC report had "exposed" what he termed the SACC's "dependence on affluent white liberal groups in Europe," and added that "black South Africa will eventually sort out the SACC

43. Cited in O. Ndibe, "To Higher Heights," *Concord Weekly*, 18 February 1985, pp. 7–11.
44. Cited in *Race Relations Survey* (Braamfontein, 1984), p. 913.

and [does] not require the might of the state to enable [it] to do so."[45]

During a special parliamentary debate on the EC report, Louis le Grange, then minister of law and order, expressed the hope that donors would henceforth realize that the SACC was not a church (which it had never claimed to be in the first place) "but merely a left-wing political activist organization which clearly enjoys hardly any support in South Africa."[46]

Of the apartheid regime's opponents, Archbishop Philip Russell, head of the Church of the Province of South Africa (Anglican), expressed his belief that whatever had happened would not "in any way destroy or impair the relationship of trust and support that the CPSA has long given to the SACC."[47]

Chris Aitken, then general secretary of the Presbyterian church, stated that he had no objection to the SACC being investigated under the Fund-Raising Act since their sources had never been a secret in the first place, but expressed alarm that the apartheid regime wanted to arrogate itself the power to decide which projects were "spiritual" and which were not, while the Rev. Fremont Louw, president of the Methodist Conference, expressed similar fears.

The Rev. David Botha, then the N.G. Sendingkerk's director of communications, issued a guarded statement in the March 1984 issue of *Econews*, saying that the apartheid regime would be "carrying matters too far to subject the SACC to the Fund-Raising Act."

The Southern African Catholic Bishops' Conference (SACBC), whose former general secretary, the popular Father Smangaliso Mkhatshwa, suffered torture and other physical abuse during more than a year of detention without trial, issued a statement which pointed out: "In a purely white milieu, talk of strategies of resistance, conscientious objection, and radical trade unions sounds disquieting. In a black milieu the topics referred to sound like very moderate Christian reactions to a situation of unbearable privation and frustration. The great problem for the SACC lies not so much in being

45. Ibid.
46. Ibid., p. 914.
47. Ibid.

prophetic about the evils it sees in South African society, as in communicating its prophetic vision."[48]

The most forthright criticism against the EC report naturally came from charismatic Bishop Desmond Tutu, then general secretary of the powerful SACC and now the CPSA's archbishop of Cape Town. In a verbal reply to the EC report, he correctly pointed out that the EC had neither the theological competence nor moral basis to investigate and sit in judgment over the SACC, a body whose church-based membership was 80 percent black, because it [the EC] did not boast of a single theologian or black commissioner. "The commissioners," Archbishop Tutu further said, "are people who benefit daily from the vicious socio-political dispensation which we want to see changed. They have spoken like whites threatened by the fear that their privileges would disappear or be significantly modified if we were to have a more just and more democratic setup in South Africa."[49] After challenging the apartheid regime to use any of its many harsh and repressive laws, he finally declared that the EC was a "thinly veiled part of the government's strategy to vilify and discredit the ANC,"[50] of which he has been an open and longstanding supporter.

Major U.S. Religious Right Groups

Now that it has failed in its attempts to destroy the SACC and prevent the South African Christian community and members of other religious faiths from becoming involved in the liberation struggle, the apartheid regime has resorted to the sponsoring, promoting and encouraging of religious right-wing groups. Many of these groups have their roots in the United States, from where they still receive support in the form of funding, training and publishing. Most of the time, this multifaceted support is covert, or at least is never openly acknowledged. But sometimes it can be provided quite openly

48. *Rand Daily Mail*, 20 February 1984; *The Star* (Johannesburg), 20 February 1984.
49. Tutu, transcript of verbal reply to the Eloff Commission Report, in *Sechaba* (Lusaka), June 1984.
50. See *Race Relations Survey* (Johannesburg), 1984, p. 912.

under different guises, the most usual being "humanitarian assistance" or "relief aid."

Though a few of the American right-wing religious groups have been operating in South Africa for some years, the first big wave of penetration occurred during 1984 and 1985. This was at the height of the Vaal Triangle popular revolts, when the Pretoria regime was hit by the most serious crisis of political and moral legitimacy since the 1976 Soweto youth revolts. This crisis of legitimacy was so deep that from September 1984 until the end of 1986 the racist regime's authority had no standing in the eyes of the majority of the South African population. The apartheid regime had virtually lost effective control over most of the country's black townships, and the revolts were even threatening to spill over into the white industrial and business areas and posh suburbs. Under these circumstances, the only way for the Pretoria regime to continue maintaining any semblance of authority was to send troops into the black townships and impose a partial state of emergency in thirty two magisterial districts on 21 July 1985. Since then, the declaration of martial law has been extended to almost all black townships and renewed each year. Indeed, it had now become a total state of emergency fully in line with the ideology of total war, total market and other totalitarian concepts.

Since military occupation, no matter how strong, can never alone be a guarantee for continued and effective control over the black townships which have become a rumbling volcano waiting to explode, the Pretoria regime has found it necessary to suppress violently the voice of the dissident churches, most of whom, with the exception of the white DRC and the large Zion Christian Church (ZCC), belong to either the SACC or SACBC. On the other hand, it has introduced the use of right-wing religious groups mainly in its propaganda campaigns, or has at least supported or encouraged their emergence, growth, and proliferation in many parts of South Africa and beyond.

The RAMBO Coalition

In only one year, 1985, David W. Balsiger, the founder of the Restore A More Benevolent Order (RAMBO) Coalition, editor of the Biblical News Service and publisher-editor of Family Protection Scoreboard, based in Costa Mesa, California, formed eleven of the many right-wing religious groups in South Africa.[51] Some of the groups set up by or under the direction of Balsiger are the Coalition for Realism, led by Claude Moller; Family Focus, also headed by Moller; Jesus Christ for Peace in South Africa, led by Mzilikazi Masiya; and the South African Action Group under Andy Goetsch. Balsiger, who is closely associated with such groups as the Wycliffe Bible Translators-Summer Institute of Linguistics (WBT/SIL), Campus Crusade, and Youth With A Mission (YWAM), and who has attacked liberation theology as "the single most critical problem Christianity has faced in its two thousand-year history,"[52] explains the reason for setting up these groups:

> As South Africa is a country strongly based on Judeo-Christian values, I merely encouraged and showed Christians how to play a more aggressive role in solving South Africa's problems instead of letting the pro-Marxist liberation theologies speak for them.[53]

Not content with ignoring the extent to which the apartheid regime has turned its back on the Judeo-Christian tradition and, indeed, has abused the Bible to justify its un-Christian and inhuman practices against the majority of the South African people, Balsiger defends it by making incredible claims, such as "in South Africa, lives are protected – not threatened – by the government."[54]

"South Africa's Judeo-Christian government," Balsiger further states, "has never instituted massacres, nor mass starvation, nor terror[55] and respects democratic rights, such as of

51. See *I.C.T. News* (Braamfontein) 5, no. 2 (June 1987), p. 2; *Crisis News* (Salt River, So. Africa), no. 26 (November 1988).
52. See editorial in *Family Protection Scoreboard: Special Edition on Liberation Theology*, Costa Mesa, Calif.
53. *I.C.T. News* 5, no. 2 (June 1987).
54. See O. Scott, "Human Rights in South Africa vs. Communist Countries," in *Family Protection Scoreboard: Special Edition*, p. 14.
55. Ibid.

Jeffrey Marishane

"worship and toleration of all religions," assembly, free press and expression, fair trial, choice of one's own career, etc. Balsiger's familiarity with some of the aspects of the LIC strategy and the understanding of his role within the general framework of this military doctrine is made clear by his attempts to explain the deaths of hundreds of thousands of innocent and defenseless people – at the hands of the apartheid regime's army, police, surrogate forces in the form of vigilante bands, secret death squads, UNITA and the MNR – by adopting the apartheid regime's psychological warfare method of attributing most of this to the deception of "black-on-black conflict."[56]

Whenever the role of the Pretoria regime's army or police force in these murderous activities is uncovered, it is excused on the grounds that they are fighting communism or terrorists. This is done even if the victim is, for example, a thirteen-year-old boy killed in cold blood on his way to church, or a seventy five-year-old disabled man in his sleep[57] or, no less serious, the detention without trial and communication of priests for long periods of time and their subjection to severe torture. According to statistics compiled by the Johannesburg-based Human Rights Commission, at least 450 clergy and church workers were detained by the South African police under various charges between June 1986 and June 1987. A list of the names of 134 of these has been compiled and published as an appendix to the book, *No Neutral Ground*, by the New York-based Human Rights Watch in August 1989. Among these, Father Smangaliso Mkhatshwa, former secretary-general of the SACBC, General Secrader, and the Rev. Abraham T. Maja, organising secretary of the Northern Transvaal Council of Churches, seem to have been the most heavily persecuted by the Pretoria regime and its black Bantustan puppets. Strangely enough, their plight also seems to have been the least reported by both the South African press and the international media.

Father Smangaliso Mkhatshwa's woes with the apartheid

56. Ibid.
57. Mathebula, "Vigilantes: State-Sponsored Violence," p. 29; T. Gqubule, "Profile of a Shot 'Terrorist': A 75-Year-Old Disabled Chief," *The Weekly Mail* (Johannesburg), 7–13 April 1989.

regime started during the historic events set off by the Soweto youth revolts in June 1976, and which reached their height in Mamelodi, where he was a parish priest, in August of that year. In that month, he was arrested and detained without trial until his release toward the end of the year. He was subsequently served with a harsh five-year banning order, which confined him to his home and also stopped him from delivering sermons to his large congregation in Mamelodi. In recognition of the service he had provided to his congregation and the more than 300,000-strong Mamelodi township community as a whole, he was appointed general secretary of the SACBC in May 1981 while still banned. He held and fulfilled his duties under this post with full honor and respect from his old congregation in Mamelodi and his new one in Soshanguve until the end of 1987, when he had to relinquish it under pressure from the Vatican.

By this time, Father Mkhatshwa had again been detained incommunicado and without trial under the total state of emergency regulations for a full year from 12 June 1986 to 11 June 1987. During this long period of detention, he was subjected to physical and psychological torture by the South African security police. Father Mkhatshwa's ordeal has caused real pain and anguish to both the Mamelodi and Soshanguve communities and his congregations there who still today regard him as their priest. Upon his release, Father Mkhatshwa refused to be cowed into silence and submission by intimidation and harassment from the security police and their paid agents. His lawyers presented the Pretoria regime with a potentially embarrassing lawsuit that could have once more torn to pieces its claims to the Judeo-Christian tradition. In order to avoid a costly and long, drawn-out lawsuit, which could only end up putting it in a situation of serious embarrassment, the apartheid authorities decided to settle the case out of court, and Father Mkhatshwa accepted the offer. Finally, an arrangement for the payment of R 25,000 (about $10,000) in damages to Father Mkhatshwa was made. He subsequently donated all of this to the cause of the poor and needy.

Father Mkhatshwa's ordeal is one of those rare cases in which the Pretoria regime has admitted its inhuman treatment of political detainees. In fact, it is not farfetched to think that the apartheid authorities were led to this decision by Father Mkhatshwa's high-profile status in Mamelodi, a township which has always prided itself on the old tradition of struggle set off by King Sekhukhuni and Mzilikazi and known to outsiders for its bustling life. Its residents, together with those from its sister townships of Attridgeville, Ga-Rankuwa, Mabopone, Soshanguve, Hammanskraal, and the squatter settlement of Winterveldt, have been daily victims of rampant racism in Pretoria which, with a policeman on virtually every street corner, is the most heavily policed city in South Africa. In the light of these experiences, Father Mkhatshwa's ordeal at the hands of the South African security police cannot be taken lightly. Nor can the call which he issued in March 1988 be overlooked:

> What the real church of Jesus Christ is saying [is] that we can no longer allow the Hitlers, Mussolinis and imperialists of this world to misuse the church for their own political and selfish ends. . . . Dare the church betray its vocation in order to ingratiate itself with Caesar?[58]

Father Mkhatshwa's experience of torture at the hands of the South African police gives us just a glimpse at what happens to political detainees in South Africa. In this particular case, the use of torture to either extract information from detainees or cow them into submission is not an aberrant act but is rather a routine method employed by the security police to achieve their aims. For instance, a study done by Don Foster[59] on political detainees between 1974 and 1984 shows that most had been subjected to various forms of professional torture. The physical torture, which would always be combined with psychological torture, involved beatings on the body: burning the soles of the feet; whippings; pulling out or burning hair; cutting the hands with a sharp knife; burning fingernails or crushing them with a brick; pulling teeth out without anesthesia; setting on fire; electric shocks; genital abuse; pulling or squeezing breasts; maintaining abnormal

---

58. Cited in *Weekly Mail* (Johannesburg), 25–30 March 1988, p. 9.
59. D. Foster, *Detention and Torture in South Africa*, cited in *New Nation*, p. 9, April 1987; *Human Rights and Repression in South Africa*.

body positions for long periods of time; forcing gymnasium-type exercises; being thrown into the air and left to fall hard on the floor; being given salted water to drink, etc. The psychological torture involved detention without trial or charge and being kept incommunicado; solitary confinement; sleep deprivation; contradictory styles of interrogation; drug administration; excrement abuse; verbal abuse; threats of violence to family and relatives; sham executions, etc. In 1987, a panel of doctors who handle released detainees issued a study which pointed out that 72 percent of those they had treated claimed to have been assaulted while in detention, and 97 percent showed signs of such abuse as bruises, lacerations, perforated eardrums, and even gunshot wounds.[60]

The Rev. T.S. Farisani's persecution by the Pretoria regime also started many years ago, in 1977, when he was detained incommunicado and severely tortured in Pietermaritzburg – the center of today's bloody vigilante war unleashed by Chief Gatsha Buthelezi's Inkatha against the democratic forces. In October 1981, he was again detained, this time by the Venda Bantustan puppet authorities and subjected to torture. In 1986, he was one of the tens of thousands detained incommunicado and without trial under the same state of emergency regulations. After having been kept out of circulation and subjected to psychological torture for more than two months, the regime was forced by public pressure to release him in February 1987.

For the Pretoria regime and its Bantustan puppets, the Reverend Farisani's sin seems to have been that he acted in the best possible way a true Lutheran should act – identifying himself with the cause of the poor black farmworkers and other rural workers, whose children and students were subjected to cruel oppression, exploitation and repression in an area strongly infested by South African army military bases, soldier-farmers, and Afrikaner Weerstandsbeweging (AWB) neofascist zealots blessed by the white DRC. Sadly enough, the ZCC hierarchy has also played some role in this by first inviting P.W. Botha to address its huge prayer meeting in 1985, and thereafter, proceeding to form a small paramilitary squad nicknamed the Moria Defense Force to suppress students in

60. Ibid.

their grievances against the Lebowa Bantustan puppet authorities. The victims of this oppression, exploitation and repression, it is important to point out, are the most vulnerable sector of the South African work force – farm and rural workers who have been rendered rootless, helpless and hopeless by the operation of such laws as the Labor Relations, Basic Conditions of Employment, and Unemployment Insurance acts, which do not cover them.

It was therefore not without reason that in December 1984, the Council of African Independent Churches (CAIC) – a body which brings together most of the independent churches under one umbrella, in cooperation with ten other independent church bodies – issued a statement of protest which in part stated:

> We in the African independent churches are the poorest and most oppressed of South African society. We are the most affected by forced removals, resettlement, migrant labour, influx control laws and economic exploitation at the factory floor, and we constitute the greater part of workers in this country.[61]

The Reverend Abraham T. Maja's troubles with the Pretoria regime, which ultimately led to his detention without trial or charge between 17 June 1986 and June 1987, can be traced as far back as October 1984. In that month, Dr. Gerrit Viljoen, then minister of cooperation, development and education, presented a complicated "land consolidation" plan, which would have had the effect of transferring two thousand hectares from the Gazankulu Bantustan to "white" South Africa, and seven thousand hectares from the same territory to the Lebowa Bantustan. The Gazankulu and Lebowa Bantustan territories are largely but not exclusively populated by the Tsonga-Shangaan and Pedi-Northern Sotho ethnic groups, respectively. The scheme was based on a claim ostensibly made by a Gazankulu chief on a piece of land lying in the Acornhoek area which, though historically belonging to the Shangaans, had for many decades been used by the Sothos without causing any conflict between the two groups. The claim led to some clashes between the Shangaans and Sothos in the area toward the end of that year.

61. Mathebula, "Vigilantes: State-Sponsored Violence."

This subsequently led to other clashes over land in the Tzaneen area at the end of February 1985. In this case, the instigator was Nelson Ramodike, then minister of economic affairs for the Lebowa Bantustan. Ramodike's sinister role on this occasion was to demand the expulsion of the Shangaans from a piece of land which apparently belonged to the Sothos by calling on them to cut down the border fence put up by the apartheid regime between Gazankulu and Lebowa. Toting a gun in a country where blacks are legally prohibited from owning firearms (unless it is to the benefit of the Pretoria regime to make an exception), and shouting tribal abuse at the Shangaans, Ramodike threatened war against them. This ultimately led to the death of one person, more than one hundred serious injuries, thirty homes destroyed, five shops burnt down, and others looted. What is important to note in this whole bloody saga is that neither the Gazankulu chief nor Nelson Ramodike has so far been asked to account for their role in it, or even to make a statement to the Pretoria government.

On the other hand, Reverend Maja, who played an important role in easing tensions between the two groups and thereby helped to frustrate the apartheid regime's plans to put them at bitter loggerheads, has been harassed, intimidated and even detained for a full year by the South African security police. At the height of the clashes, which were widely reported as another case of black-on-black conflict by both the Pretoria regime's propaganda machinery and the local opposition's press, only to be parroted later by the international media, Reverend Maja charged:

> It would certainly seem like the local politicians are being used to do the dirty work of apartheid and cause friction between the two groups. Pretoria has promised in Parliament that there would be no forced removals, so by giving backhand orders to cut the fence and stir up the people against each other, Pretoria could then step in and be seen to be the peacemaker by redefining the borders and using this as a weapon.[62]

After the Pretoria regime's plans to stir up hostilities between the two groups were frustrated, it decided to introduce

62. Ibid., p. 26.

a new element into its strategy for breaking up popular resistance to its policies in both Gazankulu and Lebowa: vigilante bands composed mainly of MNR bandits and Zimbabwean renegades. As of March 1986, the townships and villages of the northern Transvaal were subjected to a continuous reign of terror by a combined force of SADF soldiers, security police, MNR vigilante bands, and secret death squads composed of off-duty policemen, soldier-farmers and AWB neo-fascists. In one of their actions, they violently broke up a prayer meeting organized by the Namakgale Youth Congress (NAYCO) at the Lutheran church in Namakgale, a village outside the town of Phalaborwa, where the SADF has a large military base for stationing the seventh Infantry Battalion and training MNR terrorists. Mavis Malotji, a sixteen-year-old girl, was shot dead in that attack, and many people were either seriously injured or detained.

The "import" of counterrevolution in the form of the MNR to suppress the internal resistance movement against apartheid has many serious implications for the national liberation movement in South Africa and the region as a whole. Among these is showing how the MNR, initially set up with the aim of destabilizing Mozambique and harassing the Zimbabwean guerilla fighting the Ian Smith regime from behind the lines, can easily be turned around and used against the South African national liberation movement led by the ANC. Secondly, it shows how far the MNR, composed of those who were used against the national liberation movement of their own country but had their hopes dashed after it proved a useless and futile exercise, can go in wanting to change their fortunes for the better. With nothing or very little to lose, they allow themselves to be used as cannon fodder in any military adventure, no matter how small the benefits they receive in return. Used in combination with the various SADF ethnic units, such as the 111th, 112th, 113th, 115th and 121st battalions, set up respectively for the Swazis, Vendas, Shangaans and Sothos in the northeastern and western Transvaal and the Zulus in northern Natal, as well as the puppet armed forces of the "independent" Bantustans of Bophuthatswana, the Ciskei, Transkei and Venda, the MNR serves as a deadly force able to retard the progress of the national liberation struggle for many years. Thus, the SADF can succeed in using many of the Bantustans as territorial buffer zones and their paramilitary forces as a first line of defense against the movement of ANC guerrillas.

Jesus Christ for Peace in South Africa (JCP)

Unless it be thought otherwise, it is important to point out beforehand that most of the bodies set up by David Balsiger are just a coterie of small groups with no sizable membership. Their spurious membership would often be composed of one or two persons, including the group's leader and his family members or immediate circle of friends. Sometimes the same person or group of individuals would be heading what is essentially the same organization operating under different names. With the exception of a few large groups like Campus Crusade or World Vision, they would have no traceable addresses and usually operate from a post office box number. In order to conjure up an image of importance and a large following, they would assume a grandiose or high-sounding name and inflate the size of their membership. Since they do not have traceable addresses and their leaders are not in the habit of issuing membership statistics except to make wild claims, it is almost impossible to verify their real size. While their membership, from casual observation, is very small, it is unfortunate that their dishonest methods of operating do sometimes succeed in playing on the minds of some naive believers and attracting a certain measure of support, no matter how negligible, to these groups.

A case in point is the shadowy Jesus Christ for Peace Inter-denominational Movement in South Africa (JCP), wrongly thought to have been founded by the self-styled Archbishop Mzilikazi Fanie Masiya "with the help of God."[63] The first reaction to these simple words by Masiya is to ask if, in his opinion, God is an American revealed in the person of David W. Balsiger. Recently, Masiya was exposed as a former policeman who had made himself available to a mysterious group of white "businessmen" to be used as a front for promoting

---

63. See *I.C.T. News* 5, no. 2 (June 1987), 2; *Crisis News*, November 1988, p. 7.

and defending their interests abroad.[64] When his odd history was finally revealed, Masiya had no option but to admit that indeed he was a former policeman trained in counterinsurgency methods and, to use his own words, turned into a "killing machine." However, he tried to explain his decision to join the police in 1973 by saying that, faced with the prospect of long unemployment, he had no other choice but to embark on this path. Masiya has been accused of shooting at students while a policeman during the June 1976 youth revolts. Not content with the meager salary which he received from his paymasters in Pretoria, he turned to crime to make ends meet. In 1977, he was arrested, charged, and found guilty of robbery, theft, and murder. The robbery and theft charges included the pilfering of weapons from the Mabopane police station and their subsequent use in bank holdups and street crime. The murder charge involved the killing of Philemon Shisana during a drinking brawl at his home near Hammanskraal, from which Philemon operated an illegal shebeen.

Masiya was sentenced to two years imprisonment on the weapons theft charge. While awaiting trial on fourteen other charges, he managed to escape from the Pretoria maximum security prison on 25 June 1977 in the company of several other prisoners. In February 1978, he was captured in Gazankulu and given a further six-month sentence for the murder charge. He claims that he was converted to Christianity after he was released on parole in 1981. This was after he had also come across and read a book by Martin Luther King, or so he claims.

This, in short, is the personal history of a man has been presented to the outside world as a key leader of the African Independent Churches (AIC) movement and, specifically, of the Council for Apostolic and Zion Churches in South Africa, the National Christian Development Fund of Southern Africa [sic], and the Jesus Christ for Peace group, which altogether ridiculously claim a total membership of 3.5 million people and are involved in Pretoria's efforts to break the sanctions campaign against apartheid. Again strangely, these ghost

64. See E. Maluleka, "The Odd History of Sanctions Busting Bishop," *Weekly Mail* (Johannesburg), 21–27 July 1989.

organizations all operate from the same Van Erkoms Building in Pretoria Street, Pretoria, next to the headquarters of the South African security police.[65] On 16 August 1989 the 4.5-million-strong African Spiritual Churches Association (Asca), a body whose membership is made up of many of the estimated three thousand black Apostolic, Zionist and Ethiopianist churches in South Africa, denounced Masiya as an imposter who "is not even known as a Christian – let alone even belonging to any church denomination."[66] The leadership of Asca went a step further by pointing out that "in the AIC . . . there is no such thing as a bishop without a church denomination, let alone an archibishop." The statement was issued during a rally, organized on short notice because of the harsh restrictions imposed by the four-year-old state of emergency, at Tsakane Stadium, outside the town of Brakpan on the East Rand, to take a stand on "Bishop" Isaac Mokoena and Masiya's involvement in questionable activities falsely claimed to be on behalf of the AIC movement. Nevertheless, the rally was attended by almost seven thousand people, mainly from the PWV area (Pretoria, Witwatersrand and Vaal Triangle). Since both "Bishop" Mokoena and Masiya have no traceable official or home address and could not even be contacted by telephone, an open and public invitation was sent to them, but they did not attend. More rallies on this issue are still being planned specifically for Soweto and other key areas of the country.

During the Pretoria rally, Asca also questioned Masiya's easy release under remission after he had committed such horrendous crimes, and the source of his funding. Asca went further and challenged both "Bishop" Mokoena and Masiya to hold a similar rally to prove their claimed membership or to stop misrepresenting the AIC movement to the outside world.

The size of Masiya's following can perhaps be gleaned from the fact that when he launched his "million signatures" campaign against sanctions in 1988, he could only manage to bring together a group of thirty-five elderly people dressed in typical Zionist colors to support him. The march was given

---

65. Ibid.
66. African Spiritual Churches Association, statement on the Mokoena–Masiya issue, 16 August 1989, Braamfontein; *New Nation*, 25 August 1989.

unwarranted importance by the South African pro-apartheid media, including the SABC radio and television services, which provided it with wide coverage. When he finally managed to come up with 500,000 signatures in support of his bizarre campaign, it turned out that most had been written by the same person. Asked to clarify this anomaly, he foolishly claimed that his field workers had to fill in forms for those who could not write. Masiya would probably not be able to give the correct answer as to why so many black South Africans cannot read or write. If perchance he is honest enough to provide the right answer, he would most likely lose his well-paid job or, worse, be sent back to prison, not as a common criminal, but this time as a political agitator or even a communist.

Pressed to give more details about his antisanctions campaign. Masiya inadvertently revealed that this was in fact initiated by some whites, including the owner of a Johannesburg travel agency, whom he declined to identify by name. He was brought in later after, to use his words, "they realized they couldn't get anywhere overseas on their own without blacks."[67] This, understandably, only helped to throw suspicion on his antisanctions campaign, regardless of whether it is funded by South Africa-based foreign transnational corporations or not. The suspicion became even greater when Archbishop Joseph Selekisho of the United Immanuel Assemblies of God said that Masiya was ordained as a bishop by Uamca because he is the purported founder of Jesus Christ for Peace,[68] which had been set up at the initiative of a foreign citizen with a questionable background in his own country, and when *Clarion Call*, the KwaZulu government's propaganda mouthpiece, claimed that the so-called National Christian Development Fund, which he chaired, was "an anti-apartheid church alliance,"[69] which it obviously was not.

One can go further and state that in fact, it seems that the ground is slowly and carefully being laid for right-wing religious groups to play the same role in South Africa that they have been playing in Central America, the Philippines, and

67. Maluleka, "Odd History."
68. Ibid.
69. *Clarion Call* (Ulundi, KwaZulu).

other conflict areas of the world. One of the last reported initiatives taken by Masiya as leader of the little-known Council for Apostolic and Zion Churches was to send a letter to former South African president P.W. Botha, thanking him for his reforms and "negotiation process." The message was handed over to the state president's office at the Union Buildings, Pretoria, by Masiya in the company of twenty other black church leaders, including Isaac Mokoena, and in part read: "We hereby wish to thank you and your administration for the oath of reform that you embarked upon since you took over power."[70] Indeed, Masiya, and definitely not the mass of the South African people, has got a lot to be thankful for to P.W. Botha.

United Christian Action (UCA)

A group which fits almost perfectly the description of those bodies led by someone who is simultaneously the leader of several other related organizations is the United Christian Action (UCA), directed by Edward Cain. Also set up around the time that David W. Balsiger helped to establish Masiya's Jesus Christ for Peace, the UCA is an umbrella body which includes fourteen right-wing religious groups. It counts among its members "Bishop" Isaac Mokoena's Reformed Independent Churches Association (RICA); Frontline Fellowship; Gospel Defence League; South African Catholic Defence League; Christians for Partnership Association; Bet-El (Group of Ministries); Foerdergesellschaft Afrika; Rhodesia Christian Group; German-South African Friendship Association; Christian Mission International of South Africa; Christian Resistance Group; Victims Against Terrorism; Vox Africana; Veterans for Victory; the *Aida Parker Newsletter*; Signpost Publications and Research Center; Signpost magazine, etc. Ed Cain is the head of both the UCA and *Signpost* Publications and Research Center, as well as the sole editor of Signpost magazine.

Ed Cain, a Baptist missionary during Portugese colonial

---

70. *The Citizen*, (Johannesburg) 18 May 1989.

rule in Mozambique, has a long history of involvement in right-wing Christian activity in support of the Pretoria regime and against the progressive sector within the Christian churches. He is the former head of the publications arm of the Christian League of Southern Africa (CLSA) and a one-time editor of its newspaper *Encounter*. He is also a former staff member of the Christian Mission International, a United States-based group which purports to fight communism and liberation theology under the cloak of religion.[71] The CLSA was founded by Rev. Fred Shaw in 1974 to counter what he saw as a left-wing, or at least liberal, drift in the focus of the religious activities of the SACC and its affiliate churches, while *Encounter* was published in South Africa and distributed without charge to many local clergymen and a wide network of church leaders in the U.K. and aboard KLM flights operating between Jan Smuts Airport in Johannesburg and Schiphol Airport in Amsterdam. The CLSA also published *Vox Africana* as its German-language mouthpiece and distributed it to a growing number of West German Protestant church leaders who showed strong sympathies with the apartheid regime.

Not too long after its founding, the CLSA, which operated out of posh headquarters in Pretoria with a full-time staff of ten, and which never showed any signs of running short of cash, was brought under the control of the Pretoria regime. At the same time, the circulation and quality of *Encounter* were increased and improved with secret funding provided by the now-defunct Department of Information, not least of all in order to smear the WCC for its humanitarian support of southern African liberation movements. The secret funding of *Encounter* was also done out of a need to improve the tarnished image of the white DRC, whose leadership was exposed to have secretly received, in return for continued support of the apartheid system on scriptural grounds, an amount equal to £66,000 as of 1974 from the Department of Information without the knowledge of the DRC's members. Bernard Smith, author of *The Fraudulent Gospel*, was a regular contributor of articles to *Encounter*.

Until the debâcle of the Muldergate scandal, in which the

---

71. See D. Knight, *Wolves in Sheep's Clothing*, (February 1989), p. 9.

CLSA was revealed to be "Project G11-C, codename Bernard" under the Department of Information, the Rev. Fred Shaw and his colleagues denied any link with the Pretoria regime. Even on 6 March 1980, when this truth was more than an open secret, Graham Blainey, former head of the CLSA's office in London, vehemently denied the link when he stated, "We totally and completely reject the suggestion that we have been in receipt of South African government funds. The fact that individuals would attempt to use this as a smear is a demonstration of their dishonesty."[72]

However, Dr. Eschel Rhoodie, during a long series of interviews with the editor of the Dutch magazine, *Elsevier*, had already revealed that his Department of information had provided the CLSA with R 229,314.81 since the Pretoria regime took over the control of its affairs. This included R 13,200 as a salary to Rev. Fred Shaw and R 10,000 as legal defense fees in a lawsuit brought by the SACC against the CLSA and its director.

Despite his tarnished image as a former executive of CLSA, Ed Cain hopes that the UCA will be helpful in providing "liberation from a fraudulent gospel which is poisoning South African mainline churches . . . and [in] generating the necessary Christian action to prevent a Marxist takeover of South Africa."[73]

From among the leaders of CLSA affiliates, Dorothea Scarborough is the next person who perfectly matches the description of a single individual heading more than one body. She is both leader of the Gospel Defense League (GDL), which is "dedicated to the defense of biblical Christianity . . . against humanistic influences undermining Christ,"[74] and the sole editor and publisher of *Vox Africana*.

72. Cited in D. Knight, *Beyond The Pale*, pp. 113, 117.

73. Cited in "The Political Abuse of Religion," *Crisis News*, no. 26 (November 1988), p. 6.

74. Cited in K. Evans, "How Much Support for Anti-Tutu Groups? Not Much" *Weekly Mail* (Johannesburg), 8–14 April 1988.

Reformed Independent Churches Association (RICA)

Though Ed Cain is the leading figure in the UCA, the center-piece of his umbrella body seems to lie more firmly in the Reformed Independent Churches Association (RICA). Founded in 1970 by the discredited "Bishop" Isaac Mokoena with the support of conservative religious leaders from the white DRC, RICA was set up with the initial purpose of countering the African Independent Churches Association (AICA, also known as AIC movement), which earlier stood under the influence of the Christian Institute. Before Mokoena's image was damaged beyond repair in 1979 by disclosures that he had used official funds for personal benefit and had been involved in "unnatural sex acts,"[75] RICA's lifeblood was apparently the Southern Africa Theological College for Independent Churches (SATCIC), whose founder and rector was the "bishop" himself. In papers submitted by some of his colleagues to the Johannesburg Supreme Court in a bid to stop him from further exercising his post as rector, it also emerged that his corruption was not limited to the college. An internal investigation by the SACC, which had employed him in 1978 as director of church development to liaise with the African independent churches, revealed around the same time that he had forged an unspecified number of checks. After his credibility was battered by these revelations, he tried to form an alliance with the white DRC and thereafter moved on to join the CLSA. Until 20 December 1981, a CLSA leaflet claimed RICA and SATCIC as members. All this drama took place many years after he had lost his post in the AICA in the 1960s, largely because of dishonest practices.

After the Eloff Commission was instituted, Isaac Mokoena rather suddenly began to be featured regularly on the SABC television services as a "prominent South African clergyman" with a "moderate view" and opposed to the call for sanctions. For instance, he began to attack Archbishop Tutu in earnest, mainly on the issue of sanctions, in 1980. From then on, he also began expressing his support for the Reagan

---

75. See L. Kickham, "How U.S. Evangelicals Bless Apartheid," *Penthouse* (March 1988), 18–20; Knight, *Wolves in Sheep's Clothing*, p. 13; "The Political Abuse of Religion," p. 7.

administration's "constructive engagement" policy, and toured several West European countries and the United States. One of his favorite habits during such tours was to denounce leading South African clergymen such as Archbishop Tutu and the Reverend Doctor Boesak as frauds.

To strengthen his argument against Archbishop Tutu and other leading South African clergymen, he would typically claim that RICA had a membership of 4.5 million. He has gone so far as to give himself the title of "Bishop of Soweto" simply because he used to live in the huge sprawling township. Mokoena's wild claim about a membership of 4.5 million has been openly challenged by Prof. G.C. Oosthuizen of the University of Zululand's Research Institute on Black Independent Churches, whose research into RICA has concluded that RICA membership is composed of a small number of churches and can at best be counted in "only a few thousands."[76]

When one tries to enquire into who sponsors Mokoena's regular trips abroad, the standard reply is that RICA is financed by small donations from its individual members or, at most, some anonymous "businessmen." But, as shown by the case of the Muldergate scandal, the unidentified businessmen might just be covers for the secret funding of covert projects by the Pretoria regime. One small clue as to who may be behind his travels is provided by the Hennendorfer public relations firm in Frankfurt, West Germany. During several of his trips to that country, he was hosted by the firm. One of the firm's major customers is the South African government.[77] More revealing is former South African state president P.W. Botha's decision to award Mokoena with the Decoration for Meritorious Service in 1987, which he gladly accepted. The same award was also given to Gen. Magnus Malan; Prof. Wynand Mouton, the former chair of the SABC's board of directors; Mrs. Elize Botha, wife of the former state president; and Mrs. Tienie Vorster, widow of John Vorster.

One more important clue about who finances Mokoena's trips to Western Europe is provided by the London-based

76. See Kickham, "U.S. Evangelicals," p. 118; Knight, *Wolves in Sheep's Clothing*, p. 12.
77. Knight, *Wolves in Sheep's Clothing*, p. 14.

Freedom Association, a highly influential lobbying group within the British Conservative party. Founded as the National Association for Freedom (NAFF) in December 1975, it changed its name to the Freedom Association in 1979. Along with the right-wing Institute of Economic Affairs (IEA), the Center for Policy Studies, and the Adam Smith Institute, the Freedom Association was largely responsible for charting the Conservative party's economic, social, and foreign policies during the last ten years of Margaret Thatcher's prime ministership.

In April 1989, the Freedom Association sponsored Mokoena and the self-styled Archbishop Masiya on a speaking tour of the United Kingdom. In the same manner that some pro-apartheid elements set up "Bishop" Mokoena to be a competitor with Winnie Mandela for her nomination as the honorary rector of Glasgow University in February 1987, the Freedom Association arranged for them deliberately to upstage Archbishop Tutu's visit to Birmingham by a few days during the city's centenary celebrations. During a radio interview with Trevor Barnes of Radio four, Mokoena, as is his standard practice, lambasted Archbishop Tutu for his position on sanctions. He further dismissed the call for the elimination of the apartheid system as a recipe for disaster and tantamount to the institution of "black apartheid." In his view, "the solution to apartheid will come through capitalism."[78]

The Freedom Association is an elite body with a cell-like structure whose membership, according to its charter, is limited to a tiny minority of conservative members of the British aristocracy. Like its American counterparts, it operates in almost total seclusion and keeps its membership secret. Contrary to its professed goal of pursuing freedom, its rules specifically state that no branch member "shall be entitled to examine or take copies of any books or records"[79] of the branch, except the annual accounts released with the approval of the annual general meeting. Two of its leading members are Robert Moss and Brian Crozier. Moss was its

78. I. Mokoena, transcript of radio interview with Trevor Barnes on Radio four, 16 April 1989.
79. Jennings, *Enemy Within*, p. 6.

first director when it was founded as the NAFF, and has all along been editor of its publication, the *Free Nation*.

In 1979, the Freedom Association published a book entitled *The Minimum State – Beyond Party Politics*. Written by Crozier, the book opens with a forthright statement that "the era of party democracy is nearing its close" and calls for an alternative to "the system now in its prolonged death throes."[80] After writing off liberal democracy, which he also calls the "democracy of universal suffrage and political parties," he denounces the "totalist tyranny" of scientific socialism or Marxism, which he regards as the "horrible twin" of fascism. Having said this, Crozier strangely enough does not dismiss or denounce fascism, which he claims is far from an authoritarian military dictatorship. Instead, he states that though fascism can be "exceedingly unpleasant" and cannot be seen as desirable, it is nevertheless "far preferable" to the "totalitarian nightmare" of scientific socialism. In the course of this, he even denounces social democracy and the welfare state. But unlike his counterparts elsewhere, he sees "the devil" as being incarnated more by the Labor party than the Communist party in British politics. To drive this point home, Crozier categorically states that "a return to power of the Labor party would . . . be the worst political disaster that could overtake the British people."[81]

One of the central planks of Crozier's argument against either liberal democracy or social democracy, let alone any form of socialism, is that under democracy the individual's initiative to make an investigation into controversial matters suffers as a result of "the intimidatory pressures of those who think it wrong to inquire into the possibility that some races may be 'less equal' than others in inherited ability."[82] Departing from this position, he goes on to complain bitterly that "for years, it has been fashionable to denounce 'elitism,' since everybody is held to be equal to everybody else - women and men, blacks and whites, the dull and the bright, the swift and the slow, the rich and the poor."[83] As a solution to this

---

80. B. Crozier, "The Minimum State – Beyond Party Politics," (1979), cited in ibid., p. 18.
81. Ibid., p. 21.
82. Ibid., p. 18.
83. Ibid., p. 19.

question, Crozier proposes political rule by a self-perpetuating elite composed of carefully selected individuals with the necessary 'intelligence capacity' and a 'minimum state' with 'counter-subversive capacity' under which "telephone taps may be needed, and files on the activities of subversive or potentially subversive groups must be maintained."[84] It goes without saying that Crozier's select elite group of individuals with the necessary "intelligence capacity" should preferably, if not obligatorily, be white Anglo-Saxon Protestants (WASPS).

If this is so, it would seem that the only thing which Mokoena has learned from his association with such elements is to extend their racist logic to his preaching of ethnicism among South Africa's oppressed majority. For instance, in October 1986, he attacked the ANC as "a party of Xhosa-speaking people" and went on to disparage its Sotho and Tswana-speaking leaders as the movement's "stepchildren."[85] Oddly enough, he finds solace in Chief Gatsha Buthelezi, whom he holds in high esteem as the supposed leader of the six million Zulu-speaking South Africans. The ideological affinity he shares with Crozier on the need to ensure the political rule of a self-perpetuating elite can perhaps be seen by appointing himself as the life president of SATCIC, which was closed down in 1979 because of his financial mismanagement and other corrupt practices.

In October 1986, Thamsanqa Linda, the former "mayor" of Port Elizabeth's Ibhayi township in the Eastern Cape, with the support of Isaac Mokoena, Edward Kunene, and Dr. Evangel B. Malamb, founded the United Christian Conciliation party (UCCP) at a meeting in a posh Johannesburg hotel. Linda and Mokoena immediately became the joint presidents of the UCCP, while the SABC TV–2's Rev. J.E. Mglalose became general secretary, Kunene, a former "mayor" of Soweto, its treasurer, and Dr. Malamb, the public relations liaison officer. The UCCP's other leading figures were former Soweto "mayor" Sigfried Manthata, C.S. Lengene, J. Mokoena, Patrick Gaboutloeloe, and Revs. J.P.J. Khubheka and D.E. Selipe. The composition of its leadership, which includes at

84. Ibid.
85. Cited in S. Nyaka, "The Rhino-hide Bishop Thunders into Politics," *Weekly Mail* (Johannesburg) 17–23 October 1986.

least six former or actual township councillors, has led most people to dismiss the UCCP as a bunch of government stooges, and caused Azhar Cachalia, the UDF's national treasurer, to state:

> The collection of a few discredited individuals calling themselves a Christian party is a last-ditch attempt by the government to prop up a so-called moderate alternative to our people's organizations.[86]

At its launch, all four senior leaders of UCCP evaded answering controversial questions on its constitution, membership size, criteria for admission as a member, possible relations with trade unions, position on the demand for Nelson Mandela's release, etc. Thamsanqa Linda even stated that "the only person who can advocate the release of Mandela is his wife and what's more, Mandela is big enough to speak for himself."[87] Any suggestion that the UCCP had links with the Pretoria regime or some other foreign government was rejected out of hand.

But listening quietly in the back seats of its launching conference were some unlikely guests – Russell Crystal, the founder and then president of the small National Students' Federation (NSF) and Martin Yuill, the head of the Student Moderate Alliance (SMA). The target of both the NSF and its affiliate SMA has been the largest student body on the white English-speaking university campuses, the National Union of South African Students (NUSAS), and, since 1985, the End Conscription Campaign (ECC). Both NUSAS and the ECC are affiliated with the United Democratic Front (UDF), while the NSF and SMA are notorious for their persistent defence of the South African government's policy. Russell Crystal has already been exposed as a paid agent of the Pretoria regime's security and intelligence services, while the *National Student*, the magazine around which the NSF was formed, was found to have received secret funds from BOSS.[88] Russell subsequently

---

86. *Weekly Mail* (Johannesburg)
87. Cited in S. Nyaka, "Rhinos in Search of Someone To Protect," *Weekly Mail* (Johannesburg), 9–15 October 1986.
88. See "Lunatic Fringe: Anti-Conscription Rankles Night" *Resister*, no. 53 (December 1987–January 1988), p. 21: COSAWR, London. For more information on Isaac Mokoena's links with the South African security police, see L. Kickham, "How U.S. Evangelicals Bless Apartheid," *Penthouse*, March 1988.

married a U.S. diplomat and settled in the United States.

Before he solidified his links with the U.S. through this act, however, he had to prove his loyalty in the best possible way he could find, namely, organizing NSF campaigns in support of UNITA and the MNR.

One of the highlights of such NSF actions was sending representatives to an international gathering of right-wing forces sponsored by the CIA and SADF in June 1985 at UNITA's headquarters at Jamba, in southern Angola. Attending the gathering were representatives of the CIA-trained Nicaraguan Contras, the Pakistan-based Afghan Mujahdin, and the WACL. This was followed by the organization of a conference under the slogan "Youth for Freedom," which was held in Johannesburg in July 1985. Sponsored by the NSF at a cost of about R 500,000, the conference was also attended by representatives of UNITA and the Afghan Mujahdin who addressed an audience composed of right-wing elements from the United States, Western Europe, Latin America, and the South African security police. The conference also heard a message of support from P.W. Botha, who praised the activities of these groups as a positive effort to "combat pacifism, radicalism and terrorism."[89] The next year, the NSF staged a speaking tour of several South African universities by UNITA officials, but the well-publicized propaganda stunt proved to be a failure as most students refused to allow its representatives onto their campuses.

If the presence of Russell Crystal and Martin Yuill at the UCCP launch may be thought to be of no political significance, perhaps that of Prof. Colin Vale, Prof. André Thomashausen, and Graham Levin will correct any misconception. Professor Vale, from the University of the Witwatersrand's international relations department, is also employed by the training section of the Pretoria regime's Ministry of Foreign Affairs. He is in fact an accredited member of the South African diplomatic corps. Prof. Thomashausen is from the University of South Africa's (UNISA) Institute of International Law, while there is little known about Levin to this print. These three whites have been exposed as leading members of the UCCP. Rumors abound that they are the real masterminds behind the forma-

89. *The Star* (Johannesburg), 18 July 1987.

tion of the UCCP. They are also said to be the puppet masters who are "effectively in control" of the UCCP's direction.[90] Such connections would most evidently invalidate Mokoena's declaration that the UCCP "won't accept money from the government because that money stinks."[91]

At its launch in 1986, the UCCP's front leaders promised they would soon undertake a huge recruitment drive in the black townships. Doctor Malamb went so far as to claim that "because we are good people we won't need the protection of the police or the army when we go into the townships."[92] In one of the few rallies it has so far held to fulfil its promise, the UCCP called a meeting to launch a branch in Port Elizabeth in January 1988. The meeting was addressed by Thamsanqa Linda and was attended at most by a mere 130 people. According to a report given to the South African church weekly *New Nation* by a municipal policeman who attended but, for obvious reasons, declined to be named, more than sixty of the audience were members of the notorious municipal police force or "special" constables, dressed in civilian clothes.[93] The policemen were hired by Linda to attend as part of the audience and, at the same time, to protect him from the residents of KwaZakhele and other black Port Elizabeth townships. Linda was forced to run away from his home in Ibhayi township, and was virtually declared a persona non grata in the other black townships of Port Elizabeth in early 1986, after he had requested his paymasters in Pretoria to ban the UDF and threatened to deny housing to trade union members.

Soon after it had announced its intention to participate in the October 1988 black municipal elections, the UCCP decided to extend its politics of intimidation, corruption, and bribery into the churches. During the campaign before the abortive elections of February 1988 Thamsanqa Linda and Jimmy Nako, his successor as "mayor" of Ibhayi township, surreptitiously promoted the division of Zwelonka, the main body of the independent Zionist churches' ministers, with

90. See S. Nyaka, "Black Rhinos Charge . . . from White Pretoria," *Weekly Mail* (Johannesburg) 14–20 November 1986.
91. Nyaka, "Rhino in Search of Someone To Protect."
92. Ibid.
93. *New Nation*, 21–27 January 1988, p. 5.

promises of money, employment, training, and land plots. Taking advantage of the poverty and low educational levels of many members of the African independent churches, they encouraged a group of twenty religious leaders from Zionist churches to break away from Zwelonka and form the still-born United African Unity Association of Churches (UAUAC). They managed to achieve this with the connivance of "Arch-bishop" Enoch Matyana of the small Holy Healers Zionist Apostolic church in Port Elizabeth, where most Zionist church ministers do not have their own church premises and, in fact, alternate their preaching on Sundays with factory work during the week. Matyana, who holds a Standard 7 (equivalent of junior high school) school certificate and admits that self-promotion is not an uncommon feature in the Zionist churches, is no exception to the rule in this predicament facing the African independent churches. In return for the promises of money, training, and other help, Nako and Linda expected the church ministers to urge their congregations to go out and vote in the October 1988 elections.

However understandable their predicament, it is difficult to understand why Matyana, who along with millions of other black South Africans is also a victim of oppression and exploitation through the apartheid system, could expect the likes of Mokoena and Linda to deliver on their promises since it is well known that they have no real influence with the Pretoria regime.

Because of this long terrible history of double-dealing and corruption in the service to the Pretoria regime, Isaac Mokoena has been roundly condemned as a traitor not only to the Christian community but to the South African people as a whole. The last word goes to the leading members of the African independent churches movement, who in one of their many pronouncements on this issue, issued a statement in early 1985, which read in part:

> The history of the Bishop Mokoena over the last few years is indeed a tragedy to the Christian church in South Africa, especially the independent churches, and the struggle of the black people for a just and human society in South Africa. We . . . watched with dismay the unfolding of this tragic history, with Bishop Mokoena drifting closer and closer to the forces that work to maintain the apartheid regime whilst drifting further and further away from his

people. . . . We saw him . . . collaborating with the Christian League of Southern Africa, which is a far-right organization. . . . We are shocked by the lie that Bishop Tutu "promoted a war of black against black" [and his being labeled] as "communist." Only the enemy of the people, the perpetrators of the evil and satanic apartheid system, use such labels against peace-loving South Africans.[94]

Right-Wing Religion and Militarism

The fallacy of the separation of state and church in South Africa can also be seen in the role of right-wing religious thought and practice in both the SADF and the South African police force. To start with, it is important to note the role both these institutions assign to God and religion within their tasks of aggression and repression. The creed of the South African police force, which also reflects the preamble of the South African constitution, states in part:

> In humble submission to Almighty God, Who controls the destinies of nations and the history of peoples; Who gathered our forebears together from many countries and gave them this their own; . . . whereas we are conscious of our responsibility towards God and man . . . to further the contentment and spiritual and material welfare of all in our midst; we are prepared to assume our task and . . . foster sound international relations based on Christian and religious principles to realize the ideal of peaceful coexistence.[95]

The evolution of the South African state is thus seen as an act ordained by God, rather than as a process of historical development. Within this, the Bible is also viewed as the final and absolute text of God's authority over humankind, not because the Bible said so but because a group of U.S. citizens (the "Fundamentalists") decided in 1915 that this should be the central pillar of their religious faith. Accordingly, anyone who disagrees with this is showing insubordination not only to the state but to God as well, and therefore

---

94. *Ecunews*, March 1985, p. 26.
95. S.A.P. *Annual Report*, (Pretoria, 1987).

woe unto him. Aside from the hypocrisy found in the above text, the attempt to find moral justification for the European colonization of present-day South Africa and the implanting of a foreign economic system through force of arms by invoking God's mission and Christian principles, let alone the blatant distortion of history, is remarkable for its incredibility.

For its part, the SADE, in the person of Gen. Magnus Malan, states:

> Every member of the SADF has the right to belong to the church or religion of his choice. This right is respected in service matters and the member must be given the opportunity to practice his religion.... No influencing of members or proselytizing is permitted in the Defense Force. To prevent confusion and proselytizing, no interdenominational or external organization or person may perform any religious or church function within the Defense Force, nor distribute any religious literature, without the authority of the Chaplain General.[96]

Yet the SADF, which General Malan considers to be representative of South Africa's population, until 1988 had thirty-six ordained priests, all white, serving as military chaplains in its ranks. Though South Africa as a country has various religious faiths, chaplains employed by the SADF are drawn exclusively from the Christian denominations and are largely Protestant. The South African police force, which until 1987 had its chaplains recruited only from the three white Dutch Reformed Church denominations and one English-speaking Protestant denomination, has fared no better than the SADF in this respect. In fact, most chaplains are serving in both the SADF and SAP against the stated official policies of their respective church denominations. This state of affairs has very serious implications not only for the integrity of the SADF as a supposedly national defense force but also its representative nature in the eyes of the majority of South Africa's population.

Drawing upon the old Christian ideology of aggression,

96. M. Malan, *Briefing on the Organisation and Functions of the South African Defence Force and the Armaments Corporation of South Africa Ltd., to Members of Parliament* (Cape Town, 1987), p. 52.

long abandoned by most Christians, many chaplains serving with the SADF have a strong tendency to look upon it as an army of holy crusaders defending Christian civilization against evil forces. These presumably find their worldly incarnation in those fighting against the apartheid system, the "anti-Christ" ideas supposedly inherent in socialism, Islam, and any other factor which is seen as a threat to the status quo and the privileged position of the white South African minority. For instance, as early as 1979, the SADF's chaplain general issued a Christmas statement which said that the "Defense Force serves the Christ of Christmas and takes up arms to defend this Christmas patron."[97] Even the insignia adopted for use by the SADF's Chaplain Corps – the cross of the Knights of Malta – is a clear reflection of this ideology. In line with this, the worst forms of aggression against other peoples, their cultures, and religious faiths can find justification under the pretext of defending or spreading "Christian" civilization.

In its June–July 1988 issue, *Resister* published an article based on a set of lecture notes which clearly show how some military chaplains still try to find moral and religious legitimization on scriptural ground for the SADF and its military aggression. In the first set of notes, Padre D.M. Williams claimed that "the source of any authority which men may exercise over their fellow men . . . all human authority is derived authority."[98]

"The Scriptures," he added, "teach us that the existing authorities have been put there by God." After blessing the Pretoria regime in this way, Padre Williams went on to exhort the young white conscripts in military service to submit themselves willingly to the SADF and its rules, regardless of the untold damage and suffering that its acts of aggression have caused to both the South African people and those of neighboring countries, because

God is a God of order. It is His will that men lead ordered lives. . . . For this reason He has invested various institutions with

---

97. "Churches In Uniform: Defending Civilisation," *Resister* (London), April–May 1988, p. 7.

98. "With God on Their Side? The SADF's Abuse of Religion," *Resister* (London), June–July 1988, p. 8.

Jeffrey Marishane

authority so that law and order can be ensured in the home, the church, the state and the community.[99]

These are just a few examples which show how most military chaplains help the SADF promote militarism and at the same time claim moral legitimacy for its acts of aggression under the cloak of religion. During the past sixteen years, the main South African church denominations, to which many of the young military conscripts belong, have tried to change this situation by demanding the right to set up an independent chaplains service that does not fall under SADF control, but to no avail. Currently, all military chaplains are full employees of the SADF, hold military rank and receive an official salary paid by the Pretoria regime. The only churches which have so far not taken a stand against this are the three white Dutch Reformed Churches and some black independent churches. However, even if the black independent churches were to do this, the impact of their voice would be negligible, since all their members are denied the right to vote and, perhaps with the exception of the ZCC, they do not have any financial muscle. From among the white Dutch Reformed churches, a new splinter church, the Afrikaanse Protestantse Kerk (APK), which broke away from the main NGK with seventy two congregations and twenty dominees, supports the present role which military chaplains play within the SADF.

Frontline Fellowship – Veterans for Victory

As shown above, the SADF has over the years, and contrary to its own stated rules, denied many of its members the practice of their own religious faith by not making provisions for the recruitment of military chaplains from their denominations. If a military chaplain from one's denomination has perchance been recruited, the SADF would then refuse his church the right to choose the chaplain and determine the content of his sermons and lectures. Instead, the SADF has continued at will to impose on many young white conscripts

99. Ibid.

a brand of Christianity alien to that of their respective church denominations, thereby manipulating their religious belief in favor of the Pretoria regime. Worse still, it has allowed the emergence of several right-wing religious groups and even encouraged their proselytizing activities within and outside its ranks.

Foremost among such groups is Frontline Fellowship, formerly known as the Motorbike Mission. Formed in 1981 as a prayer fellowship within SADF ranks, Frontline Fellowship is led by its founder, Peter Christopher Hammond, a British citizen serving with the South African army, and is one of the groups affiliated with the UCA. Its field of activity has involved, to use its own words, "assisting persecuted churches in Mozambique, Angola, and the Cape Verde Islands; Bible distribution in communist lands; challenging South African Christians to pray for revival and missions; defending the church against the infiltration of unbiblical heresies; evangelism in war zones, etc."[100] However, Veterans for Victory, its sister organization, let its tongue slip and almost came close to the truth when it said of Frontline Fellowship: "This is a Christian Mission group, but don't be fooled by the name, Christian or Mission. These fellows go into Mozambique and Angola doing research and . . . can supply information and photos of SWAPO and other terror groups."[101]

Thus, the role of Frontline Fellowship as part of the SADF's intelligence gathering apparatus has been laid bare for the world to see. An article published in *EDICESA News* in early 1989 described Frontline Fellowship as "the pivotal organization for the deployment of South African military men and pro-apartheid mercenaries as 'missionaries' in Mozambique and throughout southern Africa." Another source says that Peter Hammond, its leader, is the clearest example of "a soldier operating in the guise of a missionary."[102]

Hammond takes great delight in illegally entering Mozambique, courtesy of the SADF and under the protection of the

100. See Veterans for Victory, *Newsletter* (n.p. n.d. [early 1987]); "Missionaries Detained by Zambia Preach to MNR," *Weekly Mail* (Johannesburg), pp. 23–29 October 1987.
101. Ibid.
102. "Far-right Military Church Group Captured – and Released – by Frelimo" *Southscan* (London), no. 41 (3 November 1989).

MNR, in search of "first-hand accounts of eyewitnesses" to prove "Frelimo atrocities" and the alleged persecution of the church in that country. While he sees Mozambique as "a world of chaos, fear, roadblocks, starvation, house searches, summary executions, burnt churches and constant warfare,"[103] he omits to mention that the terrible situation in which that country has been finding itself is more a direct consequence of the destabilization war waged by the SADF through the MNR than a sign of failure by the Frelimo leadership and the economic system that they chose to follow.

Hammond decries the "evils" of socialism and "Frelimo atrocities" but says absolutely nothing about the brutal murder of nearly 100,000 innocent and helpless civilians by the MNR. According to a report prepared by Robert Gersony, most of the killings were done through "shooting executions; knife-axe-bayonet killings; burning alive; beating to death; forced asphyxiation; forced starvation; forced drownings; and random shooting at civilians in villages during attacks."[104] In addition to this, the MNR was found to have engaged in the systematic abduction of civilians, mutilations, rape, the looting of shops and government storage facilities, and the stealing of food destined for the civilian population. The MNR is also held directly responsible for causing damage to or destroying 1,800 schools, 720 health clinics, 900 shops and 1,300 vehicles, including tractors, buses, and trucks, between 1980 and 1988. These had to be targets for military attacks simply because the MNR is resentful of the fact that they are one of the main sources of the Frelimo government's popularity among the local population.

The direct consequence of the MNR's random attacks has been to turn Mozambique into the poorest country in the world, with an annual per capita income of about $100, an infant mortality rate of nearly 375 deaths per one thousand

103. *Frontline Fellowship Newsletter*, January–February 1986, Newlands, So. Africa.

104. See R. Gersony, *Summary of Mozambican Refuge Accounts of Principally Conflict-related Experience in Mozambique* p. 21 Bureau for Refuge Programs, US Dept. of State, April 1988. For more information see W. Minter, *The Mozambican National Resistance (RENAMO) – As Presented by Ex-Participants*. Research report submitted to the Ford Foundation and the Swedish International Development Agency (SIDA), March 1989.

live births, and average life expectancies of about forty years for men and thirty-seven years for women.[105] As if this were not enough, there is currently an estimated three million people facing starvation and over one million internal refugees.[106]

At first sight, the untold damage and destruction caused to the Mozambican people and their economy may seem merely haphazard, but when Alfonso Dhlakama, the MNR's commander, sent an urgent request to his paymasters for more "war material" on 16 June 1984, Colonel Cornelius (Charles) van Niekerk, then head of "Operation Mila," replied four days later:

> Renamo must continue to squeeze Machel, but in such a way as to use as little war material as possible [and] avoid combat with the FAM [Fuerzas Armados de Mozambique], giving more attention to destroying the economy, infrastructure, and controlling the population.[107]

105. J. Mathebula, "MNR: The U.S. South Africa Connection," *Sechuba* (Lusaka), April 1989, pp. 25–26.

106. A. Meldrum, "The Most Brutal War," *Africa Report*, (New York), May–June 1988, p. 26.

107. Mathebula, "MNR," p. 25.

· 4 ·

American Evangelicalism in Zimbabwe

PAUL GIFFORD

From Rhodesia to Zimbabwe

Zimbabwe, formerly Rhodesia, was colonized by the British in the 1890s, and among those pioneers were Christian missionaries. The Christian churches can boast a proud record in health and education during the colonial years, but with some notable exceptions, like the Anglican, Cripps, and the Methodist, White, who articulated black grievances, the churches were not conscious of their role in the colonizing enterprise as a whole. An insight into this role is provided by the following comment of Cecil Rhodes himself to the parents of a Dutch Reformed missionary: "Your son among the natives is worth as much to me as a hundred of my policemen."[1]

When Britain began to dismantle its empire, white Rhodesians refused to bow to British pressure to accommodate African aspirations, and unilaterally declared independence from Britain in 1965.[2] Black resistance became open war in 1972, escalating until Prime Minister Ian Smith was forced to negotiate a settlement with black nationalists in 1979. During the years of this increasingly bloody war, the Smith government, controlling all the media, presented the struggle as a clash between Christian civilization and godless communism. Moreover, of all the nationalist leaders, it was Robert

---

1. Cited in P. Zachrisson, An *African Area in Change: Belingwe 1894–1946. A Study in Colonialism, Missionary Activity and African Response in Southern Rhodesia* (Gothenburg, 1978), p. 267.
2. In 1965 there were about 200,000 whites in Rhodesia out of a population of six million. By 1988 there were about 100,000 whites in Zimbabwe out of an estimated population of eight million.

Mugabe in particular whom they painted as an archetypal Marxist thug. Hence the consternation of white Rhodesians when, in the internationally supervised elections marking Zimbabwe's independence (1980), Mugabe won an absolute majority in parliament.

The Jesuit-educated Mugabe is not opposed to Christianity; nor are the members of his Cabinet, most of whom are also products of missionary education. Some are quite active in their churches. Mugabe appointed the Methodist minister Canaan Banana as Zimbabwe's first (non-executive) president, the highest dignity in the country. Mugabe, Banana, and government ministers have frequently called on the churches to play their full part in creating the new Zimbabwe.[3]

The response of the mainline churches since independence has been hesitant and confused. Between 1965 and 1980, Rhodesia was ostracized by the international community, and the predominantly white-led churches in their isolation largely succumbed to government propaganda. The Anglican church seemed particularly susceptible, and some of its most prominent spokesmen frequently denounced the nationalists as communists and terrorists and urged support for Smith's "Christian government."[4] These pronouncements have been responsible for the Anglican church's low profile since independence. Rhodesia's United Methodist church was headed by Bishop Abel Muzorewa, who as a party to Smith's "Internal Settlement" in 1978 actually became prime minister of the short-lived country of Zimbabwe-Rhodesia in 1979. In this role he was seen as Smith's puppet and a traitor to the black cause, and his political party was all but annihilated in the 1980 elections. However, he continued in politics until 1985, while still head of the United Methodist church. His criticisms of the government in those years, coupled with counterallegations that he was implicated in dissident activity in Matabeleland, led to open conflict with the government and compromised the Methodist church, which has

---

3. C. F. Hallencreutz, "Ecumenical Challenges in Independent Zimbabwe: ZCC 1980–85," *Church and State in Zimbabwe*, eds., C. Hallencreutz and A. Moyo (Gweru, 1988), pp. 276–89.

4. M. Lapsley, *Neutrality or Co-option? Anglican Church and State from 1964 until the Independence of Zimbabwe*, (Gweru, 1986).

been particularly unsure of itself in the new Zimbabwe. Similarly, the first post-independence general secretary of the local council of churches (now called the Zimbabwe Christian Council) was closely linked to Bishop Muzorewa. This made the ZCC also appear in a rather ambiguous light, and prevented it from acting with any confidence or authority.[5]

The Roman Catholic church came out of the liberation war in rather better shape. Though in no sense developing anything like a liberation theology, one of the bishops publicly denounced Smith's government, publications of the Catholic Justice and Peace Commission drew international attention to abuses of Smith's security forces, and by the end of the war several priests and nuns on mission stations were openly on the side of the guerillas.[6] However, in the early years of independence, the Catholic bishops denounced abuses committed by government forces in combatting dissidents in Matabeland. Although privately he may have heeded the criticism, Mugabe's official reaction was one of furious repudiation. Speaking to the combined heads of religious denominations at Easter 1983, Mugabe took the opportunity to excoriate the Catholic bishops publicly. This experience chastened, even cowed, the Catholic authorities. Subsequent government allegations that it is the Catholic Justice and Peace Commission that has fed critical material to foreign bodies like Amnesty International have not made Catholic authorities any more confident in their public leadership.

For all these reasons, the mainline churches have since independence failed to provide notable public leadership, either singly or together. While cautiously feeling their way to a new relationship with a self-styled Marxist government, they have tended to retreat to ministering to their own flocks, administering their (often considerable) plant, or involving themselves in their own development projects.

If mainline churches have preserved a low profile since independence, the same years have witnessed the advent of a particularly confident evangelical revival. This evangelical sector of Christianity includes the older free churches, but

5. Hallencreutz, "Ecumenical Challenges," pp. 265–75.
6. See I. Linden, *The Catholic Church and the Struggle for Zimbabwe* (London, 1980).

comprises mainly fundamentalists, Pentecostals and new charismatic groups which promote a pietistic, otherworldly, personal, privatized Christianity, which is often dispensationalist and characteristically has American ties. For convenience we will consider these evangelicals under three headings: the transnationals, crusades, and local groups.

The Religious Transnationals

In the years since independence, all the major American religious transnationals have appeared on the Zimbabwean scene.[7] Campus Crusade was founded in California by the Presbyterian Bill Bright in 1951. The organization is dispensationalist, personal, privatized, sees the threat of communism everywhere, is associated with conservative causes within the United States, and tirelessly promotes American interests abroad. In Latin America, its adherents see themselves as the shock troops countering liberation theology. In Zimbabwe, Campus Crusade was established in 1979 as Life Ministries. By 1988 it had a full-time ministerial staff of ten, of whom six were U.S. expatriates. Most of these Americans have been trained at Campus Crusade's international headquarters in California. Its activities in Zimbabwe include university chaplaincy, the training of local pastors, and running seminars for senior government and business personnel at Lake Kariba, Fothergill Island, Nyanga, and other resorts.

Youth With a Mission (YWAM) was founded in the United States in 1960 by Loren Cunningham, and now has its headquarters in Hawaii. In 1985 it claimed to have 5,100 long-term missionaries and 190 permanent YWAM bases, and to send out 15,000 short-term missionaries, more than any other mission. It is Pentecostal, dispensationalist, and tends to see the United States as God's champion on earth. Although YWAM came to Rhodesia in the 1970s, it closed after a short period because of the war. After independence it was reestablished in 1981 by a local couple who had previously run

---

7. For a fuller discussion of all these transnationals, both in general and within Zimbabwe, see P. Gifford, *The Religious Right in Southern Africa* (Harare, 1988).

their own ministry in Bulawayo. In 1987 YWAM had seven full-time workers in Harare (five white Zimbabweans, one South African, one North American) and six in Bulawayo (five black Zimbabweans and one North American). Its work has three thrusts. First, it is involved in evangelization, which includes helping local churches and founding churches where none existed before. Secondly, it trains would-be missionaries in its discipleship training school near Bulawayo. Thirdly, it engages in relief work, particularly along the Mozambique border. The number on short-term mission work varies; once a group of forty came for three weeks' concentrated evangelization. The advantage of such short-term work is that it can be done on a tourist visa.

The Full Gospel Businessmen's Fellowship International (FGBMFI) began in Los Angeles in 1952, founded by Demos Shakarian, a prominent California dairyman. It fosters a worldwide revival to prepare for the imminent return of Christ. It is Pentecostal, but is non-denominational and includes Catholic charismatics. President Reagan had close links with it; he claimed his ulcers were cured by FGBMFI members who prayed over him during his term as governor of California. Many prominent members of Reagan's administration belonged to it, as do many in authority in the United States military and in related industries. The FGBMFI began in Zimbabwe in 1983, founded by a South African group who controlled the Zimbabwean chapter until it became autonomous in 1985. By 1988 there were four Zimbabwean chapters in Harare, Bulawayo, Karoi and Gweru. The Harare chapter has about sixty members, of whom about 95 percent are white. Members are from a variety of professions and businesses, and most belong to local Pentecostal churches.

Jimmy Swaggart Ministries is based in Baton Rouge, Louisiana, and has been operating in Zimbabwe since January 1985. In Zimbabwe there is no strictly evangelistic mission, merely an office for Jimmy Swaggart's Relief Ministries and Jimmy Swaggart Child Care International, which exist to channel aid rather than to proselytize. However, the office does distribute Swaggart's books, tapes, and videos; the videos have had regular screening on Zimbabwean television. The office had an aid budget in 1986 of Z $2,500,000 (approximately U.S. $1,500,000), most of which went to Mozambique and

Mozambican refugees in Zimbabwe. All its activities in Zimbabwe are closely scrutinized by the Zimbabwe government, because of the suspicion that some of its activities may have been directed to helping Renamo rebels in Mozambique. These suspicions arose not just because of Swaggart's own well-publicized anticommunism, nor just because of the aid given to the Nicaraguan Contras by the American religious Right, nor just because Swaggart literature was discovered in 1985 at a captured Renamo base. They arose because in 1986 in Washington a spokesman for the pro-Renamo Mozambique Information Office stated that Jimmy Swaggart was providing aid through Assembly of God Churches in Renamo-held territory. Swaggart's aides would not comment on this claim. The Zimbabwe officials of Jimmy Swaggart Ministries insist that all such suspicions are groundless.

World Vision International grew out of American Evangelicalism at the height of the cold war, when conservative Evangelicalism was closely identified with anticommunism. Its anticommunism was still strong when World Vision began operations in Vietnam. Its seemingly limitless funds and large headquarters opposite the U.S. embassy emphasized its close links with the U.S. Agency for International Development; its willingness to report its activities to USAID led to charges of informing for the CIA. At the same time, it continually refused to join with other Vietnam aid agencies in protesting against human-rights violations or the maltreatment of refugees. Criticism of World Vision increased after attention was drawn to events in Salvadorean refugee camps for which World Vision was responsible. The publicity elicited a report from World Vision headquarters admitting some of the criticisms, but insisting that the abuses were the work of individuals in their employ, not the policy of World Vision itself.

World Vision came to Rhodesia from South Africa in 1969. In 1979 it severed its links with South Africa and became World Vision Zimbabwe. Since independence it has expanded greatly and in 1988 employed about fifty in its Harare office and another fifty in the field. This workforce comprises almost entirely black Zimbabweans, all of them evangelical Protestants. In 1986 its budget was Z $2,500,000 (approx. U.S. $1,500,000). It is involved in development, relief, and (the primary reason for all its activity) evangelism. As well as World

Vision Zimbabwe, Zimbabwe hosts a separate branch of World Vision responsible for its activity in Mozambique.

Rhema Bible Church, although not in the same league as the transnationals just mentioned, is an offshoot of Kenneth Hagin's Rhema Bible Church in Tulsa, Oklahoma. Kenneth Hagin is a prominent American media evangelist, best known for his prosperity gospel, that is, the insistence that health and wealth are signs of a true Christian. Rhema began in Zimbabwe in April 1982 with six people meeting in the pastor's home. By 1987 it had six hundred adults and 175 children attending its Sunday morning service, and three hundred adults attending its evening service. Of its adherents, about 20 percent are black. It boasts sixteen full-time employees, two bible schools, audio and videotape ministries, a prison ministry, a youth ministry (of 150), a hospital ministry, a radio ministry, and Compassion Ministries, its relief arm in Zimbabwe's four camps for Mozambican refugees. Rhema also sees itself called to work in the surrounding countries of central Africa. Rhema's Christianity is a faithful reflection of its parent body's: it is fundamentalist in Scripture, millennialist, stresses healing and tongues, practices discipling, and insists that health and prosperity are the right of every true Christian, so much so that poverty and illness disclose a deficient Christian life. Its U.S. ties are manifest. The founder and pastor of Rhema in Zimbabwe is a graduate of Gordon Lindsays's Christ for the Nations in Dallas. Rhema's two bible schools use a course devised in the United States by founder Kenneth Hagin. Rhema's Compassion Ministries have received considerable aid from Pat Robertson's Operation Blessing. Rhema's audio and videotape collections feature, along with some South African evangelists, almost all the major figures of American Evangelicalism – particularly Swaggart.

Crusades

Besides the above transnationals which have established themselves in Zimbabwe, other organizations purveying the same kind of Christianity have visited the country. Preeminent among these is Christ for All Nations (CFAN). CFAN was founded in South Africa by a German Pentecostal,

Reinhard Bonnke, who has taken his revival crusades all over the continent and as far afield as Scandinavia, the United States, and New Zealand. In 1986, to facilitate its access to all African countries, it moved its headquarters from Johannesburg to Frankfurt. CFAN conducted three revivals in Zimbabwe between 1980 and 1986. These were events of some importance, particularly the last, held in CFAN's new tent which, with seating for over 32,000 people, they claim is the biggest movable structure in the world. The third crusade in May 1986, which involved 130 local churches, was staged in conjunction with a "Fire Conference" which drew four thousand evangelical leaders from forty one African countries.

The Christianity of both crusade and conference was standard American Evangelicalism. This was obvious from the bookshop, where the material on sale comprised twelve titles by Jimmy Swaggart, eighteen by Kenneth Hagin, three by Ray McCauley (the founder of Rhema in South Africa, who flies both the South African and United States flags at his Johannesburg church), eleven by Kenneth and Gloria Copeland of Fort Worth, seven by Gordon Lindsay of Dallas, and three by John Osteen of Houston. Apart from these, and five titles by Elijah Maswanganyi of South Africa, there were only thirteen other miscellaneous titles on sale. The American connection became even clearer from the list of key speakers. Bonnke apart, the most important speakers at the crusade and conference were: Loren Cunningham of Hawaii, founder of YWAM; Ralph Mahoney of World Missionary Assistance Plan, California; Wayne Myers, now of Mexico; and both Copelands and Ray McCauley, whom I have just mentioned.[8]

Given that the revival was held in Zimbabwe, it was not surprising that overt displays of anticommunism were rare. The message was rather one of "hands-off" politics. However, it became evident soon afterwards that at least some of the speakers were hiding their full political agenda when Ralph Mahoney, on his return to the United States, published a blistering attack in his magazine on Zimbabwe, describing it as a communist tyranny, in contrast to South Africa, which he

---

8. For an analysis of Bonnke's Christianity, see P. Gifford, "'Africa Shall Be Saved.' An Appraisal of Reinhard Bonnke's Pan-African Crusade," *Journal of Religion in Africa* 17 (1987), pp. 63–92.

presented as an embattled democracy. He claimed Zimbabwe was characterized by corruption, mismanagement, police and military brutality, and anti-Americanism. By contrast, South Africa, as the only "viable prosperous capitalist country on the continent" deserved the West's support. Mahoney concluded: "May [Africa's] people find the reality of Jesus Christ . . . sufficient for their desperate needs." That plea to cling to Jesus alone and stay out of politics may seem a very apolitical message. In southern Africa, however, to stay out of politics is a decisive vote for the status quo, and thus this message is in fact a very political one.[9]

Explo '85 was a crusade of a similar kind. This satellite video conference was organized from the United States by Campus Crusade, and linked up audiences in fifty-four countries. The main speakers included Billy Graham and the California-based Argentinian Luis Palau, and during the four days of the event Campus Crusade's Bill Bright gave keynote addresses from (interestingly, given U.S. strategic interests) South Korea, the Philippines, West Berlin, and Mexico City. Campus Crusade in Zimbabwe organized the Zimbabwean end of this event at Harare's International Conference Centre, and fifty-nine local churches took part.

Maurice Cerullo, another California-based Latin American, conducted a "miracle crusade" at Rufaro stadium, Harare, in February 1985. Cerullo, with Luis Palau, was one of the founders of the Latin America Evangelical Fraternity (CONELA) set up in Panama in 1982 in opposition to the liberation-oriented Latin American Catholic Bishops Conference and the Latin American Council of Churches. Maurice Cerullo Ministries has an office in Harare which directs activities in ten sub-Saharan African countries. This office also offers a mass-circulation free correspondence Bible course in both Shona and English. In mid-1988, 1,847 were enrolled for the English course, 457 for the Shona.

Besides such mass crusades, there has been a steady stream of speakers promoting this Christianity to smaller and select audiences. For example, Ed Louis Cole of California conducted public seminars in international hotels in Harare and Bulawayo in mid-1988, and addressed various other audiences

9. See Gifford, *Religious Right*, pp. 69–70.

before going on to give similar seminars in South Africa. His Christianity was the normal American export, with perhaps a stronger than normal prosperity component. It should also be noted that in May 1988, when the Californian John Wimber visited South Africa with his message of healing and personal success, and his inattention to social structures, many evangelical churches in Zimbabwe organized transportation to his seminars in Johannesburg.[10]

Before leaving the subject of crusades, mention must be made of the multi-media *Carter Report*, staged at Harare's International Conference Centre over a period of two weeks beginning 21 May 1988. This event was preceded by an elaborate advertising campaign on television and the mass distribution of glossy leaflets. This promotion was as subtle as it was expensive; the nine thousand who queued for the first evening were not quite sure whether they would witness more than the mysteries of Near Eastern archaeology. Only after a few days did it become clear the the report was promoting Christianity; it needed a few more days to make clear that it was promoting Seventh-Day Adventism. Thus the Carter Report was different from all the ministries and crusades mentioned above, which all promoted one product, standard American Evangelicalism; this one ended up giving considerable importance to Seventh-Day Adventist emphases like sabbatarianism and a surprisingly virulent anti-Catholicism. However, this media event by J.J. Carter, a Texas-based Australian, in many important respects did reinforce the standard American revivalism with which we are concerned here, being scripturally fundamentalist (often bizarrely so), predicting an imminent return of Christ, and focusing purely on personal or "family" morality, with no concern for structural matters.[11]

Local Ministries

Since independence there has been a mushrooming of small local ministries promoting American Evangelicalism. Although

10. Wimber is Professor of Church Growth at Fuller Theological Seminary, Pasadena, California. A good example of his Christianity is J. Wimber with K. Springer, *Power Evangelism: Signs and Wonders Today* (London, 1985).

11. Copies of all Carter's presentations are available from PO Box W19, Waterfalls, Harare, Zimbabwe.

Zimbabwean, these ministries are closely linked with American organizations. For example, Harare's Northside Community Church in mid-1988 adopted a program of door-to-door evangelism called Evangelistic Explosion, using the techniques (and videos and literature) of Dr. C. Armstrong, its American creator. Different Zimbabwean ministries may often have links with the same U.S. organization. For example, it was mentioned above that the head of Zimbabwe's Rhema Bible Church studied with Gordon Lindsay's Christ for The Nations in Dallas. Another graduate of Lindsay's runs a ministry called Africa for Christ in Gweru (he gives an address in Dallas as well); this opened its own Bible college in 1987 with nine students. Also, an Harare organization called Global Literature Lifeline distributes a thoroughly fundamentalist Bible correspondence course which at any one time caters to 10,000 Zimbabweans. This body also publishes seven of Lindsay's publications, with some subsidy from Lindsay's organization, and distributes them with its own biblical material.

Zimbabwe's most notorious local ministry also has links with Lindsay. Shekinah Ministries, an offshoot of the White Assemblies of God Church at Chipinge on the Mozambican border, was discovered aiding the Renamo bandits in Mozambique in 1987. Shekinah had fully taken over the anticommunism of the American religious Right, and one of its Australian missionaries used to telephone government troop movements to the Renamo representative in Washington, for which he was sentenced to ten years in prison by a Mozambican court. Shekinah received aid from several U.S. evangelical bodies, among them Lindsay's Christ for the Nations, which provided money for a van in 1987.[12] Thus Christ for the Nations in Dallas has fairly close links with at least four independent ministries in Zimbabwe; or put the other way, there are at least four different Zimbabwean ministries propagating the Christianity associated with Christ for the Nations.

---

12. For accounts of the trial of the Shekinah missionary, see *Sydney Morning Herald*, 28 March 1988, and *Bulletin* (Sydney), 12 April 1988.

Significance

Zimbabwean churches, ministries, and revivals which promulgate this American evangelism are not only linked with organizations in the United States, but are considerably interconnected among themselves. Consider Harare's Rhema Bible Church, discussed earlier. Rhema plants churches itself; by 1987, about twelve, some in the refugee camps. Rhema establishes them and gives them six months' finance and support. These churches are called simply "Christian" and are autonomous, but the brand of Christianity is, naturally enough, Rhema's. Rhema's pastors have close personal links with the (Wesleyan Holiness) King's Church and the (Pentecostal) Christian Life Centre. Rhema took a prominent part in the 1986 CFAN crusade. Rhema pastors teach at Bishop Guti's Africa Multination for Christ Institute, Zimbabwe's biggest Bible college. It has close links with Andrew Wutawanashe, pastor of the (black) Family of God church; much of the Christian literature used in the refugee camps was written by Wutawanashe. Rhema works closely with Zimbabwe's Africa Enterprise, a subsidiary of the South Africa-based organization founded by Michael Cassidy, a graduate of Fuller Theological Seminary, in Pasadena. At least one of Rhema's pastors works in Africa Enterprise's "Go Teams" (groups of three who witness in homes or at work), and in the refugee camps Rhema uses Africa Enterprise's *"Fox Fires"* (young Bible college students who operate in pairs in rural areas). The director for sub-Saharan Africa of Morris Cerullo World Evangelism attends Rhema. The director of Zimbabwe's Jimmy Swaggart Ministries was formerly Rhema's business manager; he still attends Rhema with two others from Swaggart's Harare office. Most important, Rhema educates many local Zimbabwean pastors, whose previous theological education may have been fairly rudimentary.

Rhema is run by three elders, its three pastors. Two of these, together with the pastor of Bulawayo's Christian center, comprise the three directors of the Africa Fellowship of Christian Ministers. This fellowship is for leaders in ministry, most of whom are pastors. It meets for two days every two months; in 1987 it had fifty paid members, but it can have up to 120 at these assemblies. The meeting in November

1987, attended by well over one hundred Zimbabwean pastors, was conducted by Ray McCauley, whom we met above at the CFAN crusade. The June 1988 meeting, on the topic of money, was addressed by Californian Ed Louis Cole, a proponent of the prosperity gospel. In these ways Rhema influences local pastors. (Note that both YWAM and Campus Crusade give a similar priority to the education of local pastors.)

These ministries and churches are also all linked to the same media producers. Zimbabwe, like so many third world countries, suffers from a lack of foreign exchange. Foreign currency reserves are allocated to essential imports, and religious literature is not classified as essential. The mainline churches have access to considerable funds overseas, but they use these funds for development projects and to maintain physical plant, such as schools and hospitals; they do not import modern theology, either popular or academic, to which they give a fairly low priority. Consequently it would be hard to find in Zimbabwe, outside the university bookshop, any work of modern theology. However, Harare's Word of Life bookshop is always well stocked with evangelical favorites like Bill Bright, Tim LaHaye, and Francis Schaeffer, because its supplies are donated by the American missionaries of the Evangelical Alliance Mission (TEAM), which owns the shop. Swaggart's literature is readily available as well, brought in by his local office, and Lindsay's booklets are published locally under licence. The result is that someone interested in Christian literature can find virtually nothing else but American Evangelicalism. As regards literature, this kind of Christianity has won by default. The victory is even more comprehensive in the field of audio and video cassettes.

Members of mainline churches have not remained unaffected by this evangelical growth. They are influenced by literature and tapes, and as directors of evangelical ministries are also increasingly invited to conduct services on evenings or weekends (often involving media presentations) for mainline church groups. This influence is increasing. In 1989 a group of fourteen churches combined in a "Down to Earth" outreach program in the affluent northern suburbs of Harare, a program involving house fellowship groups and culminating in a crusade "with evangelists from Zimbabwe and elsewhere." Behind the project was the fundamentalist Northside

Community Church. The thirteen participating churches included, not surprisingly, the Church of the Nazarene, and Baptist and Pentecostal fellowships; more surprisingly, five Anglican and one Catholic parish participated. It is significant that the steering committee of eleven pastors included only two Anglicans and did not include the Catholic; the initiative came from the evangelical component, and the mainline churches followed.[13]

The Level of Awareness

Since independence, Zimbabwe has witnessed a remarkable evangelical revival. The Christianity of this revival is totally American. Most of its literature and its audio and video cassettes have come from the United States. Many of its ministers are American, and so is much of its funding. This funding is considerable, and (World Vision excepted) these evangelical bodies, unlike the mainline churches, spend little on development. Their funds go to evangelizing, or, when they go beyond that, to relief. There is nothing African about this Christianity. Inculturation is never mentioned. African culture is not to be Christianized; it is to be repudiated for a totally new existence in Christ.

The leaders of this revival are almost exclusively white, either Zimbabwean, South African, or American. This contrasts starkly with Zimbabwe's mainline churches, whose leadership is totally black. The directors of the transnationals discussed above (World Vision excepted) are white. The eleven-man (they are all male) steering committee of the Down to Earth program just mentioned is totally white. The planning committee of CFAN's 1986 Fire Conference contained twenty-one whites and one black. Its key speakers were all white, with one exception. Is it significant that elsewhere in independent Zimbabwe only the business sector is still dominated by whites?

This Christianity is not overtly anticommunist. Shekinah Ministries, as mentioned above, was proved to be aiding anticommunist Renamo forces in Mozambique. Thomas

13. *Northern News* (Harare), February–March 1989.

Schaaf, a member of Mission to Mozambique, an offshoot of Mutare's One Way Christian Centre, left Zimbabwe in 1985 to appear in Washington as a spokesman for Renamo. But they are exceptions. At first sight this Evangelicalism appears totally apolitical. It is privatized, personal, pietistic, and pays no attention to the social structures within which Christians operate, or refers to them only to insist that they do not matter; true Christianity can flourish under any system. By thus deflecting attention from any political structures, this revivalist Christianity is a decisive vote for the status quo. For this reason it is a very political Christianity.

The question naturally arises of what level of awareness this phenomenon is operating on. Is there, in the spread of this very political Christianity, a conscious strategy for political and cultural hegemony? If this book deals with the gray areas between intended and unintended political ramifications of Christian organizations, where does Zimbabwe fall in this zone? To what degree are the undoubted political effects of this Christianity consciously intended?

It must be said that there is no simple answer. The level of consciousness in this area cannot be compared to that in countries like South Africa, the Philippines, or those in Latin America, where there is an open split within Christianity. In South Africa, for example, one can hear Archbishop Tutu insisting that a true Christian must oppose the apartheid regime in the name of the Gospel; one can also hear evangelicals urging obedience to lawful authorities and resistance to communist subversives intent on overthrowing Christian civilization. Each side may denounce the other for betraying the Gospel. The clash is given prominence in the media. In these circumstances, it is obvious that Christianity assumes different and conflicting forms, which have dramatically opposed sociopolitical effects.

North of the Limpopo, however, the situation is entirely different. In nearly all of black Africa there is no comparable polarization within Christianity. There is little that could be called liberation theology against which any right-wing Christianity could appear in clear relief. Generally, anything presented as "Christian" will be accepted completely uncritically. Thus not only do Catholics attend Seventh-Day Adventist crusades, and Baptists attend Pentecostal revivals, in a way that would be impossible in the West; now Christians can be found espousing theologies which on the face of it could be called completely contradictory. Thus in most of Black Africa mainline church leaders with close links to the World Council of Churches (WCC) can be found endorsing the crusades of preachers who espouse a Christianity that undermines everything the WCC stands for. This lack of theological awareness is perhaps the major reason for the unchallenged spread of this right-wing Christianity.

Zimbabwe's Christian Marching Church of Central Africa exemplifies much of this. This Marching Church is an independent church, founded in 1954, with perhaps five thousand members in 1990. In 1981 the bishop purchased a farm near Chegutu where he opened a Bible school. To run this complex, he invited an Englishman who had previously established Benson Idahosa's Bible school in Benin City, Nigeria. (Idahosa, with close links to Christ for the Nations of Dallas, was another main speaker at Bonnke's Fire Conference mentioned above.) The Englishman belongs to a Christian fellowship, part of Britain's House Church movement; he draws a continual stream of short-term assistants to teach in the Bible school from this fellowship, as well as from related groups in the United States. The more than thirty students in the Bible school, from various denominations, thus imbibe a fundamentalist, otherworldly, dispensationalist, miraculous kind of Christianity, though in this case one derived primarily from Britain, not the United States.

The bishop of the Marching Church is prominent in the ZCC, and on his farm operates several development and training programs, including a craft workshop for women, and dairy and poultry schemes where the Bible students are trained for self-sufficiency. One might think he would have more affinity with a WCC theology than the British House Church theology of his Bible school, but in fact he does not seem to see any difference, or at least gives it no importance. He simply takes assistance from wherever he can.

This seems to be true of all church leaders in Zimbabwe, those prominent in the ZCC as well. Their priority is obtaining foreign aid for development projects – and, cynics say, furthering their own bureaucracies, status, fundraising trips, and currency holdings overseas.

In comparison with this, theological reflection has no importance at all. Even those Zimbabwean church leaders who may say they are alarmed at the growth of right-wing Christianity do nothing to educate their followers on the issues involved, or make available theological material of a socially committed or intellectually defensible kind. In January 1990 Harare's Word of Life bookshop carried seven different multivolume sets of Bible studies; all were fundamentalist, and at least four contained the entire American evangelical agenda. Apart from these, there was probably not another Bible study series to be found in the country. The result is that any Christian wanting to study the Bible will be forced, through the lack of anything else, to use one of these seven. Thus this kind of Christianity spreads because of the lack of awareness and misplaced priorities of mainline leaders.

When one turns to the foreign missionaries propagating this kind of religion, the issue is still not simple. Certainly their Christianity upholds the present system and serves the interest of its current beneficiaries, but to what extent can one postulate a conscious promoting of this Christianity precisely for its sociopolitical effects? It is true that in an officially Marxist country like Zimbabwe, these missionaries would want to save as many souls as possible from atheistic communism and subsequent eternal damnation; they might even encourage voting for more capitalist parties in elections, for example. But for most this could be a consciously religious act, and in no sense dictated by political considerations. Their activity need in no way be qualitatively different from that of many (say) Catholic priests, whom one would not easily associate with the aims of Western hegemony, at least in the sense under discussion here.

The general lack of theological and sociological awareness and the absence of any open debate affect these missionaries too. Most of them come from an American subculture where God and the United States are virtually identified, as are Satan and the Soviet Union. This is their conditioning from birth, they meet few who would challenge it, and the Bible schools they attend are not calculated to encourage critical thought.

It would be hard to posit for many of these missionaries conscious goals of social and political control; these are concepts that come from the world of the social sciences, which almost by definition Bible college products have no knowledge of. Their factual knowledge is often as deficient as their theoretical consciousness. When the present author remarked to one of these missionaries, "Your God speaks with the same voice as the chairman of the IMF," he received the serious reply, "What is the IMF?" It is quite possible that the majority are perfectly sincere when they insist that their agenda is purely religious. Their religion has undeniable political effects, but for most these are not intended *as political.* Views which in others would have to be called political, in them (because of their background and education) can be entirely religious.

Nor should too much be read into the efforts of these missionaries to educate local pastors; as mentioned above, this often forms a large part of their strategy. Of course, the net result of this is that local pastors come to subscribe to the whole evangelical package, and entire local churches are taken into the American evangelical camp. But there is no need to see this as a conspiracy or as a conscious political ploy. The mainline conception of "church" leads the mainline churches to confine their efforts within their own denomination or to direct their attention to the unchurched. These evangelicals have a different notion of church; for them the church of true believers consists of all born-again Christians whatever their denomination. Their preoccupation with local churches and pastors is perfectly consistent with their understanding of "church," and need indicate nothing sinister. It is the mainline churches' lack of interest in these churches that has made the latter particularly vulnerable to this evangelical concern.

No doubt there are Christian missionaries who have a political as well as a religious agenda, or who are explicitly conscious of the political issues wrapped up in the religious. A good example is Ralph Mahoney. In a 1987 article he deplored developments in Zimbabwe: "The nation became the object of communist interest some fifteen years ago, resulting in a ten-year civil war. The war ended tragically when the leaders of Rhodesia were betrayed by U.S. Government State Department leaders. Other Western nations broke their promises as well, and the struggling white minority could not hold out against the betrayal. A Marxist (communist) government came to power and now rules the nation."

Mahoney is equally explicit on the significance of South Africa: "If we continue to swallow the communist propaganda and believe the simplistic thesis that Africa's complex problems will be solved by destroying the only viable, prosperous capitalist country on the continent, we shall see the greatest human tragedy in human history unfold before the year 2000. South Africa is under seige now by communists. And our Western nations abandoning [sic] the peoples of South Africa but in fact contributing to the downfall of this one prosperous stable democracy."

Obviously Mahoney considers enunciating and mobilizing for political goals to be part of his religious crusade, but it would grossly distort the picture of Zimbabwe to attribute this agenda to others. In fact, twelve leading evangelicals in Zimbabwe who had been involved with Mahoney in Bonnke's Fire Conference publicly rebuked him and demanded an apology for Zimbabwe. They denounced his politics while adhering to the same theology. Perhaps this belief that one can preserve the theology of Bonnke's Fire Conference but repudiate its political ramifications indicates the lack of reflection in Zimbabwe on these issues.[14]

There remains the further question of outside manipulation of missionaries by parties with vested interests in a certain political order – manipulation by governments, intelligence agencies, business concerns and so on. Grace Halsell, for instance, has documented the decisions of both the Israeli government and the leaders of the American Jewish community to coopt American evangelicals in support of Israel.[15] Penny Lernoux has described the Banzer Plan, a Bolivian government ploy to use church factions for political interests.[16] Rhodesia itself furnishes a good example of an attempt to coopt the churches in its service. A confidential military "Directive for National Psychological Campaign" has the heading: "Target Group: Churches." Its obejective was spelled

14. See Gifford, *Religious Right*, pp. 69–70.
15. G. Halsell, *Prophecy and Politics: Militant Evangelicals on the Road to Nuclear War*, (Westport, Conn., 1986), especially pp. 145–60.
16. P. Lernoux, *Cry of the People: The Struggle for Human Rights in Latin America: The Catholic Church in Conflict with U.S. Policy*, 2nd ed., (New York, 1982), pp. 142–47.

out clearly: to get Christians "to recognize the communist terrorist as the national enemy." It stated that the churches' "full support should be sought to bring about a quick end to the terrorist war and to promote the benefits of the [1976] proposals."[17] Such examples make one wary of the possibility of similar instances in Zimbabwe, but to date there is no hard evidence of such manipulation.

Growing Awareness

Despite what has just been said, there are signs of a growing awareness of some of the issues involved here. It is interesting to note that these developments have been triggered by the government rather than the churches. The first step occurred in mid-1988, coinciding with the publication of a short treatment of the sociopolitical effects of American Evangelicalism in Zimbabwe.[18] It appears that this whole issue was discussed in cabinet, and the government, uneasy for some years, now decided to take firmer control in this area. Although reluctant to do anything which could be seen as curtailing freedom of religion, the government took immediate action in Zimbabwe's camps for Mozambican refugees, where groups like Jimmy Swaggart Ministries, World Vision, and Compassion Ministries were already working, and where similar groups were founding churches.

As the government recognized that such bodies may have a political as well as a religious agenda, it banned any new religious organizations from entering the camps. This ban was rather heavy-handed, and had the effect of excluding groups like the Catholic Maryknoll Sisters, whom no one could consider agents of right-wing subversion. The ban was eased after a time, though no foreigners are allowed to live in the camps even now.

This crisis had the effect of forcing the mainline churches involved in the camps to reflect on their activity. In Zimbabwe's eastern province, bordering Mozambique, ten different denominations formed a task force to ask the churches

---

17. See Gifford, *Religious Right*, pp. 47–48.
18. Gifford, *Religious Right*, pp. 109–10.

established in the camps what services they required from outside. The answers included more contact with communities outside the camps, training, and books. The task force was then disbanded, and the same ten churches constituted a pastoral committee to meet these needs. This has worked so well that the commissioner for refugees has decreed that all Christian groups wanting to work in the camps must operate through this body. This has effectively meant that extraneous evangelical activities have been curtailed; Christian influences within the camps are definitely mainline and no longer evangelical. The intent now is to introduce this system in the camps in Zimbabwe's other provinces.

Another consciousness-raising step, this time initiated by the churches, was a workshop in Harare in August 1989 on the subject of "Religion and Oppression: the misuse of religion for social, political and economic subjugation in eastern and southern Africa." This workshop, conducted by the Ecumenical Documentation and Information Centre of Eastern and Southern Africa (EDICESA), was attended by church leaders from the Christian councils of the twelve neighboring countries which make up EDICESA. The papers of South African participants in particular served to spread awareness of the issue to Christian leaders of the region. The proceedings of the workshop were published and given wide publicity.[19] In an extensive article in Zimbabwe's *Sunday Mail*, major church leaders, including the Anglican Archbishop, the general secretary of the ZCC, and former President Banana, were asked for their comments on the threat posed to the region by right-wing Christian bodies.[20]

Two months after this workshop, a particularly well known evangelical, Rev. Peter Hammond of Front Line Fellowship, was captured by Mozambican soldiers on 24 October 1988 when he, a South African, and six American missionaries entered northern Mozambican Tete province. They were flown to Maputo, interrogated, then released on 30 October. This

19. The proceedings, *Religion and Oppression: the Misuse of Religion for Social, Political and Economic Subjugation in Eastern and Southern Africa* (Harare, 1989), are available from EDICESA, P.O. Box H 94, Hatfield, Harare, Zimbabwe.

20. P. Deketeke and C. Chitsaka, "Exposing Churches Which Serve Two Masters at Same Time," *Sunday Mail*, 15 October 1989.

event was given wide publicity, for Hammond is a leader of an extreme fringe of South Africa's religious right, outspoken in his anti-communism, allegations of abuses in Angola and Mozambique, support for Renamo and the apartheid regime, and portrayal of the South African Defence Force (SADF) as a "missionary force."

In mid-November 1990, African churchmen gathered in Harare for the second assembly of the African Christian Peace Conference to discuss issues affecting justice and peace in Africa. Two government ministers and former President Banana addressed the meeting, and in their comments all dealt with liberation theology as distinct from oppressive religion. But it was President Mugabe's address, officially opening the conference in St Mary's Anglican Cathedral, which was given most prominence in the media.

Mugabe outlined the different sociopolitical effects of different kinds of Christianity. He called on churches to refuse to be used against progress and justice. He referred to Hammond and his other "missionaries funded by right-wing churches in America." He actually named Shekinah Ministries and Jimmy Swaggart Ministries as openly funding and supporting MNR bandits. "There are still many others who work among refugees and new settlements pretending that they are confronting communism with the Gospel. We condemn the activities of such organizations who, in the name of God, have been supporting the forces of darkness and reaction in southern Africa." He commended the role of churches in South Africa who have stood so boldly with the forces of liberation against apartheid.[21]

This publicity seems to be having some effect. One result of President Mugabe's address and his remarks distinguishing oppressive from liberating Christianity was to provoke the general secretary of the Zimbabwe Student Christian Movement to write an article in Harare's *Sunday Mail* calling on the government to ban new churches. He deplored the proliferating new churches, and called for a curb on "the regular influx of self-styled, antisocialist, get-rich-quick imported evangelists who wish to turn Zimbabwe to a procapitalist God." He called on the ZCC to work with the government in

21. See *Herald*, 16 November 1989.

banning these churches.[22] The significance of the article is that its author comes from this evangelical background himself. He admits that until he heard Mugabe's address at the African Peace Conference he had had no idea of the political role of these churches.

Thus, slowly, the sociopolitical role of American evangelical Christianity is coming to be acknowledged. However, the level of awareness is still remarkably low, and under these circumstances this evangelical Christianity is spreading rapidly. In the opinion of this author, its rapid growth owes more to this general lack of awareness than to any conscious strategy of hegemony on the part of its exponents.

22. F. Mpindu, *Sunday Mail*, 31 December 1989.

A S I A

·5·

Christian Politics in the Philippines

ALEXANDER HULSMAN

In the past few years a number of writers have expressed concern about the resurgence in activities of right-wing Christian groups in the Philippines. This essay aims to extend the focus of the discussion from the theological and political implications of these groups to a larger historical overview of the hegemonic politics of Christian churches in that country. Different modes of Christianity correlate with different modes of Western expansion. From a description of the successive colonial legacies of Spanish Catholicism and American Protestantism in the Philippines we will attempt to arrive at some answers to the question of the relationship between the impact of different religions and the development (or penetration) of capitalism. Stated in another way, does the simultaneous occurrence of evangelical Christianity and postwar U.S. hegemony reflect a particular mode or stage of Western expansion?

In the Gramscian sense hegemony refers to the cultural leadership of a class, or a leading institution, vis-à-vis the populace of a nation. Extrapolated to the level of international relations hegemony refers to the situation of one state representing the interests of an international dominant class, which has taken the lead in the establishment of a universal world order. Such an expansive hegemony appears in the more peripheral nations as a passive revolution. The dominant mode of production penetrates all these countries and extends links to other, subjugated modes of production.[1]

---

1. R.W. Cox, "Gramsci, Hegemony and International Relations: An Essay in Method," *Millennium* 12, no. 2 (1983).

The real power of a ruling class, according to Gramsci, is related to the degree in which it succeeds in striking a balance between coercion and consent. Through an integrated system of organizations and institutions ("civil society," in Gramscian terminology), norms, beliefs, and morals favorable to the interests of the ruling class are disseminated among the population. Accordingly, religion can be regarded as a component of class rule.

In many non-Western countries civil society tends to be weak and gelatinous and here the public institutions of the state (e.g., the armed forces) dominate. As a result, the United States as a hegemonic power has been able to dominate peripheral nations through a vast international civil society, a network of private and non-governmental bodies acting in the shadow of overarching (quasi-) state structures. Private institutions, interest groups, educational associations, research institutes, and religious groups became characteristic of the hegemony of postwar capitalist civil society over the formal interstate system.[2]

In the United States the growing political influence of the so-called religious Right has contributed to the shift to neo-conservatism in politics and neo-liberalism in economics through political action committees, the increased participation of conservative think tanks in policy-making, and the high media visibility of evangelical organizations which marked the presidency of Ronald Reagan. In the case of the Philippines the question arises as to how the changes in ideology in the United State have affected one of its closest allied peripheral states. Useful reports have been written on the subject with regard to Latin and Central America, while the Philippines have been left out of focus. Especially with regard to the military strategies of counterinsurgency and, more recently, low-intensity warfare, this country seems to have been a unique case.

Evangelical missions seem to have stepped up their activities in the Philippine Islands. This coincides with the closing of an era of developmentalism for the capitalist periphery as a whole. The question of whether a new Evangelicalism is

---

2. K. van der Pijl, *Class Struggle in the State System and the Transition to Socialism*, After the Crisis Series no. 4 (Amsterdam, 1988), pp. 23–24.

accompanying the Philippines' entering into a stage of neo-colonial late capitalism – just as Spanish Catholicism and American Protestantism have accompanied the local development of, respectively, colonial mercantilism and colonial capitalism – might be answered by taking into account the nature and location of evangelical activities. Moreover, that the Philippines are the only Catholic country in Asia makes it necessary to relate the influence of the evangelical movement to the power of the Roman Catholic church.

The Philippines as a Spanish Colony

Until 1903 the Catholic church in the Philippines was controlled by Spanish missionary orders; Augustinians, Dominicans, Franciscans, Jesuits, and Recoletos established their rule under the *patronato* of the king of Spain.

At the time of Spanish colonization, in 1565, Philippine society, economy, and culture were locally oriented toward extended kinship groups called *barangays*. There was no national law or administration and no military or political organization adequate to resist a European army. The Spaniards soon overran the most populated parts of the archipelago, disrupting the indigenous society by violence, by the introduction of a system of forced labor, by the creation of semifeudal fiefdoms called *encomiendas* and by depleting the food supply. By evangelization the conquistadores undermined traditional value and belief systems. As a result of the erosion of traditional patterns of authority, crime and disorder increased, villages were abandoned, and often agriculture was deliberately neglected in attempts to starve the invaders.

Under pressure from the clergy, Spain imposed a regime designed to protect the population against further destructive exploitation. The Spanish government closed the islands to foreigners and, within the archipelago, closed the countryside and the villages to all Europeans, including Spaniards, except for a small number of government officials. This blockade was partly the result of a power struggle between the clergy and the Spanish laity in the islands. For the next 250 years, until the second half of the nineteenth century, Spain governed the Philippines through friars and the descendants of the traditional indio (native) elite.[3]

In handling the many different ethnic and linguistic groups of the Philippines, the Spanish administration employed the old technique of divide and rule, and even denied the Filipinos the right to learn Spanish. Having conquered the islands at minimal cost, the Spaniards did not want to encourage the growth of a national consciousness through the introduction of a common language. Spanish colonial policy took local political autonomy away from the regional groups. From then on decisions were to be made in Manila.[4]

The artificial isolation of the islands ended when the British occupied Manila between 1762 and 1764. In contrast to the Spaniards, who used Manila simply as an entrepôt for their galleon trade between Asia and Mexico, the British started to trade in indigenous products of the islands, such as sugar and hemp. This marked the beginning of the commercial development of the countryside, as landowners began to specialize and produce for an export market. As a result new wealth began to appear in the provinces, much of which fell to a new class, which came to aspire to a Westernized lifestyle – the *ilustrados*.[5]

As Spain's own efforts at economic development lagged, British firms (and later their American counterparts) became the principal dynamic element in the economy. Spain, however, refused to recognize that a new group of cultural leaders had replaced many members of the traditional elite, which set in motion a cumulative process of alienation. The opening up of the Philippines to world trade also resulted in students going to various countries of Asia and Europe, where they became aware of the revolutionary ideas of nationalism and liberalism. The ilustrados brought these modern ideas to the Philippines, which led to further friction with the Spanish clergy.[6]

3. J.C. Thomson, P.W. Stanley, and J. Curtis Perry, *Sentimental Imperialists: The American Experience in Asia* (New York and London, 1981).

4. H.J. de la Costa, "The Development of a Native Clergy," in ed. G.H. Anderson, *Philippine Church History* (London, 1969), pp. 32–56.

5. Thomson, *Sentimental Imperialists*, pp. 56–87.

6. F. Von der Mehden, *Religion and Nationalism in Southeast Asia: Burma, Indonesia and the Philippines* (Madison, 1968).

In 1896, after years of unsuccessful reformist agitation, a group of middle-class conspirators launched an armed rebellion in pursuit of civil rights and the secularization of the parishes. The quest for appointment of indigenous clergy to the parishes was blocked by the monastic orders, which practically constituted a state within a state. Within the ecclesiastic hierarchy the monastic orders assumed an autonomous role; they refused, for example, to accept visitations from the archbishop. In the provinces they exercised so much control over the parishes and municipalities that on occasion they could force the recall of a governor-general if they disagreed with his policies. Since the friars stayed in office permanently, they had great advantage over the civil and military officials who rarely stayed in office for more than four years. The Spanish system of using missionary priests as salaried government officials was also effective in retarding the indigenization of the clergy.[7] The friars were particularly averse to well-educated Filipinos who spoke Spanish, were trained abroad, or had written about the abuses of the friars.[8]

Because of the Spanish colonial policy in the Philippines, the Catholic church's missionary objective of the formation of a corps of indigenous priests has still not been accomplished today. After four centuries of mission, the Philippines still remain mission territory.[9]

The eventual defeat of the Filipino revolutionary forces by American troops prevented the planned expulsion of the Spanish friars by the revolutionary government of 1898–1899. According to the Treaty of Paris which ended the Spanish-American War, the property of the church was to be restored. The authorities, moreover, made no statements to the effect that the land problem would be ameliorated by the new sovereign power. The revolutionaries, assuming that the new government would restore the friars to their lands, quickly transferred their hostility to the United States. There is sufficient evidence to support the notion that Filipino revolutionaries

7. J. Arcilla, "Protestant Missionaries in the Philippines," *Asian Survey*, 1988, no. 4, p. 106.
8. Thomson, *Sentimental Imperialists*, pp. 122–34. See also C.A. Majul, "Anticlericalism During the Reform Movement and the Philippine Revolution," in G.H. Anderson, ed., *Philippine Church History*, 1969, pp. 152–71.
9. De la Costa, "The Development of a Native Clergy," p. 68.

were not averse to the Roman Catholic church as such; they only wished to nationalize their religious life and institutions.[10]

Similar to what happened during the Spanish period, the institutional church was coopted by the cause of imperialism. Few in numbers, the Americans wanted to have as many allies as possible against the massive popular rebellion that had led to the ferocious American–Philippine War of 1898–1902, which followed immediately upon the Spanish-American War of 1898. During the war, the American government courted the ilustrados and leaders of the Catholic church.

William Howard Taft, the first American to become governor of the Philippines, was instrumental in establishing a good working relationship between the American government and the Vatican. The United State respected the properties of the church, and assured Pope Leo XIII that the huge haciendas of the friars would not be confiscated. Still, the Roman Catholic authorities disagreed with the Organic Act of 1902, which confirmed the separation of church and state in the Philippines. Official church doctrine steadfastly opposed separation of church and state until the Second Vatican Council of 1962–65.[11]

However, in order to defuse anticlerical and antifriar sentiment, the American government had to favor the sale of the friar estates. With this the Vatican agreed, but when it appeared that the Americans sought to introduce a secular public school system patterned after the U.S. model – thus pervaded by Protestant values – the Vatican raised objections.

These soon proved to be minor issues, however, for ecclesiastical peace and order were greatly upset with the rise of the Iglesia Filipina Independiente in 1902, a schism from the Roman Catholic church. Highly nationalist, the new church attracted a quarter of the Catholic population in the early years of its existence; sometimes whole parishes and their priests joined the schism. As a genuine people's movement, it continued the ideological momentum of the revolution against the domination of the Spanish clergy. It lasted until

10. T. Agoncillo, *A History of the Philippines* (Manila, 1960), p. 79.
11. E. Smith, "Right-wing Catholicism," (unpublished paper, Manila, 1970).

1906, when the Supreme Court of the Philippines handed down a decision in favor of the Catholic church, ordering the Iglesia Filipina Independiente to return contested church properties; thereafter the tremendous membership boom of the indigenous church began to decline.[12]

The American concept of the secular state eroded the Church's hold on government, but it did not stop the Church from exerting influence in the political sphere. Significantly, the newly arrived Protestant missionaries on numerous occasions complained that officials catered too much to the interests of the Catholic hierarchy. Among those officials were American governor-generals J. Smith (a Catholic) and W. Cameron Forbes, who succeeded Smith in 1909. The foreign Catholic missionaries succeeded in capturing a strategic position in the bitterly contested area of education. From that advanced post they were able to reestablish contact between Catholicism and the lay leadership of the nation.[13]

In 1930 Pope Pius X set forth a worldwide program of "lay apostolate," called Catholic Action. Laymen were called upon to collaborate with the hierarchy to Christianize the predominantly secular society. Efforts to instruct the laity in social encyclicals and to organize them in functional unions of workers, students, and professionals were undertaken in order to seek practical ways of influencing society. Training in Catholic Action programs was meant to prepare laymen as individuals for a responsible political role. Many of the leaders of present-day Christian Democratic parties received their inspiration and training in the Catholic Action movement of the 1930s.

Various religious orders have played a major role in educational, economic, and political affairs. Within the church, Franciscans, Dominicans, and Jesuits have had their own tradition and spiritual emphasis. Jesuits in the Philippines have built interrelated organizations concerned with research, the training of laity, and action programs in labor union organization and low-cost housing. Their major preoccupation

12. M.D. Clifford, "Religion and the Public Schools in the Philippines," in ed. Anderson, *Philippine Church History*, pp. 280–301.
13. H.J. de la Costa, *Asia and the Philippines* (Manila, 1967).

has been with the question of social change.[14] Of major importance to the development of Catholic Action in the prewar years has been the Jesuit led Social Justice Crusade, initiated in reaction to the formation of the Partido Komunista ng Pilipinas (PKP), the Philippine Communist party. As such they have been an important source of ideas for the Christian Democratic party in the Philippines. Today, Jesuits have many close allies among cabinet ministers and other high-ranking officials.[15]

American Mission and Expansion

Under the aegis of "Manifest Destiny" the United States developed its own conception of imperialism, which was not so much rooted in maintaining colonial empires as in exclusive access to overseas markets. Colonies and wars were deemed too expensive by American businessmen.

Captain Alfred Mahan, a leading architect of American overseas expansion, urged that the United States develop a battle fleet for the control of important trade routes, and support this fleet with strategically placed bases and stockpiles in the Atlantic, the Caribbean, and the Pacific. His policy was centered on the assumption that if the United State should fail to avail itself of its power to expand, it would decay from within, as it would not be able to cope with internal disarray and rebellion on the part of the culturally disoriented and impoverished masses generated by the nation's new industrial might. This complemented the views of another leading intellectual who supported a westward course of empire, the Rev. Josiah Strong, a Congregationalist minister active in the Social Gospel movement. He argued that if the United States and Britain were to join in civilizing and Christianizing the world in their image, and if America were to use its vast resources to establish a global economy of mutually beneficial exchange with itself and its new industries at the center,

14. M. Dodson, "The Christian Left in Latin American Politics," in ed. D. Levine, *Churches and Politics in Latin America* (Beverly Hills, 1980) pp. 109–34.

15. R.P. Ofreneo, "The Catholic Church in the Philippines," *Journal of Contemporary Asia* 17, no. 3 (1987).

there might be an American millennium. This matched the vision of Manifest Destiny.[16]

When in 1898 the United States occupied Manila in their war against Spain American leaders initially assumed that power in the colony would continue to be exercised by Spain, except in Manila and some other places that the United States would require for itself. The Filipino revolution of 1898 against the Spaniards, however, was surprisingly successful in that it seized control over virtually the entire archipelago outside Manila. The British government informally urged the American government to conquer the colony in order to keep out imperialist rivals, such as Germany. The American-Philippine War soon broke out.

The Filipinos adopted guerrilla tactics in the face of the overwhelming strategic power of the United States, which soon found itself tied down in a bloody conflict without the possibility of a quick victory, in spite of the fact that over half of its entire army was sent to battle.

In the United States, anti-imperialist sentiments – embodied in the Anti-Imperialist League, a heterogenous coalition of moralists, idealists, nativists, and isolationists opposed to expansion – gave way to a new moral critique of imperialism, arising from a progressive reform movement. Based on the notion that, in essence, imperialist groups were merely pawns in the hands of the world's capitalists who acted at the expense of the American workers, the reform movement posed a radical threat to imperialism.

The advocates of formal imperialism, who sought to defeat the Philippine "insurrection," realized that they would only be able to do so if they could defuse the political opposition of Filipinos to American rule. Thus, in order to neutralize the political threat to imperialism both at home and in the Philippines, the "natives" not only had to be conquered, but they had to be converted to the American cause and (Protestant) values as well.

The Americans thus developed a policy of "attraction." In order to coopt talented and reliable Filipinos, they contacted the Manila elite and, later, the provincial elites, who had once

16. Thomson, *Sentimental Imperialists*, p. 143.

hoped to dominate the revolution but found themselves instead caught in the crossfire between the U.S. Army and local guerrilla groups. After a structure for collaboration had been established, the Americans built roads, schools, and colleges, and stimulated export-oriented agriculture. There was a role in this process for the Protestant missionaries who entered the new colony in the footsteps of the army.[17]

This missionary expansion in the Philippines was part of the broader evangelical outburst in nineteenth-century America known as the Second Great Awakening. The missionary objective was to evangelize the world in one generation. Ever since the Civil War, most Protestants identified the survival and expansion of the United States with a divine plan, and they increasingly believed that American-style democracy required an evangelical base. Ideological compatibility between church and state found practical expression in missionary efforts to further the national purpose.

Most missionaries in the Philippines assumed that the aims of their government were altruistic. They also expected the government to be paternalistic, for, like most Americans, the missionaries believed that Filipinos and most other non-Western peoples were culturally and racially deficient and incapable of governing themselves. So, in general, Philippine culture was to be upgraded by infusing American material and spiritual values.

Despite the great number of Filipinos who turned to armed resistance, there were virtually no missionaries who opposed the use of force. Good relations between the armed forces and missionaries prevailed; the YMCA enjoyed the closest of relationships with military personnel, since it was a semiofficial arm of the government. Still, some American officials were indifferent or even hostile to missionaries, but those who encouraged the establishment of their missions saw their potential, at least in the short run, as a force of reconciliation and conservatism. William Howard Taft understood the value of the missions to the government very well and established lasting relationships with several of them.[18]

17. K. J. Clymer, "Protestant Missionaries and American Colonialism in the Philippines, 1899–1916: Attitudes, Perceptions and Involvement," in ed. P.W. Stanley, *Reappraising an Empire* (Cambridge, Mass., 1984), p. 146.
18. Ibid., p. 157.

The presence of American missionaries would prove to be most useful to the government's massive educational effort. The introduction of a compulsory system of public education was intended to be the cutting edge of the social and political revolution, the device that would make the difference between a literate oligarchy and an educated democracy. In the United States the public school had been more than an academic institution; it had served as a means of molding people of diverse origin into a nation. This particular American concept of the role of education in the building of a nation would be peculiarly appropriate in the Philippines with its many peoples, languages, and religions.

Under the Spaniards primary education had been in the hands of the church. A system of secondary schools and colleges had made it possible for a few Filipinos to learn Spanish and study for a profession. The revolutionary leaders accepted the American notion of education as the handmaiden of the state and the school as the training ground for citizens and patriots, though they took for granted the Spanish conception that the educated man belonged to a small privileged group. The reform of Philippine education made other changes possible. The separation of church and state, the constitutional commitment to popular sovereignty, acceptance of social mobility, participation in the electoral process – all these changes depended, in the long run, on the success of popular education.

During the American occupation education became the main route for upward social mobility, and helped to bring new social classes into being. The shortcomings of the educational system, however, were serious. Practically all education beyond the primary level remained either private or parochial; the public education system was bypassed by a parallel system of church-affiliated schools.[19]

Although the American school system was officially secular, Protestant values prevailed. Anti-Catholic sentiment had been a significant factor in the missionary concern of American Protestants. According to the Rev. J. King, the Spanish-

19. G.E. Taylor, *The Philippines and the United States: Problems* of *Partnership* (New York, 1963), pp. 243–57.

American War had been "a war between Washington and Rome."[20] The missionaries always feared that Catholics had too much influence in the Philippine schools. Many of them considered Roman Catholicism un-Christian, no better than the threat of advancing secularism to the moral values of the "unformed" Filipino character. They criticized the government for allegedly failing to uphold religious freedom and for the departure of policies from American Protestant values. Most missionaries felt that Filipinos were as yet ill-suited to bear important responsibilities, especially if these involved policy-making. Although the occupation began with assurances to the Filipinos that they were to be given a large measure of self-government, it was clear that this was to be within the confines of a policy of "benevolent assimilation." Neither President McKinley nor Taft were in favor of independence.

The period from about 1920 to 1940 was distinguished by the effort to extend popular democracy to the colonial world. The Wilsonian principle of self-determination for all peoples discredited the idea of "the white man's burden" in the public's mind. Furthermore, maintaining colonial rule became too expensive in the face of the rapidly intensifying nationalism of the indigenous elites. In order to defuse this nationalism, the United States introduced the Jones Bill (1916), calling for moderate reforms with a pledge toward eventual independence. From the 1920s until 1946, the Philippines held dominion status within the U.S. Commonwealth, so as to "prepare" the archipelago for its future independence.[21] In the early 1920s a second generation of American missionaries began to arrive. This new group had no objections to independence, but they were not a majority in the colony.

The general orientation of the American Protestant missionaries was rooted in the ideology of Manifest Destiny and the conviction that they came as representatives of the most dynamic and enlightened civilization in the world to uplift

20. Clifford, "Religion and Public Schools," p. 335.
21. The preceding paragraphs about Filipino self-determination draw heavily on P.W. Stanley, ed., *Reappraising an Empire*; see especially J. Arcilla, "Protestant Missionaries," pp. 105–12, and C. Ileto, "Orators and the Crowd," pp. 108–34.

and Christianize backward and static civilizations, as the Asian countries had been regarded ever since the Protestant missions to (especially) China in the seventeenth century. As such, the missionaries were conscious agents of cultural change and cultural domination. Their educational and humanitarian efforts proved, moreover, to be the best way to convert people.[22]

Before 1938, the primary home base of all Protestant missionaries was Europe, from where some 60 percent originated. The remainder came from the United States. In the period prior to the Second World War, a large number of Protestant sects proliferated in the Philippines, in spite of the fact that Protestants constituted only a tiny porportion of the population. Most of these sects were affiliated with the National Council of Churches of the Philippines (NCCP), which is officially related to the (ecumenical) World Council of Churches. Other denominations flocked together in the United Churches of Christ (UCCP), which was also an ecumenical organization. A third important overarching organization was the Philippine Bible Society, which encompassed more than 30 different denominations.[23]

American Hegemony

At the end of the Second World War the United States had once again occupied the Philippine islands, only this time the American conquerors were generally and enthusiastically welcomed as liberators, whereas just prior to the war they had been denounced as colonialists.

By the end of the war, the United States had officially announced that the colonial powers would have to prepare their colonies for independence. The policy of simultaneously intervening against the exclusivity of colonial economic relations and granting concessions to nationalist movements in the colonies was perhaps the best strategy for preserving the

22. D.J. Elwood, "Varieties of Christianity in the Philippines," in ed. G.H. Anderson, *Philippine Church History*, p. 359.
23. P. Armstrong, A. Glyn and J. Harrison, *Capitalism Since World War II* (London, 1984), p. 29.

damaged capitalist system as a whole.[24] Such concessions were, however, not granted to the Philippines, for here, as in Latin America, the United States did not have any imperial rivals.

The way in which the United States dealt with the question of collaboration with Japanese fascism and the anti-Japanese resistance movement would prove to be of utmost importance to postwar developments. An important segment of the Filipino elite had collaborated with the Japanese, politically as well as economically, while many common Filipinos had joined the various guerrilla groups. The American-oriented segment of the elite had taken refuge in the United States. When the tide began to turn in favor of the U.S., the collaborating elite started to contact and support some of the guerrilla groups and the American intelligence services.[25]

Most guerrilla groups were recognized by the U.S. Armed Forces in the Far East, and were called USAFFE guerrillas. They provided services for American military strategy in the Pacific, which was largely under the command of General Douglas MacArthur. A majority of the manpower of these groups had roots in the prewar Philippine Constabulary (PC); many of them had even served as PCs under Japanese rule. They simply fought for the return of the commonwealth.

MacArthur was entrusted by the American government to make important decisions independently. He consistently favored the Manila high elite, with whom he had become thoroughly acquainted during his long residence in the city before the war. To this select group belonged Commonwealth President Manuel Quezon, wartime President of the Philippine Republic José Laurel, Manuel Roxas, Andres Soriano, Joseph McMicking, Charles Parsons, and Courtney Whitney.[26]

After the war Parsons returned to the Philippines as a U.S. Navy commander. Before the war he had become closely acquainted with the archbishop of Manila, Michael O'Doherty, who had installed him as the church hierarchy's representative on the board of four banks. In 1945 Whitney – for years

24. S.R. Shalom, *The United States and the Philippines: A Study of Neo-Colonialism* (Philadelphia, 1981), p. 3.

25. B.J. Kerkvliet, *The Huk Rebellion* (Berkeley, 1977), p. 57.

26. H.J. Abaya, *The CLU Story: Fifty Years of Struggle for Civil Liberties* (Quezon City, 1987), p. 1.

MacArthur's lawyer – became the head of the Philippine Civil Affairs Unit (PCAU). McMicking was a confidant to the richest and most influential Spanish and Spanish mestizo families in the country, such as the Ayalas, Zobels, Elizaldes, Sorianos, and Madrigals. In the 1930s these had all donated generously to the Manila Falange, a flourishing fascist organization with at least 10,000 members among these families, various Spanish religious orders, and members of the church hierarchy. In a Jesuit university chapel the Falange had been blessed as an organization dedicated to Franco and the church. At the same time, a section of the governing Nacionalista party attempted to establish a one-party dictatorship under the leadership of the charismatic president Quezon.[27]

MacArthur's chief of staff, Richard Sutherland, and the American chief of intelligence in the country, Charles Willoughby, a friend of Soriano, had both expressed their admiration for Franco's Spain and Salazar's Portugal. MacArthur endorsed the Moral Rearmament movement (MRA), which rallied ideological support for American globalism and the cold war in the 1950s. MacArthur's stand was joined by Senator Truman, Chiang Kai-shek, and, in 1946, the Vatican.[28]

In 1944 President Roosevelt established a mission charged with the restoration of democratic government in the islands and the punishment of collaborators with the Japanese. The mission included MacArthur, Soriano, Willoughby, Sutherland, and Whitney. When hostilities ended, this mission replaced the (communist) Huk guerrilla leadership in the areas where it had succeeded in establishing autonomous democratic rule with members of the U.S. Army's PCAU, many of whom were USAFFE leaders. Under U.S. Army supervision, the Philippine Military Police was organized, armed, and financed as a replacement for the discredited PC and Philippine Army (AFP), with the aim of keeping the Huks at bay.

Roxas was MacArthur's handpicked candidate in the 1946 presidential elections. Roxas's ties with MacArthur, U.S. High Commissioner Paul McNutt, local conservatives, hacenderos,

27. J. P. Nederveen Pieterse, introduction to his work.
28. R. Constantino and L. Constantino, *The Philippines: The Continuing Past* (Quezon City, 1978), p. 265.

Alexander Hulsman

and business magnates contributed to his acceptance of American solutions for rebuilding the heavily damaged Philippine economy in favor of revived private enterprise. In the first years of the Roxas presidency, a number of bilateral agreements were forced upon the country, which in effect denied any substance to the independence granted on 4 July 1946. The Bell Trade Agreement gave the United States strong regulatory power over, and American businessmen preferred access to, the Philippine economy. As a consequence of two military agreements the islands became the most important outpost of American strategy in Asia and the Pacific. The United States acquired huge bases in the constitutionally neutral country and the direct supervision by the Joint U.S. Military Advisory Group (JUSMAG) over the military and intelligence services of the Philippines.

The restoration to power of the most reliable sector of the colonial elite, the measures to prevent political participation of anti-imperialist opposition groups, and, finally, the renewed imposition of free trade relations constituted the first pillars of the postwar neocolonial structure of relationships between the two nations.[29] The old Catholic elite was restored to power despite the close prewar association between the Catholic establishment and international falangism.

The close collaboration between the American government and the vestiges of Catholic power in the Philippines seems to have been a result of the pro-Vatican efforts of General William "Wild Bill" Donovan, who served as chief of the Office of Strategic Services (OSS), the wartime predecessor of the Central Intelligence Agency. When the Allies liberated Rome in 1944, Donovan sponsored a spy network in the Vatican. From there the OSS was able to obtain confidential reports provided by apostolic delegates in the Far East.[30] Donovan mobilized the worldwide political and financial power of the Catholic church with the assistance of Cardinal Spellman of New

29. R. Lee, *The CIA's Secret War in the Philippines* (New York, 1987), p. 56.
30. The fact that a relatively large number of the leading people in the mobilization of Catholic power belonged to the by-then influential community of very rich and conservative Catholics of Irish descent in the United States may be illustrative of the state of Catholic elite cohesion on a world scale during this particular period. See also the chapter in this volume by Ad van Wesel.

York. In the Philippines Archbishop O'Doherty and the Manila high elite were their chief liaisons.[31]

The return to power by the old elite prompted the PKP to renew guerrilla activities; the revived Huk movement rapidly increased in strength.

From 1949 onward, American foreign policy in Asia was geared to the containment of China. The United States started to look for an American policy in Asian garb, and for this strategy there was no better conceivable object than the Philippines. Roxas had already declared that, as far as he was concerned, the Philippines were not part of the Orient, except for its geographical location. "We are part of the Western world, by reason of culture, ideology and economics."[32]

In 1949 the Philippine government allowed the United States to build a Voice of America broadcasting station, so that it would be able to reach China, Korea, and Indonesia. The success of the Philippine "experiment" would be a great propaganda achievement in the cold war.[33]

The same year, JUSMAG was able to convince the Philippine government to adjust its defense budget in favour of centrally coordinated counterinsurgency at the expense of its prestigious air force and navy. In 1950 JUSMAG completely reorganized the intelligence services. The CIA sent Edward G. Lansdale to Manila to instruct the army and government in the methods of counterinsurgency. Ramond Magsaysay, a former USAFFE commander, became secretary of defense with the support of Lansdale, JUSMAG chief Leland Hobbs, and U.S. Ambassador Myron Cowen. Under his leadership the entire AFP and PC were reorganized into large counterinsurgency units.

In 1951 Lansdale prepared a massive campaign to generate ideological support for Magsaysay as "the man of the masses." He was portrayed as an outsider to traditional elite politics and as "the champion of democracy" in order to make him appear as the people's preferred candidate in the 1953 presidential

---

31. E. San Juan, *Crisis in the Philippines: The Making of a Revolution* (South Hadley, Mass., 1986), p. 37.

32. G. Sussman, *The Political Economy of Telecommunication Transfer: Transnationalizing the New Philippine Information Order* (Ann Arbor, 1986), p. 152.

33. J.V. Abueva, *Ramon Magsaysay: A Political Biography* (Manila, 1971), p. 106.

elections. To this end, the CIA directed and financed the creation of the National Movement for Free Elections (NAMFREL). NAMFREL rallied the support of all kinds of middle-class organizations throughout the country. Due to the efforts of the Lions, the Rotary, the Jaycees, and professionals, the Masons, the YMCA, the YWCA, Catholic Action, various women's professionals clubs, Magsaysay was able to build his own political base, separate from the existing parties.

The CIA recruited Jaime Ferrer, Eleuterio Adevoso, and Frisco San Juan to organize NAMFREL chapters and meetings nationwide.[34] Supported by a large-scale media campaign, the Catholic hierarchy, the Iglesia Filipina Independiente, the Iglesia ni Kristo (an indigenous church with some two million converts), and, financially, by interested American citizens and the Manila elite (e.g., Soriano), Magsaysay's landslide victory was carefully prepared.

Lansdale brought together the different elements for the Magsaysay campaign by using a great deal of anticommunist propaganda. This was launched by the Office of Psychological Warfare (OPW – later renamed the Civil Affairs Office) and directed toward schools, colleges, and villages throughout the country. Propaganda material for all such campaigns in Asia was supplied by the U.S. Information Service (USIS). In order to increase the dissemination of the OPW message, Lansdale secured the cooperation of the American missionaries of the Far Eastern Broadcasting Company (FEBC) and the Far Eastern Gospel Crusade (FEGC).[35]

The large number of evangelical Protestant mission groups affiliated to FEBC and FEGC reflected the steady rise of evangelical missions in the islands since 1938.[36] Their extreme pro-Americanism and their view of the world as a battlefield

34. R. Constantino, *The Philippines: The Continuing Past* (Quezon City, 1978), p. 245.
35. Affiliated evangelical missions were the Wycliffe Bible Translators, the Conservative Baptist Association, the International Foursquare Gospel Church, the intervarsity Christian Fellowship, Overseas Crusade, World Vision, the Christian Literature Crusade, the Overseas Missionary Fellowship (previously the London-based China Inland Mission), International Missions, to name a few. Elwood, "Varieties of Christianity."
36. L. Jones, conference in Amsterdam, 1988.

between the forces of good and evil made these missionaries useful manpower in the anticommunist crusade of the early 1950s.[37]

Another prong of the ideological campaign was the improvement of the image of the AFP by effective "civic action" programs in areas of Huk influence. While this was successful in encouraging many guerrillas to turn in their weapons, Lansdale broadened support for his counterinsurgency work by involving the Roman Catholic church and the Iglesia ni Kristo. The InK's authoritarian and antiunionist orientation helped win electoral support for the United States' goals. The involvement of Catholic Action in the formation of Catholic trade unions, such as the Federation of Free Workers and Federation of Free Farmers of Fr. W. Hogan, S.J., and the Ateneo de Manila's training and education of workers and entrepreneurs to prepare them for participation in trade unions with an economic instead of a political orientation, made them useful assets in the overall antileftist efforts. The success of Lansdale's operations meant the political defeat of the Huks, who were thereafter easily defeated militarily.[38]

The success of CIA operations in the Philippines convinced the American government that it had found a suitable pattern for intervention in other countries, one that would not cost any American lives, that could be executed with a fairly modest budget, and that would yield a rich harvest in terms of countering armed rebellions, installing leaders selected by the United States, and promoting American economic and strategic interests. For these reasons, Lansdale and his team were dispatched to Vietnam to start a similar operation for Ngo Dinh Diem. Lansdale used Filipino assistance because he believed that other Asians would sooner accept Filipinos than Americans as advisors and as liaisons between the CIA and local intelligence services.

Oscar Orellano, chairman of the Jaycees in the Philippines, organized Operation Brotherhood, which was to assist tens of thousands of North Vietnamese in taking refuge in South Vietnam. Frisco San Juan headed the Freedom Company, which helped organize the Diem government. The Company's

37. Abueva, *Ramon Magsaysay*, p. 108.
38. J. B. Smith, *Portrait of a Cold Warrior* (Quezon City, 1976), pp. 178–80.

humanitarian programs were executed through private Catholic relief groups. These activities enhanced the credibility of the president of South Vietnam.[39]

The CIA station in Manila kept assisting Magsaysay with all sorts of advice and projects, such as press publications in favor of Magsaysay's internal and foreign policies, the development and restructuring of communities in the countryside, and the establishment of economically oriented trade unions to fill the vacuum left by the government's dismantling of the militant, politically oriented Congress of Labor Organizations' unions, which were organized in 1945 by Huk leaders. These political programs were accompanied by a series of bilateral aid programs, arranged by voluntary relief services from the United States, such as the Cooperative of American Relief Everywhere (CARE), the Catholic Relief Service, the Seventh-Day Adventists Welfare Service, and the United Nations Children Fund (UNICEF). Thus certain "reliable" religious organizations again accompanied a military-political campaign by the United States government in its quest for hegemony in the Philippines. Compared to the cooperation between Protestant churches and the U.S. Army during the Philippine-American War, the role of missionary groups had become more important, presumably because in modern counterinsurgency the contribution of ideological and humanitarian efforts was increasingly appreciated.

Differentiation within Catholicism

Despite Magsaysay's popularity and almost total American hegemony in the Philippines, an ideological opposition remained. After the suppression of the radical mass organization, the anti-imperialist movement was taken over by the only sectors that were relatively immune to the McCarthyist witchhunts of the House Committee on Un-Filipino Activities (which was supported by high military officials), i.e., elements of the middle class and their intellectual supporters.[40]

39. Constantino and Constantino, *The Philippines*, p. 94.
40. R.P. Ofreneo, "The Catholic Church in the Philippines," *Journal of Contemporary Asia* 17, no. 3 (1987).

In 1949 Truman had allowed the Philippines a temporary degree of protectionism, and this had given rise to a small class of Filipino entrepreneurs opposed to a return to free trade. This constituted a small and fragile basis for the nationalist cause, of which Senator Recto became the chief spokesperson. He denounced his country's foreign policy and the continuation of the Bell Trade Act as manifestations of a "colonial complex."[41]

In the 1950s both the United States and the church were alarmed by the senator's proposal to recognize the People's Republic of China, for, although Recto was not inspired by communist sympathies, it clearly went against the anticommunist current of the time. Recto's critique of Philippine support of the U.S.-sponsored regime of President Ngo Din Diem of South Vietnam, a Catholic, inspired the journals and writers of the Catholic church in the Philippines to start a campaign against the influence of nationalist intellectuals of the Recto camp.[42]

Under the Macapagal government (1957–1961) the Philippines became fully integrated in a worldwide system of neocolonial industrialization. The imposition of this system was guided by the World Bank-International Monetary Fund ideology of a new economic order of free trade, rationalization of production, and competition by multinational corporations without government production. The economic changes led to an exacerbation of class contradictions and this generated a massive resurgence of nationalism in the 1960s and 1970s. Confronted by the oppressive rule of a minority of landlords, compradors, and bureaucratic capitalists subservient to foreign interests, opposition groups of urban workers, intelligentsia, peasants, and nationalist businessmen began to unite, and the tensions between the nationalist and the export-oriented bourgeoisies grew to an all-time high. The protests against American domination now became more powerful than ever before.

According to the modernization theorists who became very influential in the formulation of development policy during

41. H. J. Abaya, *The Untold Philippine Story* (Quezon City, 1967), p. 142.
42. R. B. Stauffer, "The Manila-Washington Connection," *Social Sciences and Humanities Review*, no. 2, 1983.

the Kennedy administration, modernization required an intellectual elite who would formulate new values to stimulate and guide the process of change.[43] At the time the Filipino elite was considered large enough numerically to dominate education, government service, law, politics, journalism, and the churches. Over half the key positions were held by graduates of the University of the Philippines, but an increasing number of graduates from the best parochial schools joined them. In training and outlook the educated Filipinos were still dominated by American culture (even when fulminating against it), most probably because, unlike some of their Asian neighbors, they had no substantial pre-Western intellectual traditions. With education as one of the main channels of upward mobility, Filipinos tended to be social conformists as long as society provided adequate opportunities and rewards for their talents.[44]

A modernizationist study by a group of specialists formulating policy toward the Philippines, including Edward Lansdale among others, stressed the necessity for the United States to come to terms with Philippine nationalism. It warned against the progress that the communists were making in public discourse by taking advantage of new nationalist concerns.[45]

The policy directive set forth to identify potential modernizing elites. The army was an anticommunist ally, but it was acknowledged that the political training of the army was not necessarily a safeguard against the communist stress on the social content of nationalism. Another institution that was nationwide in its organization and anticommunist in ideology was the church, but it had long ceased to have an ideological monopoly. For these reasons the small middle class came to be regarded as the most important alternative source of constructive political dynamism in the country, one which the United States would have to support ideologically and materially.[46]

43. G. Kolko, *Confronting the Third World: U.S. Foreign Policy 1945–1980* (London, 1988).

44. G. E. Taylor, *The Philippines and the United States: Problems of Partnership* (New York, 1964), p. 160.

45. G. E. Taylor, Ibid., pp. 243–57.

46. Ibid.

The Lansdale group criticized the Macapagal government for limiting itself to heavy investments in the advanced technological sector and not giving sufficient emphasis to agrarian problems, which would avoid the pitfalls prepared by the communists. This was regarded as an obstruction to a real alliance of the middle class with the peasantry. Government programs in public health and social welfare and "civic action" by the army (clearing land, constructing roads, building schools) all formed part of attempts to engage the peasantry in rural development. The same holds for the start that had been made in applying science to agriculture by the newly established Rice Institute, designed to become the leading institution in guiding the so-called "green revolution" for all of Asia.[47]

These middle-class efforts were considered all the more necessary because the landed families were declining in political influence. Their wealth had come from sugar, copra, land rent, and political influence. Culturally they tended to be pro-Spanish and to maintain close ties with the Catholic hierarchy. The big processing industries, sugar and copra, were deceptively modern in that they used capital and sold in foreign markets, while the crops were still grown on small lots instead of big plantations. The traditional pattern of landlord-tenant relations, of paternalism and dependence, therefore tended to persist. A variety of factors, including socialist trade unionism, had changed the relationship and, as the 1961 elections showed, the sugar block could not deliver the vote anymore.

Some of the younger members of this class of wealthy families used their money in business ventures. Many had received their education in the best parochial schools of the Philippines and the United States, and for some members of this urban high society Catholicism was beginning to serve as the base of a caste system.[48] This group differed from the main body of intellectuals who considered association with any Catholic organization incompatible with intellectual life.

This wealthy, well-connected, urban elite was regarded by

47. Ibid.
48. M. Kalaw Katigbak, "The Filipino and His Faith," *Progress Magazine,* 1959, p. 220.

the Lansdale study group as able enough to provide "everything from the economic dynamism of the robber-baron type to political leadership of a high order." It was a link between the oligarchy, the church, and a part of the middle class.[49] American policy aimed at securing hegemony for the North American concept of development through this particular segment of the modern Philippine urban elite, whose loyalty would be rooted in the modern Catholic social doctrine that developed during the early sixties.

The social struggle in the Philippines intensified. The anti-leftist trade unionism instigated by the church would, in this plan, have to make way for Philippine political parties that might resemble West German and Italian models more than American ones. The desired objective of American policymakers would thus be the creation of Philippine Social democrats or Christian socialists.[50] To this end the United States pursued a policy of moral, political, and material support to the middle class, involving the coordination of American political and economic measures, which then would have to be integrated with American policy toward the military establishment.

The Vietnam War shifted the attention of the United States away from economic matters and the prevention of a leftist revival towards the integration of the Philippines into this increasingly important conflict. The nationalist bourgeoisie had few other means to express its opposition to American hegemony, and the Vietnam War thus became the focus of a much larger American-Philippine conflict.[51]

The emergence of leftist and other secular movements in the early 1960s confronted the church and its social institutions with the necessity of formulating a new approach to the social question. The hierarchy then identified the traditional patriarchical extended family system and the disturbingly gross inequality between the rich and the poor as major obstacles to development. It also identified nationalism as a threat to the attraction of much-needed foreign investments.

---

49. Taylor, *Problems of Partnership*, pp. 268–76.
50. Ibid.
51. G. Hawes, *The Philippines State and the Marcos Regime* (London, 1987), p. 136.

The evolving program for social action stated emphatically that it was aimed at the prevention of a violent resolution of the contradictions within the Philippine society. To this end it was necessary to create at least a semblance of equality and justice, so that the country would not follow the paths of other Catholic countries like Cuba and Vietnam. In the following decade or so the church engaged in reformist initiatives. While the hierarchy itself confined its action to educational expansion, the initiative for social action passed on to the lay organizations created after the Second Vatican Council.

Before martial law put an end to their existence, there was a whole spectrum of lay organizations, such as the Christian Socialist Movement (CSM) headed by Raul Manglapus, the Federation of Free Workers (FFW) headed by Johnny Tan, the Philippine Congress of Trade Unions (PHILCONTU) led by Ed Nolasco, the Federation of Free Farmers led by Jeremias Montemayor, and others. The movements mentioned here succeeded the earlier Catholic social vanguard, Catholic Action, and they were equipped with modern Catholic social doctrine.[52] These groups all had historic links with clerical elements, especially Jesuit, whose Spanish predecessors had enthusiastically supported the Franco regime. One of these predecessors was the rabidly anticommunist and Jesuit Social Justice Crusade of the 1930s which had been organized in reaction to the formation of the PKP and the socialist movements it had led. It was the Philippine version of the profascist clerical movements in Spain and other European countries.[53]

The new Catholic social vanguard also shared a disposition towards parliamentary struggle, as opposed to the national democratic movement, which came to advocate armed struggle. A third characteristic was its explicit attempt to build a following on the foundation of traditional clerical loyalty while using the slogan of "revolutionary Christendom."[54]

52. R. Yu and M. Bolasco,, Church-State Relations (Manila, 1981), p. 64.
53. A. Salinga, "Who's Afraid of the Democratic Left?" Asian Philippine Leader, 15–22 September 1972.
54. J. M. Sison, "Mr. Manglapus and Christian Socialism," Free Press (Manila), 7 December 1968.

During the late 1960s some of these organizations became involved in political action and mass rallies. The FFF especially gathered the harvest of the social network of leaders and centers of social action in the episcopates established by the hierarchy in 1966. The confrontation of the hierarchy with liberal capitalism and modernization policy in the Philippines took place under the intellectual guidance of Manglapus, Augusto Kalaw, Araneta, and Montemayor: the future leaders of Christian Democracy in the Philippines.[55]

The hierarchy's effort to reach the lower strata of society by sponsoring the reformist initiatives of the so-called Christian moderates, or Christian Socialists, can be seen as a modern version of the *cursillo* movement, modeled on its predecessor Franco's Spain, which sought to gain adherents among higher and lower government personnel and the upper and middle classes.[56] The Christian Socialists reflected international Christian socialism and the Christian democratic parties of Latin America in their search for a "third road" between capitalism and socialism, in order to prevent the establishment of socialism.[57]

When, after 1969, the hierarchy seemed to waver in its attention to political reform, a majority of the members of the reformist youth organizations defected to the radical camp, leaving the ecclesiastical camp in a state of disarray. Jesuit attempts to regain control over the new movement by supplying it with a coherent ideology and financial support failed, as did attempts by Manglapus, the FFF, and the Ateneo de Manila to establish an overarching countermovement. The Student Christian Movement, followed by radicalized priests, nuns, and seminarians, would establish Christians for National Liberation (CNL) in 1972.

The aim of CNL was to counterbalance the deceptive position of the church, which, according to then-CNL chairman Ed de la Torre, was a consequence of the church's obsession with order and anticommunism, and of its fear of irrelevance. This made the church "part of the problem." In short, he stated that "[the Church] will be channeling the

---

55. Yu and Bolasco, *Church-State Relations*, p. 70.
56. Sison, "Mr. Manglapus and Christian Socialism."
57. M. Dodson, "The Christian Left in Latin American Politics," pp. 143–44.

antifeudal, anti-imperialist force into 'junior capitalism' . . . and ideologies like social democracy as the Christian political choice."[58]

Such criticism from within the Roman Catholic church inspired persecution during the Marcos era, part of it supported by conservative clerical elements. A number of conservative laypeople had direct roots in the Philippines' old dominant landowning class, but their new status as agricultural or urban capitalists or bureaucrats made them paradoxically part of a "modern" elite.

Modernization and Evangelism in the Marcos Era

The period of conflict over models of national development ended on 21 September 1972, when President Marcos inaugurated the "national security state." With the support of the IMF, the World Bank, and the U.S. Chamber of Commerce, Marcos presented his plans for "development from above" as a "nationalist alternative." For the United States this seemed a way to stem the tide of anti-Americanism.

Authoritarian modernization became the official policy of the Marcos technocrats. Its primary goal was a shift to export-led industrialization (EOI): relying on foreign borrowing and investments, and export markets beyond their control, the technocrats geared industrial production to the markets of advanced capitalist countries. The United States supplied military and economic support to increase the state's capability for creating the necessary cheap and docile labor force.

Agricultural modernization consisted of the imposition of state monopolies on traditional export crops, such as sugar and coconuts, under the supervision of political trustees (cronies) of the president. Very important for the mass of the rural population was the introduction of the green revolution in the cultivation of rice and other subsistence crops. The promise of this "revolution" was the ending of food scarcity through the development of high-yield seedlings. As it turned

58. E. de la Torre, "Church and Liberation in the Philippines," *Impact*, 23 September 1972, p. 38.

out, this depended on the utilization of an expensive techno-logical package consisting of irrigation, oil-based fertilizers, and chemical pesticides. For the Marcos regime – as for other Third World regimes – the green revolution was a political tool for gaining support. For the U.S. government it was a way to stem agrarian unrest. The Philippine rice economy was to be a model for emulation by other developing coun-tries.[59]

In general, the Philippine agrarian subsistence economy has developed from a precapitalist system of production to one that is thoroughly commercialized, where the relations of production between those who own and control the land and the instruments of production and those who do not are dominated by market considerations. This transformation has occurred even in areas where tenancy relationships (generally regarded as indicating traditional, feudal relationships) still persist. The phenomenon of landlessness is inextricably linked with the commercialization of rice farming; landless workers already constituted 75 percent of total labor force in 1976. Many of the new rural capitalists come from the feudal landlord class. As the traditional structures are shattered by the forces of the Green Revolution, the external linkages between the village and the global capitalist system become more important in determining the direction of politico-economic changes in rural areas.[60]

The Philippines became the World Bank's chief focus of interest in Southeast Asia for telecommunications develop-ment. As the largest American military, propaganda, and intelligence installation in the Pacific outside the continental United States, the Philippines provided the West with a vital necessity in carrying out cold war policies.[61] American mili-tary assistance made a dramatic leap forward after the decla-ration of martial law. The transfer of sophisticated police and military equipment, together with extensive American train-ing for Philippine military and police officers, has been aimed

59. A. Tapem, *Grains and Revolution: the Politics of Rice in the Philippines* (Quezon City, 1983).
60. Ibid.
61. W. Bello, *American-Sponsored Low-Intensity Conflict in the Philippines* (San Francisco, 1987), pp. 70–129.

at stemming internal dissidence and insurgency.[62] The expansion of U.S.-supported militarism in the Philippines did not begin with martial law, but was an extension of the U.S. war in Indochina, spilling across the South China Sea.

Marcos's conversion to "global village" theory helped set the agenda for cooperation among the state apparatus, the transnational corporations, the military, funding agencies, commercial banks, and local capital in the transfer of infrastructure technology for corporate communications. In setting up export processing zones (EPZs), Marcos, along with many other Third World rulers, explicitly endorsed the world capitalist model of export-oriented production. The Philippine government's plan for integrating the telecommunications system included phasing out its own commercial participation in favor of the private sector. The overall thrust of economic development favored foreign investment in "nontraditional" export enterprises which require a communications network to support them.

Television broadcasting now reaches primarily into middle and upper-class households, and, while difficult to quantify, almost certainly spreads certain foreign values. Large-scale commercial concentration characterizes radio and television broadcasting. Of the country's 257 radio stations in 1978, 86 percent were commercial, and 83 of the stations were owned by 5 people. The training of personnel to occupy the available positions in the telecommunications industry (unskilled jobs and junior management positions) has for a large part been conducted by Jesuit schools and colleges in the Philippines. Some of the largest telecommunications and electronics firms in the country are owned by the San Miguel (Soriano) and Zobel-Ayala groups, successors to the powerful Filipino Falange families.

Next to the Voice of America (1000 kW), the most powerful frequencies in 1978 were:
1. RPN (a Benedicto enterprise, 50 kW in Manila),
2. Radio Veritas (foreign religious, 50 kW),
3. Far Eastern Broadcasting Company (foreign religious, 50 kW),

---

62. Ibid., pp. 30–31.

4. the National Media Production Center (Philippine government, 50 kW),
5. the state-run University of the Philippines (Manila, 50 kW), and
6. the U.S. Armed Forces station in Subic Naval Base (25 kW).

One communications scholar reports that CARE made a major contribution not only to the expansion of commercial broadcasting but also to anticommunism, donating to Philippine barrios thousands of transistor radios which then-President Garcia had requested to support his administration's counterinsurgency campaign.[63]

The most important communication technology to be introduced in the Philippines, which is seen by many as the technology to unite all other technologies as part of the "postindustrial revolution," is computer-based telecommunications. Without it, the expansion of the transnationalized economy on which subeconomies like the Philippines are based would be unthinkable.

As one of the primary capitalist subcenters in Asia, the Philippines have served as a haven for foreign – particularly American and Japanese – investment, with the provision by investors of reliable satellite and cable circuits as part of the package. The primary beneficiaries of this large investment in telecommunications have been the transnational corporations (TNCs), their joint venture partners, and the Marcos government. The U.S. military is the largest single end user of aggregate Philippine international circuits. American bases in the Philippines were staging areas for U.S. air and naval combat in Vietnam. The Southeast Asia regional headquarters of the CIA and Defense Intelligence Agency maintain at Clark Air Force Base a regional telecommunications relay station and information-gathering centers for Indochina and southern China.[64]

The implementation of this economic rationalization plan is guided by neoliberal and World Bank designs of develop-

---

63. Sussman, in *Telecommunications Transfer*, has written extensively on telecommunications in the Philippines. The preceding paragraphs have drawn from pp. 125–27, and p. 60, respectively.
64. Ibid., p. 241.

ment. A new direction in national education was established in 1969 with the creation of the Presidential Commission to Survey Philippine Education (PCSPE), which brought planning teams from the World Bank and the Ford Foundation together with U.S.-trained Filipino technocrats (among them Bernardo Villegas, one of the country's most influential economists, and a known member of the powerful Catholic elite network, Opus Dei), as well as a number of American Jesuits.[65]

The Catholic hierarchy supported the modernization policy of the Marcos dictatorship wholeheartedly during the first decade of its rule. The hierarchy's attitude towards the repressive regime changed into one of "critical collaboration" only after the increase in state violence against church people and the attempt of the government to take over valuable real estate from the Archdiocese of Manila.[66]

With World Bank financing, the National Manpower and Youth Council was set up to create regional training centers, which over a ten-year period (1969–1978) provided 85 percent of its graduates with vocational, agrarian, and industrial skills, as compared to less than 3 percent with management training. Management education has usually been the preserve of elite universities like the Jesuit Ateneo School of Business, the foreign-subsidized Asian Institute of Management, and the University of the Philippines School of Economics.[67]

In the specific case of the transfer of telecommunications technology to the Philippines, a would-be new "Brazil," technological developments in transportation and communication have helped lead to such an "increasing subdivision of work processes," according to one major study, "that a worldwide industrial reserve army has been created with consequences in the Third World favoring extremely low wages, long work weeks, high labor intensity (forced productivity), rapid labor turnover capacity, and optimal exploitation of

65. E. Villegas, "Notes on the Labor Code and the Conditions of the Industrial Working Class in the Philippines," The Philippines in the Third World papers, No. 23, Third World Studies, University of the Philippines, June 1980, pp. 7–8.

66. San Juan, Crisis in the Philippines, p. 29.

67. Sussman, *Telecommunication Transfer*, p. 159.

labor according to sex, age, skill, submissiveness, etc."[68]

The increasing capitalization and commercialization of agriculture has economically marginalized an enormous mass of the rural population. For many rural people there has been no choice but to migrate to the cities in order to look for some way to make a living as street vendors, prostitutes, shoeshine boys, or as low-paid factory workers. The vastly deteriorated situation has left a great number of people in very insecure living conditions, with no roots in a traditional form of society, making them possible recruits for such other-worldly religions as evangelical Protestantism – as has been the case in the impoverished rural south of the United States itself.

These types of religion had made inroads in the Philippines ever since the early days of American colonization. After 1945, more than 150 of 350 separately organized Christian bodies in the archipelago had their origins abroad or had foreign ties (financial support, personnel, literature). The vast majority of Protestant missionaries (some 75 percent) represented such independent missions. While maintaining their independence, these mission boards set out to build wider organizational relationships. In addition to the Overseas Ministries of the National Council of Churches of Christ (USA), there were at least three distinct associations of mission agencies through which independents coordinated their efforts: the Interdenominational Foreign Mission Association (IFMA), the Evangelical Foreign Mission Association (EFMA), and the Associated Missions of the International Council of Churches of Christ (TAM–ICCC), all of which became well represented in the Philippines. These developments may be regarded as proof of the liveliness of Christianity in the Philippines.

The differences between these independents and the mainline, ecumenical Protestant churches had already sharpened prior to martial law; in 1965, a new, rival national council of churches was founded by a number of strong independent denominations and service organizations from abroad, called the Philippine Council of Fundamental Evangelical Churches (PCFEC).[69]

68. F. Froebel, J. Heinrichs and O. Kreye, "The New International Division of Labor," *Social Science Information* 17, no. 1 (1978), pp. 126–29.
69. Elwood, "Varieties of Christianity," pp. 366–86.

The most obvious reason behind the formation of this fundamentalist equivalent of the NCCP was the fear among independents that the NCCP might declare itself the official voice of Protestantism before the government and become the accrediting body for foreign missionaries, and the suspicion on the part of conservative Protestants of a "theological compromise" with Catholics (in 1963 the Iglesia Filipina Independiente became a member of the NCCP). They also believed that the mainline denominations were guilty of a "social compromise," disregarding the principle of spiritual separation from worldliness.[70]

Starting in the early 1970s these "religious transnationals" became more and more interconnected; ties were made with such U.S.-based evangelical bodies as the Moral Majority, the Religious Roundtable, and the Religious Voice. These large organizations and ten or so others make up the so-called New Religious Right and were financed by state organizations, major trusts, and wealthy individuals in the United States, and by donations from North American evangelicals. In the 1980s these groups developed campaigns along with the New (political) Right, which supported the hard-line policies of the Reagan administration.[71]

In the United States the Christian New Right has shown how media access is a critical resource in Evangelicalism as a social movement.[72] In the Philippines foreign religions have been particularly active in radio broadcasting – radio being the primary mass medium in the islands – to the extent of dominating it.

Since the late 1970s there has been a high level of activity among evangelicals in broadcasting and satellite-relayed messages in the Philippines. One of the fastest growing foreign-based evangelical churches has been the Church of the Latter-Day Saints, or Mormons. In the United States this church has been very active in satellite communication; the Mormons even have advanced plans for the launching of their own satellite within a few years. Satellite expansion by

70. Ibid.
71. Ibid.
72. J.K. Hadden, "Religious Broadcasting and the Mobilization of the New Christian Right," *Journal for the Scientific Study of Religion*, vol. 26, no. 1, 1987.

the Mormon church has been envisaged for the Philippines, Mexico, and a number of other Third World countries.[73]

Until now evangelical broadcasting has been able to make use of the telecommunications facilities created for conducting the war in Indochina, and for the purpose of "nation-building" during the martial law era (that is, counterinsurgency). These facilities have been opened for commercial use primarily by the U.S. Army and secondarily by U.S.-based TNCs. Daily religious television broadcasts in the Philippines are made by preacher-politician Pat Robertson's Christian Broadcasting Network (CBN is the largest noncommercial Television network in the USA), the Jimmy Swaggart Ministry (Pentecostal), Rex Humbard's Cathedral of Tomorrow, John Alexander's Intervarsity Christian Fellowship, the Jerry Falwell Ministry (Falwell is a leader of the Moral Majority and was a personal advisor to President Ronald Reagan), and a number of others.[74]

Much of the evangelicals' influence in the Philippines seems to be in religious broadcasting. This is hard to qualify, but a recent announcement by the Catholic church that it wishes to engage in television broadcasts in the near future while it simultaneously denounces the practices of born-again Christians in metropolitan Manila might well be an indication of the church's envy of the successes of its religious adversaries. The evangelical outreach groups and relief services in the Philippines cater mainly to the urban and rural poor. It is estimated that there are no more than three thousand Protestant missionaries in the Philippines, and thus it might be reasonable not to overrate the effect of their presence on religious life, except for the Mormons and the indigenous Iglesia ni Kristo, which have become the greatest church builders in the islands.[75]

The evangelical missionary activities in the Philippines seem to be largely aimed at the cities' newly urbanized populations: those groups marginal to society as a whole. Despite

73. J. Heinerman and A. Shupe, *The Mormon Corporate Empire* (Boston, 1985), pp. 55–56.
74. S.P. Formizella, "On Electronic and Para-Churches," occasional paper, 1987, NDF Library Utrecht.
75. From author's interview with Ed de la Torre, January 1989.

four centuries of Catholicism the Philippines remain a large target for missionaries in Asia. The shortage of religious staff (one priest for some six to eight thousand parishioners) still leaves room for non-Catholic evangelicals;[76] evangelical churches are thus active not only among the poor in the cities but in the rural areas as well.

Right-Wing Forces Behind Aquino

Something of the Catholic political and social orientation can be grasped from the events surrounding the shift of power from Marcos to Christian Democratic-backed Corazon Aquino. An important number of right-wing neoconservative-oriented Catholics managed to take a very strong position in the Aquino government. This so-called "Jesuit Mafia" was headed by the late Jaime Ongpin, one of the tycoons of the Philippine electronics industry and a devout member of Opus Dei. He was one of the many prominent Catholics in the telecommunications and electronics sectors of the Philippine economy.[77]

Ongpin and fellow Opus Dei members were educated in elite Jesuit schools. For elitist Catholics, however, the association with Jesuitism alone had proven to be insufficient after the internal division of the early 1970s between progressives and conservatives within the church and the religious orders, including the Jesuits. Like many European counterparts, the estimated three thousand Filipino elite Catholics began to take refuge in the conservative order of technocratic-oriented elite laymen, Opus Dei.[78] Ongpin was a typical member of the Catholic urban elite, and a leader of the Makati Business Club, an organization made up of about two hundred executives of Philippine corporations.

The electoral policy of the united opposition, which profited from the enormous wave of indignation following the summary killing of Senator Benigno Aquino, was largely controlled

76. Von der Mehden, *Religion and Nationalism*, p. 90; idem, *Religion and Modernization in Southeast Asia* (New York, 1986), pp. 60–95.

77. M.M. Magellona, "A Contribution to the Study of Feudalism and Capitalism in the Philippines," in ed. Magellona, *Feudalism and Capitalism in the Philippines* (Quezon City, 1982), p. 91.

78. *Far Eastern Economic Review*, 19 March 1987.

by elite politicians of a staunch Christian democratic orientation, supported throughout by the archbishop of Manila,
Jaime Cardinal Sin. He staunchly defended Marcos's rival for
the presidential elections in February 1986, the wife of the
martyred senator, Corazon Aquino Cojuangco, also an outstanding member of the Philippine elite. She had been
groomed for her role as leader of the united elite opposition
by Ongpin, Cardinal Sin, and a number of politicians who
had united in the resurrected Christian Socialist Movement
of longtime Christian democratic leaders Raul Manglapus and
Aquilino Pimentel. After the downfall of Marcos the new
cabinet would be entirely assembled by Ongpin and Joaquin
Bernas, S.J., the president of Ateneo de Manila University.[79]

The informal influence of Father Bernas was substantial; he
and Joe Concepcion (the president of the Republic Flour Mills
Corporation and a member of Opus Dei and the Businessmen
Bishops Conference of the Philippines) selected the team that
was to write the new constitution. The United States urged
that Ongpin get a free hand in reorganizing the economy. He
was helped by economist Bernardo Villegas and Villegas's
assistant, Jesus Estanislao, both members of a think tank
named the Center of Research and Communication, which is
sponsored by Ateneo and Opus Dei (and the CSU's scientific
bureau, the Hans Seidel Stiftung in Bavaria, Germany). Bernas
accompanied Corazon Aquino to a seminar in Singapore
organized by Opus Dei economists in 1986.[80]

As soon as the elite appeared to be united behind Aquino,
who handsomely profited from her husband's charisma as a
martyr, most American diplomats began to opt for a shift of
power from Marcos to a moderate government so as not to
estrange the Philippines by defending the bankrupt government of a very unpopular dictator. Stephen Bosworth, U.S.
ambassador to the Philippines, and Cardinal Sin were instrumental in uniting the Corazon Aquino faction of the elite
with the Salvador Laurel faction; this was crucial, for it meant
that Aquino would be able to make use of the latter's huge
political machine. Bosworth and Sin had convinced Laurel

79. *Philippine Daily Inquirer*, 23 March 1986.
80. Ibid.

that he would have to be satisfied with the vice presidency instead of the presidency because he would never be able to attract as many sympathizers as Aquino. In the United States Michael Armacost, third man at the State Department and former ambassador to the Philippines, and Stephen Solarz, chairman of the powerful House Committee on Asian and Pacific Affairs, contacted the whole Filipino political emigre community, including CSM leader Raul Manglapus.[81]

The success of the so-called February revolution was in large part due to the electoral strategy, especially after the mass democratic movement, the National Democratic Front, urged the people to boycott the 1986 snap elections, thus making it impossible for this leftist movement to claim the electoral overthrow of the Marcos regime. The electoral strategy was largely executed by the also-resurrected National Movement for Free Elections; NAMFREL was headed by Jose Concepcion and supported by the Church hierarchy, united behind the seemingly moderate position of Sin.[82]

Crucial to the final decision of the Manila anti-Marcos movement to support the rebellion of the Enrile-Ramos factions of the AFP at Camp Aguinaldo and Camp Crame were the broadcasts of Radio Veritas, which was church-owned and sponsored at the time by the Asia Foundation (a financial channel for the CIA) and the Archdiocese of Bonn, Germany.[83]

The rebellion of the Reform the Armed Forces Movement, as well as American diplomatic pressures to reform the Philippine government by replacing the Marcos clique with a reformist government, were in large part inspired by the considerable headway that the communist insurgency had been able to make: from a band of barely one hundred rebels in 1969 it had, by 1984, become an organized army of some 25,000 armed guerrillas. The problem for the military in countering guerrilla support at the village level was caused by the military's organization at the municipal level. Thus, despite

81. L. Komisar, *Corazon Aquino: The Story of a Revolution* (Manila, 1988), p. 84.

82. R.L. Youngblood, "The Corazon Aquino 'Miracle' and the Philippine Churches," *Asian Survey* 27, no. 12 (1987), p. 1251.

83. Ibid., p. 1249.

outnumbering the guerrillas by a ratio of ten to one, the army was not capable of stemming the rebel tide.[84]

The Aquino government renewed the struggle against communism in 1987 with the decision by the new president, Minister of Defense Rafael Ileto, and Minister of Local Governments Jaime Ferrer (former chairman of NAMFREL during the Magsaysay years) to dismantle the paramilitary Civil Home Defense Forces and some 260 private armies in order to create the New Civil Home Defense Forces (consisting of the same – cheap – manpower).[85]

The anticommunist crusade was joined by a whole network of religious groups, most of which were branches of religious New Right sects and organizations in the United States. Prominent among them was Causa International, the political arm of South Korean Reverend Sun Myung Moon's syncretic Unification church. In March 1987 Causa organized a seminar in Manila for businessmen, military officers, professors, sugar planters, religious groups, and anticommunist fanatics from all over the country. The new vice president of the Philippines, Salvador Laurel, and his wife are known members of Causa Philippines. So is the president of the De La Salle University of Manila, Andrew Gonzalez.[86]

Another such organization active in the crusade was the World Christian Anti-Communist Crusade, led by Australian John Whitehall, who lives in the United States, and who visited the Philippines at about the same time that John K. Singlaub of the World Anti-Communist League came to the Philippines to meet with rightist Filipino businessmen, politicians, and military officers to urge and help them organize vigilante groups. Whitehall was personally involved with KADRE, a vigilante group from Cebu with some two thousand members. In 1987 more than two hundred vigilante groups and some seventy fanatical religious sects were counted, with an estimated total of 40,000 members. They assisted the military by launching a terrorist offensive against leftist leaders (communists and unionists, to be sure, but also leftist

84. *Far Eastern Economic Review*, 17 February 1986.
85. *Manila Chronicle*, 13 April 1987.
86. *Globe* (Manila), 23 March 1989.

priests and church workers, active in religious self-help and relief communities).[87]

Peter Brock stated a few years ago that there exists an international transconfessional revivalist religious tendency vulnerable to cooptation by the people and organizations who were conducting low-intensity conflict in the Philippines in the 1980s. Low-intensity conflict is in essence a reactive doctrine to revolutionary forces, which has brought together different strands of anti-communist and conservative organizations and volunteers.

Religious groups typical of this tendency have free and voluntary adherence, a tendency to exclusivity, and an intense community life. They tend to regard themselves as God's elect or chosen people to the exclusion of all others in a dualistic and chaotic world marked by the struggle of Good/God and Evil/Devil, which is the starting point for anticommunist activism.

The progression to militant anticommunism is not automatic, however; leadership and a theological and moral framework for activism must be provided.[88] Gen. Fidel Ramos, the Philippine Chief of Staff, provided such leadership when he said: "It's total war. This insurgency is primarily political and only incidentally military. If communism seems to succeed, it is because of civilian support: we have to use the people to teach them how to say no to communism." Calling for an integrated approach to combating insurgency, Ramos proposed the need to "closely coordinate with the middle forces, civilian authorities, religious and civic groups [to] reform the social, political, and economic systems, improve intelligence, intensify civic action, and extend public information."

A noted scholar on the conflict in the Philippines wrote that "public diplomacy and information-disinformation campaigns have been the hallmark of U.S. LIC practice under the Reagan administration. In Central America and for a U.S. audience, struggle on the ideological front has been given as much attention and significance as other, material elements

---

87. P. Brock, *A Study of Church Response to a Society in Crisis: Christian Revivalism and Low-Intensity Counterrevolution in the Philippines* (Quezon City, 1988), pp. 22–38.
88. Ibid., p. 36.

of counterinsurgency practice, and 'image' has been at least as important as facts on the ground."[89]

In Brock's perspective a number of foreign-based anticommunist crusaders and some indigenous militant Protestant sects (and also some Catholic elite organizations and persons) are examples of religious groups committed to counterrevolutionary politics. Others, such as the Philippine Council of Evangelical Churches, represent groups closer to the middle ground, opposing revolution, yet unsure whether political activism is called for. U.S.-based fundamentalist television ministries can be regarded as attempting to assert ideological and theological hegemony over the indigenous revivalist movement, and to control it through institutionalization as an outgrowth of this television ministry. Religious motives are primary in their activity, but a secondary one is the cause of the political hegemony of the United States.[90]

Generally there is a tendency towards Manichaeism, which may be a reflection of the larger dichotomy in the world between "democracy" and "totalitarianism" or, within the Philippines, between "developed areas" (the enclaves of modern production and infrastructure) and the "backward areas" (those large parts of the country that seem to have been written off with respect to development and increases in the standard of living). In the army, evangelicals, Protestants, and Catholics have become actively involved with Values Formation Courses (VFCs), in order to give officers the necessary morale for the battle against the New People's Army. The mainline Protestant UCCP, the Center of Communications and Research, the Full Gospel Businessmen's Fellowship, and various evangelical organizations have organized VFCs to form "soldiers of God" active in military-civil operations.[91]

The United States has been active in humanitarian and civil projects through the Americares Foundation, which has ties with the Knights of Malta, an extreme rightist and elitist

89. General Ramos was quoted in the *Far Eastern Economic Review*, 26 May 1989. S. Miles wrote "Low-Intensity Conflict: Sowing the Seeds of Grassroots Fascism in the Philippines," for the *AMPO Japan-Asia Quarterly Review* 19, no. 3 (1987), p. 3.

90. *Simbayan* (Manila), no. 2, 1987.

91. *Far Eastern Economic Review*, 12 March 1987.

Catholic organization, of which only some very wealthy elite figures in the Philippines are members (for example, some members of the Soriano family).[92] Americares has coordinated humanitarian efforts with the U.S. and Philippine armies.[93]

It has been reported that certain evangelical sects and aid agencies have received government funding. Evangelicalism, as a large freewheeling movement of endlessly splintering sects, offers many possible entry points for CIA infiltration. The State Department and the CIA use the sects to wage a campaign of deculturation and ideological bombardment. The Summer Institute of Linguistics has been hiding its proselytizing work among tribal populations behind supposedly scientific activities. The strength of evangelical sects as CIA conduits lies in their capacity for propaganda among the most marginalized people in the remotest ethnic and rural areas. Most suitable for this work are the large interdenominational umbrella organizations, because they are interrelated and have vast networks that can coordinate evangelizing activities, and they maintain consistent access to mass media.[94]

For the past several years, American evangelicals have conducted "crusade" rallies throughout the Philippines, successfully drawing large crowds. For the poor, especially in rural areas, the rallies can be a form of entertainment, a chance to hear amplified music and lively speakers; in other words, an escape from the routine of daily life. The rally is a form of propaganda. Other American evangelical missions have travelled throughout the islands organizing evangelical churches and "humanitarian aid" distribution, and for a series of crusades and seminars for Bible study group leaders. Just as left-wing Basic Christian Communities have used Bible study groups to develop ways of applying the Gospel to daily life, the evangelical study groups allow leaders to preach the parts of the Bible that stress obedience to authority and resignation to material deprivation.

Traditional counterinsurgency theory prescribes the use of paramilitary and psychological operations in tandem with "civic action," a military term for "humanitarian" projects

92. Lee, *The CIA's Secret War*, p. 68.
93. Van der Pijl, *Class Struggle*, p. 22.
94. *Philippine Daily Inquirer*, 22 November 1986.

designed to improve the image of the government or military forces. Rather than use uniformed Filipino soldiers to distribute food baskets, a more positive result might be generated by using independent agencies which espouse the same ideas.[95]

Several evangelical sects and parachurches have been active in missionary efforts among students. After the Second World War, Bill Bright's Campus Crusade for Christ and a number of other crusades came to the Philippines (and a large number of other Third World countries) to conduct evangelical work among students, as did organizations like Youth for Christ. The most recent manifestation of this kind of missionary concern has been the establishment of evangelical duplicates of student organizations, especially those with a leftist or critical leaning; these duplicates as a rule even carry the same initials as the "originals" so as to profit from the familiarity of these initials with respect to aspirant members.[96]

The increase in evangelical missionary activity as well as the moderate Catholic programs of the lay apostolate, such as the creation of Basic Ecclesiastical Communities as a Jesuit-inspired counterweight to the informal and critical Basic Christian Communities inspired by the left-wing of the Church, have been directed toward the rural population in an effort to decrease the effects of the structural shortage of priests.[97]

As such, it is a movement designed or simply used as a means to increase the contact of the hinterland population with the church and the forces of the modern world.

Among the urban population and in the field of communications, evangelical groups have been relatively successful in recent years, to where they inspired the Catholic hierarchy to start to develop its own communications facilities and technology, and their own Catholic version of missionary renewal.

---

95. S. Diamond, *Spiritual Warfare: The Politics of the Christian Right* (Boston, 1989).

96. "Right-Wing Vigilantes and U.S. involvement in Report of a U.S.-Philippine Fact-Finding Mission to the Philippines, 20–30 May 1987," *Amnesty International Report*, London, June 1987, pp. 38–39.

97. J. Veldman, "De Strijd om de Kerk" (unpublished paper) Nymegen, occasional paper.

Epilogue

In conclusion we would like to emphasize the implications of the existing organizations and projects for the question of hegemony. Churches and sects played an important role in the colonial history of the Philippines. From a position of total domination, the Catholic Church retreated in the face of the anti-Spanish rebellion of the last quarter of the nineteenth century. After the United States intervened in this conflict, however, liberal demands for democratic reform resulted only in a few cases in democratic and secular political changes. The old order remained more or less intact, as did the Catholic church. Still, most historians of American colonization have referred to the case of the Philippines as a liberalizing and modernizing enterprise, and the humanitarian efforts of American evangelical organisations have always been stressed. The reproduction and renewal of a feudal-style elite has been a common feature in many colonies, as it has been in the imperialist states themselves.

The foundation for the postwar independent Philippine state was laid during the commonwealth era. Through prewar ties with the Filipino elite, the United States was able to establish an almost totally pro-American government and ruling class. When a group of critical politicians and intellectuals began to question this state of affairs, elements from the United States and the U.S.-dominated army launched a McCarthyite anticommunist crusade, which was joined by the Catholic hierarchy and by some U.S.-based evangelical missions. The religious efforts were notably aimed at curbing the rise of a critical intelligentsia.

The postwar neocolonial ties between the United States and the Philippines were increasingly cast in the form of the participation of the islands' elite in the institutions and informal organizations of an international and global civil society. The aim was to modernize and develop the backward society and economy, albeit in a dependent manner. The simultaneous military, economic, cultural, and political integration of the newly independent country in the global capitalist system had been applauded for various reasons and under varying circumstances by the mainline religious communities in the islands as the only road to progress, until a new, broad, and critical emancipatory movement came into existence during the 1970s and 1980s.

Since then the churches have been forced to reformulate the Christian position on the effects of economic development on poverty in the Philippines. The Catholic church has tried to counter leftist movements within its ranks by passing the formulation of the Catholic view on social questions onto the institutions of Christian democracy; this has resulted in the "moderate" versus "radical" position, or the "democratic socialist" versus "national democratic" stand. The church hierarchy has thus been able to remain "above politics," all the time stressing the importance of spiritual renewal. It is also important to note the connection between the Christian democratic movement and the powerful Catholic segment of Philippine industrialists and professionals. They have been crucial for the insertion of modern Catholic social and political doctrine into the everyday political and economic life of the country.

The position of the mainline Protestant churches and their humanitarian stand with regard to social questions has been more severely challenged by the takeover of the Protestant mission by evangelicals than by the Catholic church. As a result, the American government collaborated much more closely with the Catholic hierarchy and the evangelicals than with the mainline Protestant establishment and the humanitarian Catholic left wing when it renewed its anticommunist struggle during the 1980s. It might therefore be safe to conclude that the strands of Christianity that tend to abstain from any real involvement in the social-humanitarian politics of a country like the Philippines, i.e., the modern varieties of traditional Catholicism and other-worldly Evangelicalism, are preferred to varieties of emancipatory Christianity by the strategists of Western hegemony.

· 6 ·

The History of a Metaphor: Christian Zionism and the Politics of Apocalypse

JAN P. NEDERVEEN PIETERSE[1]

> I give you the end of a golden string:
> Only wind it into a ball, –
> It will lead you in at Heaven's gate,
> Built in Jerusalem's wall.
>
> — William Blake, "Jerusalem," 1804
>
> To stand against Israel is to stand against God.
>
> — Rev. Jerry Falwell, *Listen America*, 1980

I n the 1970s and 1980s, after prolonged slumber, the themes of Christian Zionism returned to the front pages. Fundamentalist preacher Jerry Falwell pointed out that "God deals with nations in relation to how nations deal with Israel." One of the foundations of this belief was Genesis 12:13: "I will bless those that bless you and curse those that curse you." Pentecostalist preacher Jimmy Swaggart concurred:

> I feel that America is tied with the spiritual umbilical cord to Israel. The ties go back to long before the founding of the United States of America. The Judeo-Christian concept goes all the way back to Abraham and God's promise to Abraham, which I believe also included America.[2]

When it came to Israel Pentecostalists and fundamentalists were in complete agreement. These statements were made in

---

1. I would like to thank Maxim Ghilan for his helpful comments.
2. Quoted in A. Dehmer, *Unholy Alliance: Christian Fundamentalism and the Israeli State* (Washington, 1986), p. 7.

the context of a powerful strategic relationship between the
United States and Israel, a relationship which carried global
ramifications. Moreover, the auspicious backdrop of these
utterances was Israel's 1982 invasion in Lebanon and the
bloodletting and devastation involved in that war. More than
anytime in recent history this period saw a frightening
conjunction of apocalyptic beliefs and power politics. The
president of the United States, the world's leading nuclear
power, confiding his belief in the "Armageddon scenario"
was part of this conjunction.

Since August 1990 the theme of Armageddon has come
back into popular attention, at least in the United States, in
the wake of the Gulf crisis. "At bookstores across the United
States, sales of Bibles, prophecy books and books warning of
Armageddon have soared since August 2, when Iraq invaded
Kuwait."[3] The theses of Christian Zionism have been reiter-
ated, along with the notion of the "final battle" to take place
at the valley of Meggido in northern Israel. Several new books
are being published on the theme of Armageddon, also in
anticipation of the turn of the millennium.[4]

This essay steps back from these episodes to take a broader
view of Christian Zionism. Christian Zionism is an aspect of
the wider phenomenon of apocalyptic Christianity. In apocalyptic Christianity the restoration and conversion of the Jews
have often been regarded as signs of the end time and of the
imminence of Christ's return. The end time, or apocalypse,
ushers in the millennium, the thousand-year reign of Christ
returned to establish a kingdom of peace, the fulfillment of
Christian aspirations, and so apocalyptic Christianity is syn-
onymous with millennial Christianity. The central metaphor
for the millennium and the attainment of Christian aspirations is Jerusalem, Zion, or the New Zion.

Christian Zionism proper, of course, develops only after
the development of modern political Jewish Zionism in the
late nineteenth century. Yet, the notion of the "restoration"
of the Jews to Palestine as a political project was first ad-

3. E. McDowell, "World Is Shaken, and some Booksellers Rejoice," *New
York Times*, 22 October 1990. Cf. *Chicago Tribune*, 14 October 1990.
4. P. Robertson, *The New Millennium* (New York, 1990); J.f. Walvoord,
Armageddon, Oil and the Middle East Crisis, rev. ed. (New York, Zondervan,
1991); G. Jeffries, *Armageddon – Appointment with Destiny* (New York, 1990).

vanced by Christians. This notion has a long and involved history. Its development may be viewed as a drama in three acts, involving (1) the relations between Puritans and "Israelites" in the seventeenth century, (2) between the nineteenth-century Evangelicals and Jews, and (3) between American Evangelicals and Israel in the twentieth century.

Each of these episodes saw different negotiations of the apocalypse and different readings of the metaphor of Zion. The line of inquiry which occupies us here is how the Christian apocalyptic relates to the politics of hegemony, and what correlations exist between religious attitudes and patterns of hegemony.

In his study of Seventh-Day Adventists, Jonathan Butler distinguished between three different responses among evangelical millennialists.[5] One attitude is the *apolitical apocalyptic*, when people are "dead to the world" and choose to ignore all political questions and involvements.

A more common response among American millennialists is the *political apocalyptic*, characterized as follows by Timothy Weber:

> Many premillennialists adopt the rhetoric of political discontent to substantiate their conviction that the world is getting worse, that political institutions are falling apart, and that everything is sliding toward destruction. . . . Instead of fleeing from the world like the practitioners of the old apolitical apocalyptic, they keep one foot within it so that they can prove to themselves and the skeptics around them that everything really is as bad as they say it is. Their actual political involvement, however, is rather peripheral and insignificant.[6]

A third type of response Butler terms *political prophetic*. This is when millennialists actually do become politically involved and active. Christian Zionism, by its character, belongs to the latter categories.

Two questions will occupy us in the present context: Under what conditions does the apocalyptic turn political? Under

---

5. J.B. Butler, "Adventism and the American Experience," in ed. E.S. Gaustad, *The Rise of Adventism* (New York, 1974).

6. T.P. Weber, *Living in the Shadow of the Second Coming: American Premillenialism*, 1875–1982, 2nd ed. (Chicago, 1983), pp. 235–36.

what circumstances does Christian millennialism become an expression of social and political criticism, as among seventeenth-century Puritans, and when does it become a rhetoric of domination, as among contemporary evangelicals? Phrased otherwise, how is it that the prophecy of a kingdom of peace can turn into a rhetoric of conquest and domination, a device of expansionist warmongering? When is Christian utopianism emancipatory and when does it become a discourse of domination?

How does a utopia become conservative? Karl Mannheim examined this kind of problem in his work, *Ideology and Utopia*, in which he discussed different forms of the "utopian mentality – the chiliasm of the Anabaptists, the liberal humanitarian, the conservative, and the socialist-communist.[7]

The objective of this essay is to formulate a conceptual framework for the analysis of religious metaphor, specifically Christian millennialism and the Christian discourse of Zion. Much of the history of Christian Zionism is told in readily available sources,[8] so I can restrict myself to a brief account, expanding on the elements which are important to the present problematic, going into specifics to highlight the dynamics of this religious discourse.

Prologue: Politics of Apocalypse

Christian Zionism is a specific expression of the Christian apocalyptic and should be dealt with as part of that tradition. It belongs to an extended chain reaction, of which the Reformation, the Enlightenment, Jewish emancipation, nineteenth-century Evangelicalism and imperialism, and twentieth-century Evangelicalism and United States hegemony rank among the significant moments.

As Ernst Käsemann put it in an oft-quoted phrase, "Apocalyptic was the mother of all Christian theology."[9] The belief

---

7. K. Mannheim, *Ideology and Utopia* (1929; English trans., New York, 1936).
8. See R. Sharif, *Non-Jewish Zionism* (London, 1983); B. Tuchman, *Bible and Sword: England and Palestine from the Bronze Age to Balfour* (London, 1957); Y. Malachi, "Christian Zionism," in *Zionism* (Jerusalem, 1973).
9. Cited in B. McGinn, *Apocalyptic Spirituality* (London, 1980), p. 19.

in the Resurrection and the Second Coming of Christ is fundamental to Christianity. But from the start it has been subject to a variety of interpretations and it has thus given rise to different forms of apocalypticism.

Christianity, like Judaism and all messianic religions, inspires a forward-looking, linear view of history, that is, a view of history as a salvific process, a process of transition from bondage to freedom. *How* this transition is to take place – gradually or suddenly, by divine intervention, the intercession of the church or human development – is itself a central question to the Christian negotiation of time and history. To the extent that subsequent views on progress and evolution are secular versions of this underlying sense of history, of this basic scenario,[10] this question is echoed in the context of different discourses, for instance, in the argument between evolution and revolution. The latter represents, so to speak, a secular apocalyptic.

An early expression of Christian millennialism was the movement known as Montanism in the second century A.D., described as follows in Norman Cohn's classic study of Christian millennialism, *The Pursuit of the Millennium.*

> In A.D. 156 it happened in Phrygia that a certain Montanus declared himself to be the incarnation of the Holy Ghost, that "Spirit of Truth" who according to the Fourth Gospel was to reveal things to come. There soon gathered round him a number of ecstatics, much given to visionary experiences which they confidently believed to be of divine origin. . . . The theme of their illuminations was the imminent coming of the Kingdom: the New Jerusalem was about to descend from the heavens onto Phrygian soil, where it would become the habitation of the Saints. The Montanists accordingly summoned all Christians to Phrygia, there to await the Second Coming, in fasting and prayer and bitter repentence.[11]

Millennialism was well entrenched in early Christianity, in accordance with the Book of Revelation, where Judgment Day and the return of Christ were expected to happen "shortly." Irenaeus, bishop of Lyon in the second century and a leading theologian, included millennial views as part of Christian

10. See, e.g., R.A. Nisbet, *History of the Idea of Progress* (New York, 1980).
11. N. Cohn, *The Pursuit of the Millennium*, rev. ed. (Oxford, 1970), p. 25.

orthodoxy in his treatise, *Against Heresies*. He was in good company, with Tertullian and many others. A radical change of views began to take shape in the third century when Origen, probably the most influential among the early theologians, attempted to discredit millennialism. Origen, as Cohn observes early in his book,

> began to present the Kingdom as an event which would take place not in space or time but only in the souls of believers. For a collective, millennarian eschatology Origen substituted an eschatology of the individual soul.

> When in the fourth century Christianity attained a position of supremacy in the Mediterranean world and became the official religion of the Empire, ecclesiastical disapproval of millenarianism became emphatic.[12]

This was taken further in Augustine's work, *City of God*, or in how the church interpreted it. Writing in the fifth century, Augustine identified the City of God with the "People of God" from Adam to the birth of Christ and, in at least one place, with the church: "The City of God, that is, God's Church."[13] This thesis, that the church already embodied the millennium, remained church orthodoxy until the sixteenth century.

Irenaeus's treatise was henceforth censored by the church to delete the sections which approved of millennialism, so effectively that they were not recovered until 1575. But, as Cohn notes in the same part of his book, this only meant that millennialism, while expurgated from church doctrine, lived on in the underworld of popular religion.

Thus, some of the dynamics of the politics of apocalypse are apparent already at this early stage: the apocalyptic may be part of orthodoxy until orthodoxy has "gained the world," the apocalyptic is subversive of authority unless authority is subversive of prevailing hegemony; the apocalyptic is subversive yet may also be harnessed by authority. When religion was politics, theology was a political science.

12. Cohn, *Millenium*, p. 29.
13. Augustine, *City of God*, ed. D. Knowles (Harmondsworth, U.K., 1972), Book 13:16, p. 524.

The church performed a balancing act between, on the one hand, millennial sects which were a voice of social protest and gave a worldly meaning to the promise of redemption, and, on the other, mystical views which so interiorized the quest for redemption that the role of the church was minimized as well.

Yet, on certain occasions, the church also partook of, or harnessed, the millennial fervor. The "holy war" of the Crusades was such an instance. A great many pilgrimages were made in 1033, the millennium of Christ's passion. This and the apocalyptic atmosphere of the eleventh century formed part of the backdrop of the First Crusade. Besides, the Crusades carried a different meaning for the church hierarchy and the knights than for the common people, the *pauperes* who took part, driven by the bad harvests before 1096 and by the *prophetae* who preached the Crusades. To them the Crusade meant a militant mass pilgrimage, a collective *imitatio Christi*, and some believed that the words of Psalm 147 referred to them: "The Lord doth build up Jerusalem; he gathereth together the outcasts of Israel."[14]

The importance of Jerusalem as the Holy City had declined after A.D. 590 when the papal throne became the seat of Christian authority. Rome took precedence and the bishop of Jerusalem, although recognized as the ecclesiastical successor of St. James, the brother of Jesus, only ranked fifth in the rearrangement of the Catholic hierarchy. Still Palestine as the Holy Land continued to hold an important place in the spiritual geography of medieval Christians as a site of pilgrimage.

When Christian pilgrimages were blocked after the Muslim Turkish conquest of Palestine, Jerusalem again became the center of Christian concerns. What was at stake was not merely the earthly Jerusalem but the heavenly city of Jerusalem as described in Revelation (21:10ff) and Tobias (13:21ff). It was the center of the world, placed, in the words of Ezekiel (5:5), "in the midst of the nations and countries." As such we find it on numerous late medieval world maps.[15]

14. See H.E. Mayer, *The Crusades* (Oxford, 1965; reprint 1984), pp. 11–13; Cohn, *Millenium*, pp. 61ff.
15. S.P. Colbi, *Christianity in the Holy Land: Past and Present* (Tel Aviv, 1969).

The Jerusalem of the Crusaders was not regarded as "Jehovah's house." Quite the contrary, it was from the Crusaders that the first cries of "Hep, hep!" (*Hierosolayme est perdita*) were heard, the signal for pogroms from the Crusades to Hitler. Christianity at this stage was as much anti-Jewish as it was anti-Muslim.

It is significant for understanding the historical affinities between Christendom and Western imperialism that Jerusalem was the aim of the first European movement of expansion outside of Europe and the first European colony overseas: the Kingdom of Jerusalem. This is overlooked in all the histories of European imperialism which erroneously begin the era of European expansion in the fifteenth and sixteenth centuries.[16] It is telling also that it was named the Kingdom of Jerusalem, and not the the Kingdom of Israel, or Palestine.

It is likewise significant that America, the "New World" "discovered" in the era of European reconnaissance, has been viewed and described in terms analogous to the Holy Land. It became the site of New Spain, New England, New Amsterdam, and New France, but, above all, it has been regarded as the New Zion, the New Jerusalem – the fulfillment of millennial hopes and dreams. Joachim of Fiore in the twelfth century had prophesied a third age of the world in which all men would live in voluntary poverty, in joy, love and freedom, without pope or emperor. Columbus on his way to Cathay and the Indies also thought of himself as a Joachimite messiah, ushering in the Third Age "of the spirit."[17]

Through the Late Middle Ages popular movements had preserved the millennial creed. It revived among the flagellants, the Waldenses and Albigenses, the Lollards and Taborites. Friedrich Engels recognized them as precursors of socialism; he also remarked on the similarities between early Christianity and the workers' movement. But his concern was to establish not the continuity but the difference between utopian and scientific socialism, between millennial

16. Cf. J.P. Nederveen Pieterse, *Empire and Emancipation* (New York, 1989), ch. 5.
17. A Calder, *Revolutionary empire: The Rise of the English-speaking Empires from the Fifteenth Century to the 1780s* (New York, 1981), p. 10. See also M. Reeves and W. Gould, *Joachim of Fiore and the Myth of the Eternal Evangel in the Nineteenth Century* (Oxford, 1987).

and post-Enlightenment efforts to change society. The risings of oppressed peasants and the urban poor, "like all mass movements of the Middle Ages, were bound to wear the mask of religion."[18]

The Anabaptists in Germany and the Low Countries engaged in revolutionary action in pursuit of the New Jerusalem, in the Peasant War in Thuringia (1525), in Strasburg (1533), and in Münster (1534). This last was the New Jerusalem of Thomas Münzer and Jan van Leiden, where peasant risings and urban anticlerical class warfare took on a chiliastic form. Ernst Bloch, as part of his project to revive the tradition of the utopian left, devoted a study to Thomas Münzer. In many accounts the Anabaptists figure as a classic case of chiliastic radical politics.[19] Modern socialism, as Karl Mannheim notes, often dates its origin from the time of the Anabaptists.[20] Here the New Jerusalem serves as a radical metaphor of the classless society, utopia on earth.

Act One: Puritans and Israelites

The earliest English theologian to advocate Jewish restoration in Palestine was Rev. Thomas Brightman in 1585. While his work attracted little public attention, one of his students, Sir Henry Finch, a legal officer of the king, developed a large following. He authored a treatise called *The World's Great Restauration or Calling of the Jews and with them of all Nations and Kingdoms of the Earth to the Faith of Christ* (1621).

This thinking formed part of a much larger line of discourse. It goes back, first, to the English claim of a special place in the Catholic church on account of the idea that Christianity was brought to England by Joseph of Arimathea. "The mainspring of the development of the Joseph legend," notes Barbara Tuchman, "lay in the ever-present British

18. F. Engels, "On the History of Early Christianity," in K. Marx and F. Engels, *On Religion* (Moscow, 1976), p. 276.
19. E. Bloch, *Thomas Münzer als Theologe der Revolution* (Munich, 1921); L.G. Jansma, "De Wederdopers in de Nederlanden en Noord West Duitsland (1530–1535)," in eds. L.G. Jansma and P.G.G.M. Schulten, *Religieuze bewegingen* (The Hague, 1981).
20. Mannheim, *Utopia*, p. 211n.

jealousy of Rome. . . . In the person of Joseph, England's desire to bypass Rome and to trace the sources of its faith directly to the primary source in the Holy Land could be satisfied."[21] This goes some way toward explaining why it was in England that the restoration movement first took shape.

More important, however, was the momentum of the Reformation. In distancing themselves from Rome, the reformers moved closer to the Scripture, in particular the Old Testament, and to the people of the Old Testament, the Israelites. This proximity became a mark of purity, in contrast to the corrupted and idolatrous Church of Rome. The closer the Protestants resembled the Israelites, the closer they would approach the original faith. The fashion for Old Testament nomenclature for both infants and places (notably in the New World), is but one sign of this outbreak of Hebraism.

> Guy, Miles, Peter, and John gave way to Enoch, Amos, Obadiah, Job, Seth, and Eli. Mary and Maud and Margaret and Anne lost out to Sarah, Rebecca, Deborah, and Esther. A Chauncy family of Hertfordshire is recorded whose six children were named Isaac, Ichabod, Sarah, Barnabas, Nathaniel, and Israel. The Bible was ransacked from beginning to end; there seems to have been a particular liking for the more obscure or outlandish examples, like Zerrubabel or Habbakuk and even Shadrach, Meshach, and Abednego.[22]

The Hebraic model was, of course, only one of several "cultures" in circulation – Roman Catholic culture with its saints, cathedrals, and icons (the City of God), which overlapped with the culture of feudalism with its knights and military ethos; the classical culture of the Renaissance humanists; and Protestant culture with its scriptural emphasis and Judaizing strain. Roman Catholicism prevailed in the western Mediterranean world, Protestantism north of the Alps, while classicism with its vogue for Latin and latinized names was an elite culture that was shared north and south.

From sixteenth-century England the Restoration movement spread to other European countries and America. It flooded the Protestant world with tracts and publications, although it

21. Tuchman, *Bible and Sword*, p. 11.
22. Ibid., p. 85.

was not to have political effect until the nineteenth century.

The profound importance of the Reformation for the development of modern politics, for nationalism and state formation, is well established. Koenigsberger referred to the religious groupings in sixteenth-century Europe as the first modern parties.[23] Michael Walzer discussed the state as a Christian discipline and radical politics as "the saints' creation," referring to the Puritans.[24] Christopher Hill discussed the role of the Puritans in the political upheavals of seventeenth-century England, also known as the Puritan Revolution.[25] This epic is accordingly tightly interwoven with the vicissitudes of European politics. The Hebraic model also prevailed among Cromwell and the New Model Army. Cromwell and his officers

> literally consulted Scripture for guidance and precedent. A council of war included prayers and Bible reading. Cromwell speaks of himself as "a man who is called to work great things in Israel," of the Stuarts as "having troubled Israel for fifty years," . . . of England as "our British Israel" and "our English Zion."[26]

They even referred to extremists on their own side as 'dissenting Rabbis'.

Thus for the Puritans, Israel and Zion were radical metaphors, part of a political prophecy which they militantly implemented. Christian millennialism had come into the *mainstream* of political change. It would only be a matter of the other signs of the end time manifesting themselves for the millennium to take shape. One such sign was the conversion of the Jews. This was accordingly "one of the most serious theological concerns of the seventeenth century."

23. H.G. Koenigsberger, "The Organization of Revolutionary Parties in France and the Netherlands during the Sixteenth Century," *The Journal of Modern History* 27, no. 4 (December 1955).

24. M. Walzer, *The Revolution of the Saints* (1965; reprint New York, 1976); cf. D.–E. Mendes Sargo, "Martin Luther, Thomas Müntzer, and the Birth of the Modern State," *Social Compass* 36, no. 1 (March 1989).

25. C. Hill, *The Century of Revolution, 1603–1714* (1961; rev. ed., New York, 1980); "God and the English Revolution," in eds. J. Obelkevich, L. Roper, and R. Samuel, *Disciplines of Faith* (London, 1987).

26. Tuchman, *Bible and Sword*, pp. 86–87.

For quite a few Protestant leaders the Reformation itself indicated that the culmination of Christian history was at hand. For some Counter-Reformers the purification of the church indicated that the final act of world history would shortly occur. Other developments such as the Thirty Years War, the Turkish invasion of central Europe, the Puritan Revolution, the preaching of the gospel in America, Asia and Africa all reinforced this expectation. And, because of this heightened feeling that the scenario set forth in *Daniel* and *Revelation* was going on before one's very eyes, many theologians predicted that the conversion of the Jews was imminent.[27]

The intensified contacts between Protestants and Jews engendered by this expectation developed in particular in seventeenth-century Holland. Since 1604 Puritans had come to settle in the Dutch Republic, where they encountered Sephardic Jews, refugees from Portugal and Spain. After a sojourn in Antwerp, where the Spanish arm eventually also reached, many of them settled in Amsterdam. A new millennial project began to take shape in contacts between two religious refugee groups meeting in a nation which itself owed its existence to a religious revolt. Elements of this project, according to R.H. Popkin, were

> (a) to make Christianity less offensive to Jews, (b) to make Christians understand and appreciate actual Judaism as practiced in the seventeenth century, and (c) to enable Jews to understand Judaism so that they could see that Christianity is not in conflict with Judaism, but is, rather, the fulfillment of it. If these three goals could be achieved presumably the Jews would join hands with the Christians, and would march together into the Millennarian world in which the Jews (converted or properly informed) would be recalled to their place in Providential history, to their physical place in the Holy Land, which would be rebuilt and would be the center of the Messianic Kingdom.[28]

Again the conversion and restoration of the Jews went together. In this respect the Reformation differed from previous

27. R.H. Popkin, "Some Aspects of Jewish-Christian Theological Interchanges in Holland and England, 1640–1700," in eds. J. van den Berg and E.G.E. van der Wal, *Jewish-Christian Relations in the Seventeenth Century* (Dordrecht, 1988), p. 4.
28. Popkin, "Some Aspects," p. 5.

attempts to convert the Jews, as in Spain and Portugal, which did *not* include a restoration program. The Reformation and the return to the Old Testament meant that the Jewish experience again figured on the millennial map. This itself was a commitment born out of oppression and insurgence:

> The Puritans' mania for the Old Testament developed directly out of their experience of persecution by the Established Church. The church hounded and harried them, even to the gibbet, because of their refusal to acknowledge any authority other than the Bible and their own congregation.[29]

Indeed, the psalms and biblical places most significant in Protestant worship tend to be those of persecution and protest. In the experiences of the Jews in bondage in Egypt, exiled in Babylon, oppressed by Rome, they saw their own fate mirrored. The precedent of the *Exodus* as a metaphor for liberation, as in contemporary liberation theology, was established in the struggles of the Reformation against the church, the Inquisition and the Spanish Habsburg empire. As in biblical times, Rome and the empires of the epoch were again the forces of oppression. The profound identification of the Protestants with the Jews of the Scripture was an emancipatory, at times even insurgent, identification. Every reference to the Old Testament, every name, every symbol, thus stood for a consciousness of defiance – defying pope and emperor.

This was a perspective shared by the Puritans and the Dutch alike. As Simon Schama documents with a wealth of examples, comparisons with the Israelites and the Exodus as the metaphor for liberation from the Spanish yoke abound in the literature of the Dutch Golden Age.[30] As Jacobus Lydius wrote in 1668:

Above all else I thank him

Who made Holland Jerusalem.

---

29. Tuchman, *Bible and Sword*, p. 80.
30. See S. Schama, *The Embarrassment of Riches. An Interpretation of Dutch Culture in the Golden Age* (London, 1987), pp. 94–125.

The encounters of Puritans and Jews in the Dutch Republic gave rise not only to theological interchanges but also to a concrete political program. English Puritans in Amsterdam drew up a "Petition of the Jews for Repealing the Act of Parliament for their Banishment out of England," which was presented to the British Council of War in 1649. (The banishment referred to is the order of expulsion of the Jews of 1292.) A year later the chief rabbi of Amsterdam, Manasseh ben Israel, published his book *Spes Israel*, translated and printed in England as *The Hope of Israel*. He advocated the extension of the Jewish diaspora to England in order to complete the worldwide dispersion believed necessary before the ingathering of the exiles could begin. Was it not written in the Book of Daniel, "And when the dispersion of the Holy People shall be completed in all places, then shall all these things be finished"?

Thus the Sephardic reading of the signs of the times was compatible with the millennial expectations of the Puritans. Added to this millennial convergence was a convergence of interests:

> The business and commercial class, almost exclusively Puritan, was particularly jealous of the Dutch who had seized the opportunity to push into first place in the Levant and Far Eastern trades and in the carrying trade with the European colonies in the Americas as well. Dutch success was aided by Jewish merchants, shipowners, and brokers of Amsterdam, who brought in business through their Hispanic and Levantine connections. Their value was not lost on Cromwell, particularly as there were several Marrano families in England who had already been of use to him.[31]

Contact between the British Council of State and the Amsterdam Sephardic community was established in 1650, and in 1655 Manasseh personally led a delegation to London to present his *Humble Address to the Lord Protector*, arguing that the Jews were scattered throughout the world "except only in this considerable and mighty Island" and "that before the Messiah shall come and restore our Nation, that first we must have our seat here likewise." He next took up "profit which is a most powerful motive" and pointed out how useful the

---

31. Tuchman, *Bible and Sword*, p. 89.

Jews could be as channels of international influence and trade.

After lengthy deliberations the legal barrier against the reentry of the Jews into England was lifted, and the Jews thus became a factor in the Anglo-Dutch rivalry which erupted just at this juncture, after the adoption of the Navigation Acts.

The Sephardim had played an important part not only in the economic expansion of the republic but also in its political history. In the sixteenth century, while still in Antwerp, they had served as intermediaries between the Dutch insurgents against the Spanish Habsburg empire and the Ottoman Porte. Turkish financial and political aid had helped the insurgents led by William of Orange.[32]

Now Cromwell sought their capital as well as their connections and services as "intelligencers," who would bring him information on the trade policies of rival countries and on royalist conspiracies abroad.[33] The Sephardim had performed similar functions for the Dutch, notably in developing trade relations with the East and West Indies.[34] No doubt this had been a factor in the Dutch ability to take over the trading empire of the Portuguese. It may now be argued that a factor in the ability of the English to outpace the republic over the course of the seventeenth century and several Anglo-Dutch wars was the allegiance of the Jews who came to settle in London after 1655.

At this juncture began the gradual metamorphosis of the millennial metaphor from an emancipatory utopia to a hegemonic utopia. This parallels the shift in the societal position of the bearers of the utopian message; in England, the Puritans, outsiders under the Stuarts, had become insiders under Cromwell. And in a global context, England moved from the periphery of the European balance of power to the hub of the newly emerging Atlantic network; it was an

32. Discussed in J.P. Nederveen Pieterse, *Transnational Alliances and the Dutch Revolution: The Politics of the Transition from Feudalism to Capitalism* (Binghamton, N.Y., 1982, unpublished mimeograph).

33. C. Roth, *A History of the Jews in England* (Oxford, 1978); Tuchman, *Bible and Sword*, p. 89.

34. H.I. Bloom, *The Economic Activities of the Jews in Amsterdam in the Seventeenth and Eighteenth Centuries* (1937; reprint Port Washington, N.Y., 1969); V. Barbour, *Capitalism in Amsterdam in the Seventeenth Century* (Ann Arbor, 1963).

ascending nation on its way to becoming a contender for world hegemony.[35]

The metaphor of Israel and the New Jerusalem did not necessarily change but the social and political location of the forces using it did, shifting from the periphery to the center, from persecution to power. Or, it may be argued, for the radical Protestants the metaphor did undergo alterations in meaning and emphasis, from a myth of liberation to a myth of achievement. The metaphor of the reformed Christians as a spiritual Israel may be interpreted as a Protestant version of the Augustinian thesis in the *City of God*, in a Hebraic guise. A new career for the metaphor began. The Protestant nations henceforth became the leading powers in the development of empire and capital, while the Mediterranean, Catholic powers were eclipsed. This is the career taken up in Max Weber's work on the Protestant ethic and modern capitalism.

Let us linger for a moment on the fate of the metaphor in the eighteenth century. It did not play a part in the French Revolution, which shied away from things Jewish as it did from Christian symbolism; its leading metaphors were of masonic inspiration or referred to the Roman republic. Yet, it is General Napoleon Bonaparte who was the first statesman to advocate the restoration of the Jews. The occasion was the siege of St. Joan of Acre, following his retreat from Egypt. At Ramle, twenty-five miles from Jerusalem, on 4 April 1799 he issued a proclamation addressed to the Jews, "the rightful heirs of Palestine":

> Israelites, arise! Ye exiled, arise! Hasten! Now is the moment, which may not return for thousands of years, to claim the restoration of civic rights among the population of the universe which have shamefully been withheld from you for thousands of years, to claim your political existence as a nation among nations, and the unlimited natural right to worship Jehovah in accordance with your faith, publicly and most probably forever.[36]

Bonaparte called on the Jews to join his banner and offered

---

35. Cf. N. Bousquet, "From Hegemony to Competition: Cycles of the Core?," in eds. T.K. Hopkins and I.M. Wallerstein, *Processes of the World-System* (Beverly Hills, 1980).

36. See Sharif, *Non-Jewish Zionism*, pp. 50–54.

them the "warranty and support" of the French nation in regaining their patrimony so that they could "remain master of it and maintain it against all comers." He did not have the opportunity to keep his promises because he was defeated at Acre by the English and by the Ottoman pasha of Acre. Nonetheless, as Bichara Khader notes, it was a "strategic" promise by which Bonaparte sought to obtain the support of the Jews in the ongoing battle, not least that of Haim Farhi, the Jewish vizier of the pasha.[37]

Again the metaphor forms part of an imperial stratagem. The millennial hopes of which the restoration of the Jews are part had now begun to serve as an imperial beacon beckoning to panoramas of power. A moral, spiritual geography now began to interact with an actual imperial geography. Napoleon built on an older French aspiration for dominion over the Levant, which dated back to Louis XIV, and followed in the footsteps of Choiseul, who a generation earlier had hoped to gain control of Egypt and Arabia, and to win spheres of influence in Syria, Mesopotamia, and Persia, in order to wipe out the British in India. Bonaparte also saw Egypt as the vantage point from which England could be destroyed.[38]

The proclamation to the Jews was forgotten and buried under the rubble of failure, but Jerusalem was not. Chateaubriand travelled there in 1806, and his *Itinéraire de Paris à Jérusalem* became a bestseller. Jerusalem continued to figure among the central metaphors in European eighteenth and nineteenth-century discourse, as in the work of Alexander Pope.[39] For William Blake Jerusalem represented the center of the spiritual world.

England! awake! awake! awake!

Jerusalem thy Sister calls!

Why wilt thou sleep the sleep of death

And close her from thy ancient walls?[40]

---

37. B. Khader, *Anatomie du sionisme et d'Israël* (Algiers, 1974), pp. 22–23.

38. One of the literary metaphors which attracted the French in these ambitions had been, again, a Hebraic metaphor, the rustic imagery of Eden. E.W. Said, *Orientalism* (1978; paper, Harmondsworth, U.K., 1985), p. 137.

39. C. Hill, *The Experience of Defeat: Milton and Some Contemporaries* (London, 1984).

40. Jerusalem, plate 77, lines 80–83; cf. Sharif, *Non-Jewish Zionism*, pp. 34–35, 43–46.

The metaphor recurs, often in conjunction with the question of Jewish emancipation, in the work of Lessing (*Nathan der Weise*), Lord Byron, Walter Scott, William Wordsworth, and Robert Browning. Among the Romantic poets the Jews and Palestine became a topos, like slavery and abolition, blacks and Africa.

Act Two: Evangelicals and Jews

In 1792 James Bicheno, an Anglican cleric, published *The Signs of the Times* in which he drew parallels between the prophecies of Daniel and Revelation and the events of his day. The French Revolution and the disenfranchisement of the French Catholic Church seemed to him a clear fulfillment of the 'Fourth Beast' foretold in Daniel, and more tribulations would surely come.

Thus we come to the next episode in the genesis of Christian Zionism, the role of the millennial metaphor among the evangelicals in nineteenth-century England. The Evangelical Revival is usually dated from 1790. The importance of Evangelicalism in the formation of the Victorian frame of mind is a familiar theme; evangelical principles were peculiarly suited to the exigencies of an increasingly complex industrial society.[41]

Evangelicalism, often termed neo-Puritanism, brought with it a revival of Puritan themes, including the millennial metaphor and the preoccupation with Jewry. One of the early spokesmen of the metaphor was Rev. Louis Way, an Anglican clergyman who founded the London Society for Promoting Christianity among the Jews (1809). Again the restoration of the Jews in Palestine was a requirement for the fulfillment of biblical prophecy, and again contemporary events were carefully charted to indicate the imminence of Jesus' return. Several M.P.s and writers such as Samuel Taylor Coleridge were among Way's followers. Henry Drummond, M.P., gave a structure to reemerging British millennialism by organizing annual con-

---

41. I. Bradley, *The Call to Seriousness: The Evangelical Impact on the Victorians* (London, 1976).

ferences at his estate, Albury. The conference of 1829 issued a summary of their doctrine, which constituted an elementary outline of premillennialism:

1. This "dispensation" or age will not end insensibly but cataclysmically in judgment and destruction of the church in the same manner in which the Jewish dispensation ended; 2. The Jews will be restored in Palestine during the time of the judgment; 3. The judgment to come will fall principally upon Christendom; 4. When the judgment is passed the millennium will begin; 5. The second advent of Christ will occur before the millennium; 6. The 1260 years of Daniel 7 and Revelation 13 ought to be measured from the reign of Justinian to the French Revolution; 7. The vials of wrath (Revelation 16) are now being poured out and the second advent is imminent.[42]

The French Revolution formed part of the apocalyptic ambience of the turn of the century, which had prompted the reopening of the books of Daniel and Revelation. In this light, neo-Puritanism in England forms part of a counterrevolutionary rampart. The millennial metaphor, once a revolutionary metaphor for the early Puritans, had been transmuted to a counterrevolutionary bulwark, with the Bible serving as a solid defense against the infidel French *philosophes*.

Another current which took shape in this period was the British Israelite movement whose origins can be traced to an 1840 book by a Scotsman, John Wilson, *Our Israelitish Origins*. For the Puritans the identification of Albion with Zion carried a spiritual meaning, just as the identification of the Dutch Republic with Israel did for the seventeenth-century Dutch. Now, however, the argument was that the British peoples are the 'Ten Lost Tribes' of Israel, not in a spiritual sense, as with the Puritans, but racially. This matched the trend of the times, in which racism took on the status of science and "race" came to be widely regarded as the key to the understanding of history. Edward Hine's book, *Identification of the British Nation with Lost Israel* (1871), carried the argument further.

(Today the Netherlands Israel League argues that the true Israelites, and therefore the true "chosen people," are the white

42. E. Sandeen, *The Roots of Fundamentalism* (Chicago, 1970), p. 42.

Jan P. Nederveen Pieterse

Jan P. Nederveen Pieterse

West Europeans, Americans, and South Africans.[43] The World-wide Church of God in California propagates the views of the British Israelite movement in the United States.[44])

Influential as a popularizer and missionary of the premillennial doctrine was John Nelson Darby (1800–82), a Scotsman who left the Church of Ireland to establish the Plymouth Brethren. He developed the doctrine of the "rapture" (based on 1 Thessalonians 4:5–11) and his teachings carried a significant Christian Zionist component. His numerous visits to the United States and Canada accelerated the popularity of the doctrine among American evangelicals.

The step from political apocalyptic to political prophecy was a small one. It was made by Lord Ashley, the seventh Earl of Shaftesbury, the lay leader of the evangelical movement ("I am an Evangelical of the Evangelicals," as cited in Tuchman, *Bible and Sword*, p. 182). Lord Ashley played a key part in the social issues of the day. As a Tory social reformer he had been instrumental in bringing about the adoption of the Ten-Hour Bill, and he played a part in the English abolition movement, which had evangelical beginnings. But the cause he cherished most throughout his life was that of the conversion and restoration of the Jews. It was in no small part due to his incessant propagandizing and lobbying that the British consulate in Jerusalem was established in 1838 – the first consulate of a European power in Palestine – followed by the joint Anglo-Prussian bishopric of Jerusalem in 1841. Palmerston next instructed the consulate to extend British protection to the Jews of Palestine.

These were not merely acts of religious dedication but also of political strategy. They dovetailed closely with British ambitions in the area. For the setting of the metaphor at this stage, as it had been for the French a century earlier, was that of empire. The millennial metaphor now coincided with the imperial horizon and this called for a land bridge to Asia and India.

It was Shaftesbury who first coined the ominous phrase, "A

nation without a country for a country without a nation." The Zionists were to transpose his words to "A land of no people for a people with no land." In 1839 Shaftesbury made a plea for Jewish settlement in Palestine under the protection of the major powers. The Times, a year later, deemed "the proposal to plant the Jewish people in the land of their fathers," with international support, a subject for "political consideration."[45]

Thus, step by step the plot thickened. The message of the metaphor and the frontiers of empire moved closer and closer. Continuously through the century new plans for Jewish restoration were drawn up and now expedited, then delayed by the zigzag exigencies of British policy in the area, vis-à-vis the Porte, Egypt, and rival European powers. This vacillating process has been well described and need not be detailed here.[46]

Jewish emancipation (which in England only passed in 1858) was not long in being followed by a tide of political antisemitism. This in turn was the key to the development of modern political Jewish Zionism (as against religious Zionism with its much longer history). Christian Zionism and Jewish Zionism would henceforth move in tandem. This was a mélange of utopias at different developmental stages, a rendezvous of what for Christians had become an imperial utopia with what for Jews was an emancipatory utopia. Indeed the bearers of the utopia occupied different societal niches: Christians settled well within the domain of empire and Jews on its margins.

An example of this cooperation is Rev. William H. Hechler (1845–1931), chaplain to the British embassy in Vienna and an ardent supporter of the early father of Zionism, Theodor Herzl. For nearly thirty years Hechler provided political support and contacts to Herzl and lobbied for the Zionist cause. It was not until the Balfour Declaration in 1917 that the British commitment to Jewish restoration in Palestine became an overt and eventually irrevocable statement of policy. Lord Balfour himself was a premillennialist and Christian Zionist.

45. I. Finestein, "Early and Middle 19th-Century British Opinion on the Restoration of the Jews: Contrasts with America," in ed. M. David, *With Eyes toward Zion*, vol. 2 (New York, 1986), p. 80.
46. E.g., R. Sanders, *The High Walls of Jerusalem. A History of the Balfour Declaration and the Birth of the British Mandate for Palestine* (New York, 1984).

He was also known for his antisemitic attitudes and favored the settlement of Jews in Palestine rather than in England.[47]

This brings us to the question of the relationship between Christian Zionism and antisemitism generally. The Christian restoration movement always had been an instrument in the context of Christian prophecy: the Jews were to be restored to Palestine in order to bring Christ's return nearer. The restoration movement, as Barbara Tuchman put it, "was not for the sake of the Jews but for the sake of the promise made to them." A related question is to what extent nineteenth-century Christian Zionism and antisemitism can both be regarded as reactions to Jewish emancipation.

There is a certain parallel with the movement for the abolition of slavery, some of whose adherents (for instance, Harriet Beecher Stowe, the author of *Uncle Tom's Cabin*) made the emancipation of blacks conditional upon their return to Africa. Liberia and Sierra Leone, established as colonies for freed slaves, owe their existence to this project. A back-to-Africa movement also developed among blacks, largely in reaction to white racism, just as Jewish Zionism grew in reaction to antisemitism.

In right-wing circles, such as the British Israelite movement and the Netherlands Israel League, antisemitism tends to be vociferous: theirs is an interpretation of the Bible which excludes Jews so as to claim and monopolize the "promise" made to them for certain gentile peoples. The overlap or affinity between certain forms of Christian Zionism and antisemitism has imparted a cynical aspect to the cooperation of Christian and Jewish Zionists on the part of Jews.

When Zionism eventually found support in Britain it was not for want of trying elsewhere. Why not, for instance, in Germany? Indeed the project was not convenient to German imperial interests at the time ("The Ottoman Empire receives its rifles from Mauser, its cannon from Krupp," commented The *Times*). Beyond this, however, were cultural differences. German Christians did not support the Zionist project,[48] even

---

47. C. Sykes, *Two Studies in Virtue* (New York, 1952), *quoted in What Is Western Fundamentalist Christian Zionism?* rev. ed. (Limassol, Cyprus, 1988), p. 7.
48. See D. Stewart, *Theodor Herzl* (London, 1974), p. 275.

though the notion was not entirely without German advocates. The strongest reaction against Jewish emancipation took place in Germany and the longest record of antisemitism is the German one,[49] while the millennial metaphor never played as significant a part in Germany as it did in the Anglo-Saxon world.

The Balfour Declaration was adopted after a hundred years of evangelical lobbying, over three hundred years (from the first restoration proposal in 1585) after the millennial metaphor entered the stream of British history. From a metaphor of defiance it had become a statement of imperial policy.

Act Three: American Evangelicals and Israel

Let's praise the Lord and pass the ammunition.
— Nathan Perlmutter, 1982[50]

The millennial metaphor was part of the founding myths of America. In the light of European classical culture the New World was viewed as the "new Golden Land."[51] Through the monumental volumes of Theodore de Bry on the *Grands voyages* (1590–1634) stretches the leitmotiv of America as Eden.[52] To the Pilgrim Fathers and Puritans, however, America was Israel and the New Zion, the promised land. John Winthrop expressed their sentiments in a sermon he preached aboard the ship *Arbella*, as it made its way to Massachusetts Bay in 1630: "We shall be as a city upon a hill, the eyes of all people are upon us."[53]

The millennial metaphor prospered on American shores. Was this not an exodus, daring the dangers of the ocean, planting a settlement in the wilderness, "planting a new

---

49. E. Kahler, "The Jews and Germany," in *The Jews among the Nations* (New York, 1967).

50. N. and R.A. Perlmutter, *The Real Antisemitism in America* (New York, 1982), p. 172.

51. H. Honour, *The New Golden Land: European Images of America from the Discoveries to the Present Time* (New York, 1975).

52. B. Bucher, *Icon and Conquest* (1977; English trans., Chicago, 1981); cf. J. Rabasa, "Allegories of the *Atlas*," in ed. F. Barker, *Europe and Its Others* (Essex, 1984), pp. 1–16.

53. In R. Shaull, "The Death and Resurrection of the American Dream," in G. Gutiérrez and R. Shaull, *Liberation and Change* (Atlanta, 1977), p. 107.

heaven and a new earth"? Two scriptural metaphors of liberation merged, the Exodus and the New Jerusalem, heralding
the New Age. At the same time, the paradox or the flip side
of the Exodus manifested itself in the New World, by virtue
of the failure of success. For the Exodus is also but the passage between Egypt and Canaan. And the Canaanites, who
happen to inhabit the promised land, are "excluded from the
world of moral concern."[54] Deuteronomy 20:17–18 is quite
explicit: they are to be killed, men, women and children, and
their idols destroyed.

> But thou shalt utterly destroy them; namely, the Hittites, and the
> Amorites, the Canaanites, and the Perizzites, the Hivites, and the
> Jebusites; as the Lord thy God hath commanded thee: that they
> teach you not to do after all their abominations.

Phrased rather politely in the words of a Jewish American
historian:

> The American frontier psychology was much like the frontier
> psychology of the Israelites during the Age of Judges in the Old
> Testament. The problems of the Israelites in settling Canaan were
> akin to the problems the frontiersmen faced in subjugating the
> American wilderness.[55]

So wherever the millennial metaphor could be geographically
implemented because of an "open frontier" the logic of emancipation would give way to the logic of conquest. This was
the case with the Puritans who confronted the native Americans, with the Boers in South Africa who encountered the
Bantu peoples, with the Jews who settled in Palestine. The
flipside of the Exodus is the tale of settler colonialism. "The
door of hope" for one people is the gate of damnation for
another.

   Nonetheless, or rather, because of this, the metaphor flourished in the New World and formed part of the credo of
Manifest Destiny which beckoned Americans toward the
western frontier and eventually overseas.[56]

---

54. See M. Walzer, *Exodus and Revolution* (New York, 1985), p. 141–42.
55. M.I. Dimont, *The Jews in America* (New York, 1978), p. 53.
56. See A.K. Weinberg, *Manifest Destiny* (1935; reprint Chicago, 1967).

During the eighteenth century the dominant views among American evangelicals were postmillennialism and the Second Coming, personal conversion, and America as the New Israel. In the first half of the nineteenth century the holiness doctrine and Millerism swept the east coast, followed by a broader Great Awakening and emphasis on revivalist preaching and biblical prophecy. This paved the way for Darby and premillennialist teachings from England to take hold in the wake of the turmoil of the Civil War (1860–65). From 1867 to 1920 the Bible and Prophecy Conference Movement provided a forum for Darby and other premillennialists, and by the 1880s premillennial dispensationalism and Christian Zionism had become part of the American millennial package, widely adopted by evangelicals as well as mainstream Protestant leaders.

If we examine the social context of American revivalism, it was again social upheaval, the Civil War, which formed the backdrop for the revival of apocalyptic politics and the millennial metaphor, particularly among those who found themselves on the losing end of social change. The era which saw the rebirth of apocalyptic politics in the United States, the Reconstruction period and its aftermath, also saw the birth of the Ku Klux Klan and the lynchings of blacks and Indians in the South and the West.[57] In England the rebirth of the millennial metaphor early in the century had been part of a reaction to the turmoil of the French Revolution, a defensive cultural rampart. In both cases the metaphor took on a conservative, defensive character, in comparison to its earlier articulations in the sixteenth and seventeenth centuries. Then social upheaval had also formed the setting for apocalyptic politics, the Peasant War in Germany, the Reformation, the Thirty Years' War, but then the metaphor, among Anabaptists and Independent Puritans, presented itself in avowedly offensive, "progressive" modes, as a metaphor of social revolution, not counterrevolution.

In the United States, the major popularizer of Christian Zionism as a political prophecy was William E. Blackstone, author of the bestseller *Jesus is Coming* (1881). Blackstone

---

57. See J. Williamson, *The Rage for Order: Black-White Relations in the American South since Emancipation* (Oxford, 1986).

organized the first American lobby for the creation of a Jewish state in Palestine and initiated an intensive campaign which had the support of U.S. senators, the Chief Justice of the Supreme Court, and business figures such as John D. Rockefeller, J.P. Morgan, and Charles B. Scribner. The campaign called on President Benjamin Harrison and later, on President Wilson to work for the creation of a Jewish state in Palestine. When Herzl began discussions with the British government on the possibility of establishing a Jewish colony in Uganda or Argentina, Blackstone sent him a Bible with all passages referring to Israel and Palestine underlined, with clear instruction to the effect that only Palestine could be the site of the Jewish state.

The publication of the Scofield Reference Bible in 1909, an edition with notes and commentary based on premillennial dispensationalism, was a milestone in institutionalizing premillennialism and thereby Christian Zionism. A series of pamphlets published between 1910 and 1915 titled "The Fundamentals" further institutionalized the premillennial doctrine, spreading it beyond the circle of evangelicals into the mainstream Protestant denominations.

At the same time, for black Americans, the metaphor had been, at least since the eighteenth century, the central glyph for emancipation – Exodus stood for redemption from slavery, Jesus was a code for freedom, and the churches founded by black communities named after scriptural places all stood for sites of sanctuary in the land of oppression. The Zion churches of black congregations reflected the momentum of emancipation and resistance against white domination.[58]

Zion churches were also established in America by other alienated groups. Dissident groups such as the Mormons undertook their own exodus, which ultimately brought the Mormons to Utah. Here the Zion metaphor has been solidly institutionalized; institutions of the Church of Jesus Christ of Latter-day Saints in Salt Lake City include Zion's First National Bank, Zion's Savings Bank & Trust, Zion's Cooperative Mercantile Institution, and Zion's Securities Corporation.[59]

---

58. J.U. Young, *Black and African Theologies* (Maryknoll, N.Y., 1986), p. 20.
59. L.J. Arrington and D. Bitton, *The Mormon Experience: A History of the Latter-day Saints* (New York, 1980).

Another well known instance is Zion City founded in Chicago in 1896 by John Alexander Dowie, an evangelical missionary of Scottish descent. The Christian Catholic Apostolic Church in Zion, as its full name runs, "drew the bulk of its following from the impoverished urban communities of the industrial Midwest: a population itself alienated from such experiences of self-determination and rational achievement as were celebrated in nineteenth-century American Protestant ideology."[60] In the early 1900s a link developed between Zion City in Illinois and a "Zionist" initiative among black South Africans, mainly migrant workers in Johannesburg and Natal, which was the start of a proliferation of Zionist churches in South Africa.[61]

Earlier in Britain, while Albion was identified as Zion and millennial Jerusalem was sited in "England's green and pleasant land," Zion served for dissident groups as a portable metaphor in the continuing pursuit of more immediate utopias, and they established other Zions in Britain[62] – Zions within Zion, so to speak. In America, itself a Zion settlement, this process of the reproduction of Zions repeated itself.

Among black Americans the discourse of Christian liberation had developed in conjunction with the radical Puritan current of the Quakers who, by the mid-eighteenth century, initiated the antislavery movement, joined later by Methodists and other popular currents of Christianity, which subsequently grew into the abolitionist movement.[63] This has been an emancipatory Christianity and continues to be so today (after an interlude of passivity in the black church between 1914 and 1945), commensurate with the fact that black emancipation continues to be on the agenda.

This current fed into the Pentecostal movement, which had its beginnings not in the South, as did fundamentalism, but in the West (particularly in Los Angeles), among lower-class urban people who adopted the charismatic forms of

60. J. Comaroff, *Body of Power, Spirit of Resistance: The Culture and History of a South African People* (Chicago, 1985), pp. 177–84.
61. B. Sundkler, *Zulu Zion and some Swazi Zionists* (London, 1976).
62. W.H.G. Armytage, *Heavens Below: Utopian Experiments in England* (Toronto, 1961).
63. T. Witvliet, *A Place in the Sun: An Introduction to Liberation Theology in the Third World* (Maryknoll, N.Y., 1985).

worship of blacks. Pentecostalism thus stemmed from a tradition in which the emancipatory momentum of the metaphor prevailed and which, accordingly, represented the other side of the coin of the fundamentalist tendency, which was precisely a Southern rampart *against* emancipation, the emancipation of blacks in the South, and against the influence of Northerners and Yankee liberalism.

For many evangelicals and fundamentalists the birth of the state of Israel in 1948 was confirmation of the premillennial doctrine and the imminence of Jesus' return. In the wake of Israel's lightning victory in 1967 and its capture of Jerusalem, L. Nelson Bell, Billy Graham's father-in-law, wrote in the evangelical journal *Christianity Today*:

> That for the first time in more than 2000 years Jerusalem is now completely in the hands of the Jews gives a student of the Bible a thrill and a renewed faith in the accuracy and validity of the Bible.[64]

Thus the next phase of the metaphor set in: the restoration of the Jews being accomplished and Jerusalem regained, now the penultimate stage of the millennial scenario was thought to be at hand.

For Israel, 1967 was a turning point as well, in both domestic and foreign policy.[65] David came out of the Six-Day War transformed into Goliath. When international pressures began to mount for Israel to retreat from the territories occupied since the war, Israel faced the choice of either retreating or expanding and chose to follow the latter course. Israel shifted its alliances accordingly. Its relationship with the United States, one of covert cooperation since the 1950s, became overt and, over the years, increasingly strategic in character.[66] The United States took over France's role as Israel's chief arms supplier.

Israel's relations with social forces *within* the United States shifted as well, from the "liberal coalition" including Demo-

64. Quoted in *What Is Western Fundamentalist Christian Zionism?*, p. 9.
65. See, e.g., U. Davis, *Israel: Utopia Incorporated* (London, 1977); W. Stevenson, *Strike Zion!* (New York, 1967).
66. The literature on relations between Israel and the United States is extensive, e.g., S. Green, *Taking Sides: America's Secret Relations with a Militant Israel, 1948–1967* (London, 1984); and *Living by the Sword: America and Israel in the Middle East, 1968–1987* (London, 1988).

crats and blacks, toward a more right wing ensemble of forces. When the National Council of Churches endorsed the United Nations resolution that Israel should withdraw from the occupied territories, it was the signal for the American Jewish Committee to begin discreet talks with evangelical church leaders. Rabbi Marc Tannenbaum of the American Jewish Committee later described the episode:

> The evangelical community is the largest and fastest growing block of pro-Israeli, pro-Jewish sentiment in this country. Since the 1967 War, the Jewish community has felt abandoned by Protestants, by groups clustered around the National Council of Churches, which, because of sympathy with third world causes, gave an impression of support for the PLO. There was a vacuum of public support to Israel that began to be filled by the fundamentalist and evangelical Christians.[67]

When in the 1970s a stream of publications and television evangelists proclaimed premillennialism and Christian Zionism, the theme of apocalypse became increasingly prominent. Such books as Hal Lindsey's *The Late Great Planet Earth* became bestsellers, popularizing the premillennial and Christian Zionist perspective in an apocalyptic setting.

At this juncture several forces within the United States began to come together. The New Right, itself a merger of Goldwater radicals and neoconservatives, engaged in an alliance with the evangelicals. This political momentum also healed the historical doctrinal splits among the evangelicals, between fundamentalists and Pentecostalists, charismatics and Baptists.

The New Right came out of a political culture in which the millennial metaphor had long served American hegemony and expansion in the name of Manifest Destiny. Richard Hofstadter referred to the American Right as "a secular and demonic version of adventism," always "manning the barricades of civilization."[68] Richard Viguerie, one of the coordinators of the right-wing coalition, matched the profile: "I

---

67. Quoted in H. Haddad and D.E. Wagner, *All in the Name of the Bible* (Brattleboro, Vt., 1986), p. 21.
68. R. Hofstadter, *The Paranoid Style in American Politics and Other Essays* (New York, 1965).

work twelve hours a day 'to save the western world.'"[69]

The thesis of "Gramscism of the Right" appears to be valid with respect to Israel's shift of allegiance from the American Protestant churches to the evangelicals. It is a cultural strategy clearly motivated by political expedience. But with respect to the coalition between the New Right and the evangelicals, the thesis does not hold because of the preexisting affinities in terms of political culture between the American Right and the evangelicals. They already shared secular and religious versions of the same metaphor, which sanctified America and American imperialism. This cannot be regarded as a matter of "using" culture for political ends, because the political agenda itself reflects a common political culture.

At a meeting in Washington in 1975 of evangelical leaders and Menachem Begin, the leader of the Likud block, the evangelicals pledged their support to Israel. Jerry Falwell stated,

> We proclaim that the Land of Israel encompasses Judea and Samaria as integral parts of the Jewish patrimony, with Jerusalem as its one and indivisible capital.... Israel stands as a bulwark of strength and determination against those, who by terror and blackmail, threaten our democratic way of life.[70]

In 1976 Rev. Jerry Falwell was awarded Israel's Yabotinski award by Menachem Begin. This was but one token of the bond between the American evangelical right and Israel.

Nineteen seventy-six is on record as the year of the ascendancy of Christian Zionism. A combination of events unfolded which placed Christian Zionism in the mainstream of the political process. In the United States, Jimmy Carter, a "born-again" Southern Baptist, was elected president, drawing on the evangelical vote. In Israel, Menachem Begin and the Likud block came to power in 1977 on a revisionist Zionist platform utilizing biblical imagery. The triangular relationship between the New Right, the evangelicals, and the Israel lobby now emerged on the forefront. This coalition agreed on many policy issues, in particular the priority of Israel.

---

69. Quoted in T.J. McIntyre, *The Fear Brokers: Peddling the Hate Politics of the New Right* (Boston, 1979), p. 158.

70. Quoted in W. Granberg-Michaelson, "The Evangelical Right and Israel: What Place for the Arabs?" ADC Issues (Washington), no. 6, 1982.

When President Carter called for the creation of a Palestinian homeland, alienating the evangelical and New Right voting blocs, this coalition sprang into action, initiating a national campaign against Carter's support for Palestinian rights. A costly series of full-page advertisements in major American newspapers entitled "Evangelicals' Concern for Israel" was signed by leading evangelicals. This contributed to the momentum leading to Ronald Reagan's election to the presidency in 1980.

It had been precisely to avoid the issue of Palestinian rights that the American Jewish Committee and other Zionist circles in the United States had opted for a coalition with the evangelicals and the New Right, because no support for Israel's expansionist policy had been forthcoming from the mainline Protestant denominations united in the National Council of Churches. This alliance also brought the Israel lobby close to the antisemitic undercurrents among American evangelicals.

Nathan Perlmutter, the director of the Anti-Defamation League of B'nai Brith in the United States, stated, "I'm deeply grateful for this alliance," while at the same time redefining antisemitism not as prejudice against Jews but as criticism of the "Jewish state" of Israel.[71] The Jewish Zion thus had a career similar to that which the Christian Zions had had previously: it has become an imperial project, with *Eretz Israel* being equivalent to Greater Israel.

The years of the Reagan administration are now often referred to as the "decade of indulgence."[72] While this refers to economic policy it can be extended to political rhetoric and to theology as well. When the Moral Majority and other agencies of the evangelical right were catapulted center stage they broadcast their message of apocalypse. The focal area of the apocalyptic scenario was the Middle East or, to be exact, Armageddon in Israel's Valley of Meggido. The time had come for the "dark side of the force," the flip side of the metaphor, to emerge. Amid the upbeat slogans of the Reagan presidency – "Morning in America," the magic of the marketplace,

71. Dehmer, *Unholy Alliance*, p. 8; Perlmutter, *The Real Antisemitism*.
72. L. Bentsen, "Energy policy: Can Bush Do Better Than Reagan?" *International Herald Tribune*, 15 August 1990; S. Blumenthal and T.B. Edsall, eds., *The Reagan Legacy* (New York, 1988).

supply-side economics – an eerie note was struck. Armageddon was at the door. This was both unreal and threatening. It was threatening because it was unreal. An unreal message in the hands of the occupant of a real position, the presidency of the United States, seemed to make unreality reality's norm.[73]

At this juncture apocalypse emerged as a topos in American popular culture, ranging from visions of urban catastrophe to privatized forms of apocalypse or cultivated disaster, whether through drugs or sadomasochism.[74] Immanuel Wallerstein in 1980 spoke of "the socialist revolution in which we are living" as "the only alternative to Armageddon."[75]

Twentieth-century Armageddon theology is an amalgam of different prophecies merging the destinies of America and Israel, just as earlier the destinies of Britain and Israel had been fused in the nineteenth-century British restoration movement. At this stage different phases of the metaphor came together. In the publications of the Worldwide Church of God in California, such as *The Plain Truth*, published by Herbert Armstrong, and in his book *The United States and Britain in Prophecy*, several themes, which through the history of the metaphor had represented different strands of belief, are fused in one large apocalyptic panorama, which is at the same time an imperial fantasy. Following in the tradition of the British Israelite movement, this work proclaims that all the promises made in the Bible to Israel have in fact been fulfilled for Britain and the United States. They have been fulfilled for the Saxon peoples who are the true Israelites (the Jews are merely the descendants of the tribe of Judah), so that these nations are "lifted above all nations." In this re-

73. This episode is discussed in, e.g., G. Halsell, *Prophecy and Politics: Militant Evangelists on the Road to Nuclear War* (Westport, Conn., 1986); L. Kickham, "The Theology of Nuclear War," *Covert Action Information Bulletin* 27 (1986); A. Lang, "The Politics of Armageddon: Reagan Links Bible Prophecy with Nuclear War," *Convergence*, Fall 1985.

74. See, e.g., Adam Parfrey, ed., *Apocalypse Culture* (New York, 1987); Gore Vidal, *Armageddon? Essays 1983–1987* (London, 1987); "The Work Energy Crisis and the Apocalypse," *Midnight Notes* 2, no. 1 (Jamaica Plain, Mass., 1980).

75. I.M. Wallerstein, "'The Withering Away of the States,'" *International Journal of the Sociology of Law*, no. 8, 1980, and *The Politics of the World-Economy* (Cambridge, 1984), p. 57.

reading of the Scripture, modern imperial history is presented, detailed, and documented, as the inexorable fulfillment of ancient prophecy. With imperial grandeur thus grounded spiritually, imperial paranoia sets in, for the "Great Tribulation" will fall on Britain and America first.

> God will use a Nazi-fascist Europe to punish Britain-America. Then He will use the communist hordes to wipe out the Roman Europe. We are entering a time of world trouble – utter WORLD chaos![76]

Notable in this example is the division between Europe on the one hand and Britain-America on the other, the labelling of Europe as "Roman," and the term "hordes" in conjunction with "communist," invoking the imagery of the Huns and Mongols.

These and other instances of metaphoric exuberance merge several themes: the state of Israel as a step toward the fulfillment of the end time scenario; the United States and Great Britain as New Zions, spiritually wedded to Israel; the notion of the Anglo-Saxons as the actual Israelites, which is the theme of the British Israelite movement; and the privileged status of the evangelicals as true believers who thus form a spiritual Israel, destined to be taken away through "rapture" at the planetary endgame.

Evangelical support for Greater Israel has not been merely a matter of propaganda. Evangelicals became important financiers for both the Likud block and the West Bank settlement movement.[77] On the West Bank, American church groups, primarily Southern Baptists, used an institution called the Temple Mount Foundation to support Israeli extreme-right groups who planned to "blow up the Dome of the Rock and Al Aqsa mosque and then just lay claim to the site." This led to several incidents and near-crises in 1985, 1986, and 1990.[78]

76. H.W. Armstrong, *The United States and Britain in Prophecy* (1967; reprint Pasadena, Calif. 1980), p. 171. This work has gone through several new editons.

77. R.I. Friedman, "Terror on Sacred Ground: The Battle for the Temple Mount," *Mother Jones*, August-September 1987, p. 40.

78. L. Rapoport, "Slouching towards Armageddon: Links with Evangelicals," *The Jerusalem Post*, 17–24 June 1984; A. Keller, "Temple Mount Escalation," *Israel and Palestine*, January-February 1986.

The International Christian Embassy in Jerusalem (ICEJ) opened its doors in 1980 to serve as a focal center of worldwide evangelical support for Israel. "The timing of the opening," according to a report by the Middle East Council of Churches, "was designed to offset the effect of several embassies withdrawing from Jerusalem to Tel Aviv in protest against Israel declaring Jerusalem as its 'eternal capital.'" The report summarizes the activities of the Embassy:

> The Embassy engages in a number of projects which appear to have close collaboration with Israeli political leadership. Among these are: lobbying (particularly in the United States), promotion of Israeli products, sale of Israeli bonds, annual rallies such as the Feast of Tabernacles, lobbying for Soviet Jews to settle in Israel, blood donations for the Israeli defense forces, promoting Christian Zionism in the West.[79]

The Embassy which also broadcasts a radio program "A Word from Jerusalem," has "embassies" in more than twenty countries.

The Embassy is one among many evangelical organizations active in Israel and the occupied territories. Much of their work is concerned with Christian tourists and Arab Christians. At times the evangelical presence has given rise to friction and conflict with Israelis who object to Christian missionary and proselytizing activities among Jewish people.[80] Jewish nationalists resent being excluded from any quarter of Jerusalem. Jerusalem has since long become a battleground of conflicting claims sacred and secular.[81]

The objections of religious Israelis to Christian missionary activities among Jews are not without significance. Ultimately the Christian Zionist scenario calls not simply for the restoration of the Jews but also for their conversion as a precondition for the end time. As a consequence, the alliance of Jewish and Christian Zionists can only be a tactical bond for ultimately their objectives clash with one another.

It is noteworthy that we find similar combinations of American evangelical organizations and Israeli forces active on

79. *What Is Western Fundamentalist Christian Zionism?*, p. 11.
80. H. Shapiro, "The missionaries come out," *The Jerusalem Post*, 1984.
81. M. Benvenisti, *The Torn City* (Jerusalem, 1976).

the side of American interests on several frontiers of hegemony in the Third World. The Iran-Contra affair put American-Israeli covert cooperation on the front pages.[82] The involvement of "muscular Christianity" on several of these frontiers adds another dimension to the pattern; for instance, in Honduras and Nicaragua, during the conflict between the Contras and the Sandinistas, and in parts of southern Africa and Latin America.[83] The ICEJ's "embassy" in Honduras has been active in support of the Contras, in collaboration with Gospel Crusade Inc.[84] This suggests that to a certain extent this is not simply an incidental alignment of forces, either culturally or politically, but part of a larger pattern of cooperation and, in effect, a global network.

When Israel's expansionism turned northward, into southern Lebanon, the American evangelicals followed, as if another missionary frontier had opened. George Otis of High Adventure Ministries, operating out of Van Nuys, California, established Voice of Hope and King of Hope radio stations and a Star of Hope television station in southern Lebanon, with the encouragement of the Israeli government and funding from American televangelist audiences. Major Saad Haddad, Israel's strongman in the area, has been allowed free access to the stations' facilities. Otis's aspiration has been to make Lebanon a "true Christian state," while his broadcasts to Israel serve to prepare "the Jewish souls to recognize Jesus as their Messiah – before the coming battle of Armageddon."[85]

In April 1982 the Star of Hope television station "in southern Free Lebanon" was taken over by Pat Robertson's Christian Broadcasting Network (CBN). Pat Robertson explained that when Israel gained possession of Jerusalem in the Six-Day War, this was "the most significant prophetic event of our lifetime. . . . the time of the Gentiles was nearly over. Soon God would be moving towards Israel. And CBN was

82. E.g., J. Marshall et al., *The Iran-Contra Connection* (Boston, 1987).

83. See B. Beit-Hallahmi, *The Israeli Connection: Whom Israel Arms and Why* (London, 1988); J.P. Nederveen Pieterse, *Israel's Role in the Third World: Exporting West Bank Expertise* (Amsterdam, 1984). Cf. other contributions in this volume.

84. D. Preusch and J. Hunter, "Christian 'Embassy' funnels funds to Contras," *The Guardian* (New York), 31 August 1988.

85. Dehmer, *Unholy Alliance*, pp. 9–10.

going to be a vital part of that move. I knew it."[86] In his *700 Club* television program Pat Robertson repeatedly discussed the situation in Lebanon, often repeating a prediction he had made in January 1982:

> I guarantee you by the fall of 1982, that there is going to be a judgment on the world, and the ultimate judgment is going to come on the Soviet Union. They are going to be the ones to make military adventures, and they are going to be hit.[87]

On numerous occasions Pat Robertson urged his *700 Club* audience, while superimposing the telephone number of the White House on the screen, to write or call President Reagan and encourage him to continue his support for the Israeli invasion of Lebanon. Recently Robertson's station has operated under the name Middle East TV, still in Israel's *cordon sanitaire*, broadcasting such children's programs as *Super Book* and *Crusader Robot*. "Hel-lo-I-Am-Cru-sa-der-Ro-bot. I-Am-Your-Friend."[88]

Denouement

When reviewing the history of the metaphor of Zion in terms of our central question, the correlation between religious attitudes and patterns of hegemony, one key distinction to make is between counterhegemonic and hegemonic patterns. When attitudes are counterhegemonic, the metaphor applies to the apocalypse of the old powers, the *dies irae* is directed against the status quo. When they are hegemonic, the metaphor is held to apply to the power of one's own group, whose destiny is viewed as a fulfillment of millennial promises. There are, of course, different nuances within each pattern but there is no need to go into these in the span of this brief essay.

In its early stages, the overall meaning of the millennial metaphor tends to be counterhegemonic. Thus, according to the theodicy of Irenaeus, millennial hopes are legitimate, part of orthodoxy, and because they might arise anywhere, they

---

86. Quoted in Granberg-Michaelson, "The Evangelical Right."
87. Dehmer, *Unholy Alliance*, p. 14.
88. In J. de Gier, "De pacificator," *Intermagazine*, October 1989, p. 24.

may be termed a "polycentric" vision, which therefore is also subversive of central authority.

With the establishment of the Roman Catholic church, the metaphor is transformed into a hegemonic discourse with the church as the City of God and the embodiment of the millennial promise. This renders the metaphor subject to ecclesiastic politics. The metaphor is as centralized as the church is, in which the Bishop of Rome over time is transformed into the Vicar of Christ, and the papacy becomes a formula for merging spiritual and temporal power. The millennial metaphor thus becomes an imperial vision for an imperial church, an orthodoxy which held fast until the sixteenth century.

Among the millennial movements of the Middle Ages the counterhegemonic meaning of the metaphor was retained, counterhegemonic both vis-à-vis the church and hierarchy and vis-à-vis temporal powers. The metaphor serves as a utopia and a metaphor of defiance. By and large at this stage the defiance tends to be diffuse. Thus, during the Middle Ages, hegemonic and counterhegemonic versions of the metaphor coexisted, in the church on the one hand and among popular movements on the other. A middle ground, subject to recurrent negotiation, was occupied by, for instance, the Franciscans' and Savonarola's uses of the metaphor. The Albigensian Crusade and the Holy Inquisition represented hegemonic operations of the church to stamp out counterhegemonic or "heretical" tendencies and discourses.

With the onset of the Reformation, the metaphor was radicalized and turned counterhegemonic in a more focused manner, particularly among the Anabaptists. For a brief period in Munster, the Anabaptists managed to establish a "liberated zone," at which juncture the metaphor became *locally* hegemonic, a New Jerusalem, a Kingdom of God ruled by Anabaptist leadership, which, on the other hand, remained counterhegemonic in relation to the wider political and social structures.

For the Puritans the metaphor carried different meanings, reflecting their diverse experiences. For English Puritans it served as a counterhegemonic metaphor of defiance which later, with Cromwell, turned into a metaphor of reconstruction. The metaphor of defiance was retained among such

Puritan "left" currents as the Seekers, Ranters, Levelers, Diggers, Fifth Monarchists, and Quakers, and among utopian dissidents.

For the American Puritans, the metaphor guided them from Egypt to Canaan, through the Exodus as the journey of transition, and accordingly, from a discourse of defiance of Old World constellations it became a formula of hegemony for the New World, turning from counterhegemonic to hegemonic. From an exemplary utopia (the city upon a hill) the New Zion became a mode of domination for settler colonialism and subsequently an alibi for empire. Again, as in England, the counterhegemonic current survived as well, for instance among the Quakers of Pennsylvania and the Amish of Iowa, and the scenario repeatedly played out among dissident groups *within* the United States, such as the Mormons, who established their New Zion in Utah.

For the nineteenth-century evangelicals, the metaphor was from the start hegemonic, a counterrevolutionary rampart against the French Revolution and Enlightenment culture, a disciplinary formula for the "society of normalization" that took the form of Victorian England. This history ranges from 1792 (Bicheno's *Signs of the Times*) to its imperial consummation in the Balfour Declaration of 1917. In its latter form the metaphor was not merely conservative but offensive, it operated in an imperial setting and acquired the character of a hegemonic project, concretely, that of the settlement of the Jews in Palestine.

For American evangelicals in the South, for whom the metaphor came to play a central role most notably between 1867 and 1920, premillennialism served as a hegemonic discourse in the wake of Reconstruction, as a barrier against further black emancipation and incursions of Northerners. That is, it was counterhegemonic in relation to the domination of the North and hegemonic within the South itself. It thus paralleled and coincided with the aversion toward blacks, Catholics and Jews. This defensive, hegemonic stream led to the "fundamentalists" of 1910–1920. As in England, the metaphor also took on the character of an imperial (or semi-imperial) project, marked by the congressional endorsement in 1922 of Jewish settlement in Palestine.

The independent black churches in America and Pentecostalism have represented a counterhegemonic movement in which the metaphor stands for emancipation. For Pentecostalists, this changed gradually as they conformed to the rising tide of cold war Christianity and adjusted their discourse accordingly. A case in point is the shifting rhetoric of the Jehovah's Witnesses; over the years their discourse shifted from being anti-establishment in the 1930s, to a pro-free world position in the 1950s, and adoption of the Armageddon scenario in the 1980s.[89]

In the postwar period of American boom and of cold war, the hegemonic version of the metaphor spread among Southern Baptists and beyond, culminating in the evangelical alliance of fundamentalists and Pentacostals with the New Right in the 1970s. In this period, marked, in terms of Christian Zionism, by 1948 as the year of the establishment of Israel, 1967 as the year of Greater Israel, and 1977 as the year of the Likud policy of *Eretz Israel*, the metaphor underwent a metamorphosis from a hegemonic to an expansionist discourse, and ultimately, in prophecies such as Hal Lindsey's, to an apocalyptic script of "imperial madness."

Throughout the metaphor's recent history, its counterhegemonic version also has been alive and well in the circles of liberation theology, in the Peace Council of the National Council of Churches, and on the evangelical Left.

These meanderings of the metaphor raise several questions. How is it that a single metaphor can engender such a bewildering variety of political projects and attitudes? Is the heterogeneity of political articulations to be sought merely in the diverse and shifting societal loci of the users of the metaphor, or does the metaphor itself change meaning or emphasis in the course of its sojourns? Can any particular reading of the metaphor be regarded as "true"?

The diverse history of the millennial metaphor tells us something, first, about the intrinsic ambiguity of prophecy and the unstable relationship between prophecy and power. A change in the fortunes of the metaphor's users is likely to result in its reinterpretation. Besides, this particular metaphor

89. See J.F. Zygmunt, "Prophetic Failure and Chiliastic Identity: The Case of Jehovah's Witnesses," *American Journal of Sociology*, vol. 75, no. 6, May 1970, pp. 926–48.

itself charts an emancipatory scenario which, once a stage of attainment is arrived at, implies a shift of emphasis to a different moment of the metaphor. The moments of the metaphor include the following:

1. *Departure* — The *apocalypse* of the status quo as harbinger of a future millennium, represented as the New Jerusalem.
2. *Journey* — The Exodus as the passage through the wilderness between the old hegemony (Egypt) and the new (Canaan, the Promised Land, or the New Jerusalem).
3. *Arrival* — The point of arrival represents utopia realized, the millennium attained, the *City of God* or the *New Jerusalem*. The metaphor in the present tense. Again the *apocalypse* may recur, either as the paranoia of power, or as the prerequisite for the attainment of a further stage or confirmation of the millennium.

The sociopolitical significance of the metaphor at the first and second stages tends to be counterhegemonic and at the third stage hegemonic.

The dynamic of the metaphor interacts with the dynamic of the social forces who use it and rally behind it. This relates to processes of social change over time as well as to the shifting relations of the metaphor's users with other forces in social space. The latter introduces another form of ambiguity. The metaphor can carry multiple meanings, counterhegemonic and hegemonic, at *the same time*, depending on which social relationship is being considered. We can differentiate between *local, regional, national*, and *global* configurations, all which of course coexist simultaneously. A constellation that is locally hegemonic may be counterhegemonic in relation to the regional constellation of forces, and so forth. These dynamics of time and space contextualize the metaphor.

This ambiguity of discourse with an emancipatory momentum changing into a configuration of domination is not an unfamiliar theme.[90] It is the key difference between Martin Buber's *Pfade* in Utopia, a work that emphasized the moment of departure, and Ralf Dahrendorf's *Pfade aus Utopia*, which emphasized the moment of arrival, of utopian achievement.[91]

90. Cf. Nederveen Pieterse, *Empire and Emancipation*, ch. 15, "Dialectics of Empire and Emancipation."
91. M. Buber, *Pfade in Utopia* (Heidelberg, 1950); R. Dahrendorf, *Pfade aus*

Time and again decolonization processes have witnessed the metamorphosis of a counterhegemonic ideal (departure) into a hegemonic political formation (arrival) – from white sahib to brown sahib. The history of socialism, from the First International to the Third, from the labor movement (departure) to the achievement of "real existing socialism" (arrival), similarly exemplifies this drama. The history of modern Zionism, from departure to arrival, again echoes the tale of aspiration *versus* achievement.[92]

With respect to Christian Zionism, one of the key problems at a deeper level appears to be the tension between the *particularist* foundations and *universal* aspirations of Christianity. The momentum charted in the Bible is that of the development of a tribal religion with a jealous God, to a creed of universal aspiration, a "Gospel for the gentiles." By turning to the Old Testament (also known as the "Jewish Bible") the Reformers reinvoked the tribal roots of Christianity. This retribalization of Christianity found expression in the routine references in Protestant discourse to the "tribes of Israel" (the lost tribes, thirteenth tribe, and so on). With it came a new view of Jews not as a religious community but as the Jewish nation, a shift which paralleled the development of nationalism among gentiles. The dual usage of the "Israel" metaphor, as the purified community of Christians *and* as the "Jewish nation," reproduced the friction between particularist and universal dimensions of the creed at every juncture.

When the metaphor became a beacon and a target on the imperial horizon the element of particularism became acute. "The very idea of the Restoration of the Jews to Palestine as a nation," Regina Sharif observes, "has been a popular theme throughout four centuries of modern European history."[93] Christian Zionism has been a potent force in establishing the notion of a Jewish nation in Western culture, and in connecting it to Palestine. It continues to be an important element of pro-Israeli attitudes in the West. Meanwhile, on the

---

Utopia (Munich, 1967). Cf. J.P. Nederveen Pieterse, "Het utopisch bewustzijn: Beschouwingen over utopie en revolutie," *Sociologische Gids* 20, no. 1 (1973).

92. E.g., G.V. Smith, *Zionism: The Dream and the Reality. A Jewish critique* (London and New York, 1974).

93. Sharif, *Non-Jewish Zionism*, p. 133.

dark side of the metaphor is the erasure of the Palestinians from history, since for them there is no place in the script of the promised land. Likewise, on the other side of the millennial preoccupations with Jerusalem are anti-Arab and anti-Islam prejudices, for the universalism of the Gospel is not without its boundaries.

Even so, while some form of Christian Zionism has been widespread in the Protestant world, it does not mean that there has been a unified Christian attitude towards Palestine and Israel. The evangelical perspective is but one among several. There are also different attitudes towards Israel in Judaism, where religious attitudes range from total support of the state of Israel and the Zionist project to total rejection. Presently Reform and Conservative Judaism are virtually barred from establishing a presence in Israel;[94] only Orthodox Judaism, certain tendencies of which are Zionist while others, such as the Hasidic, reject the state of Israel, is represented in Israel.

The problem of universalism is not specific to Christianity. Is it possible to develop a universal metaphor from a single center, a single standpoint? The universalism of the Roman Catholic church, of the Renaissance and the credo of humanism, of the Englightenment and the claims of reason, entails similar dilemmas and paradoxes.

At the end of the road we arrive at the limits of the metaphor itself. Is it meaningful to discuss and negotiate the degree of validity or error of any particular application of the metaphor, if in the end the metaphor itself breaks down? Does this, in the last resort, call for a different epistemology, a discourse of discourses, a metadiscourse, and a commensurate politics? Does it call for an awareness of the uses and abuses of metaphor, lest the invocation of a metaphor of liberation also activate the principle of the fairy-tale-in-reverse, that is, princes turning into frogs?

If this history illustrates the contingency of religious discourse in relation to political forces, the reverse is also indicated – the role of cultural capital in shaping patterns of hegemony.

94. E. Ein-Gil, "Religion, Zionism and Secularism," *Khamsin*, no. 8, 1981.

EUROPE

· 7 ·

Catholics and Politics in Western Europe

AD VAN WESEL

With the downfall of the papal state in 1870, the Catholic church, the most durable institution of power in the Western world, lost the capacity to exercise worldly power. Ever since, the church, often through affiliated Catholic institutions, has been confronted with and participated in secular struggles for cultural hegemony and political power. From the late nineteenth century on, the church first confronted classical liberalism, which besides the principles of free trade and progress endorsed the principles of the Enlightenment, such as democracy, cultural freedom and the separation of church and state. In the twentieth century the church came up against such non-Christian ideologies as communism, fascism, and Nazism as competitors in the struggle for cultural leadership. For most of the time since the downfall of the papal state the position of the church can be characterized as defensive. More often than not, the church was forced to make concessions to secular politics and trends in society.

Simultaneously, however, the church and Catholic organizations sided with the interests of liberal capitalism in the struggle against anticapitalist political organizations and tendencies. For instance, during elections the church served the interests of the liberals by forbidding Catholics to vote for left-wing parties. This de facto political alliance was also embodied in social networks in which conservative Catholics served as intermediaries between the church and the interests of liberal capitalism. In addition, political mediation between Catholic values and liberal capitalism crystallized in the Christian democratic parties. But they, too, had to accommodate to secular trends.

During the late nineteenth century friction arose within the church itself with the rise of modernism. Modernism is that current in theology which recognizes the value of non-Catholic thought for solutions to human problems. It represented the attempt to reconcile Roman Catholic tradition with democracy and modern science and philosophy. The term is also used to define a tendency in art and philosophy which broke with traditional values and conceptions. In the 1970s cultural modernism was one of the main topics on which neoconservatives in search of a conservative "cultural hegemony" focused their criticism.[1] Both artistic and theological modernism were condemned by Pope Pius X in the encyclical *Pascendi* in 1907.

The condemnation of modernism was only implicitly revoked at the Second Vatican Council (1962–1965). In order to adapt to the process of secularization, the council tried to find ways to bring the church closer to the people. Among the most important results of the council was the recommendation of lay participation in religious work, which was condemned in *Pascendi*. The council also paved the way for the rise of liberation theology, which was in part based on a profane class analysis, and for an opening to the Left in general. However, after the election of John Paul II, the Vatican put an end to its policy of reconciliation with communist regimes, and started to condemn liberation theology and other liberal currents within the church. This change in policy coincided with a conservative shift in the world of secular politics.

The convergence of the conservative offensive by the church with the rise of (neo-)conservatism in politics over the last decade will be the main focus of this chapter. Because this chapter is meant to be an introduction to the relationship between the church and secular politics and the (un)suitability of the church as an instrument in the quest for cultural hegemony at a specific stage of capitalist development, a brief historical overview of the relationship between the church and Catholic institutions with other institutions of economic and political power has been deemed necessary. From the

---

1. D. Bell, *The Cultural Contradictions of Capitalism*, 2nd ed. (New York, 1979), p. xxxiii.

historical prespective of cooperation and tension between the church and secular power, we hope to show that the convergence between the changes in the policies of the church and the recovered strength of Christian Democracy in Western Europe, and the attack on the Keynesian welfare state and left-wing and liberal forces, has not been totally accidental.

The Church Versus Modern Ideologies

After the occupation of Rome by troops of the new Italian state in 1870, the risorgimiento process was concluded and the secular power of the papal state had come to an end. With the loss of its secular power, the church was reduced to an institution of spiritual and moral authority. Although Catholic values and dogmas were preserved as leading principles of the Italian, as well as of many other, European states, the moral authority of the church was increasingly challenged by the emergence of modern ideologies, such as liberalism, socialism, communism, and humanism. In this context, the policy of the church became a mixture of confrontation and adaptation to secular thought and politics.

In the latter part of nineteenth century, the rise of modernism and the rivalry between the Roman Catholic church and the liberal state gave birth to a new ideological current within the church, namely, integralism. Integralism rejected modernist thought and all social and political activities other than those conceived in Catholic inspiration. In the long run, integralists seek to eliminate all social and political movements based on other inspirations.[2] As an antipluralist movement, integralism implicitly rejects the division between church and state. Nowadays integralist tendencies are strongest in the ranks of the lay movements Opus Dei and Communione e Liberazione; among conservative Catholics in Poland and France; and within several *correnti* (currents) of Christian Democracy in Italy.[3] The centralist policies of Pope

2. D. I. Kertzer, *Comrades and Christians: Religion and Political Struggle in Communist Italy* (Cambridge, 1980), p. 101.
3. R. E. M. Irving, *The Christian Democratic Parties of Western Europe* (London, 1979), p. 77.

John Paul II have also been considered integralistic.[4]

The relationship between the church and the state was most hostile in Italy, where popes even excommunicated rulers of the state. The basis for tension between the Catholic community and the Italian state had been laid even before the occupation of the papal territory by the 1867 encyclical *Non Expedit*, which forbade Catholics to participate in political parties or to vote in elections.[5] After the turn of the century, the growing force of socialist movements led the Vatican to relax the doctrine of *Non Expedit*; in 1904, Pope Pius X gave permission to vote in "critical areas" where socialist candidates had to be defeated. In 1919, the ban on Catholic participation in politics was lifted altogether.[6] The dispute between the Vatican and the then-Fascist government of Italy was finally settled in 1929, with the conclusion of the Lateran Pacts. According to these pacts the Vatican was granted territorial sovereignty on its premises in exchange for the recognition of the Italian state. Moreover, the Lateran Pacts guaranteed the legal recognition of the former Catholic lay movement, Catholic Action, a guarantee which proved to be vital to its surviving the fascist dictatorship.[7]

In its attempts to deal with modernism and liberalism, the church followed different strategies. The majority of the higher clergy continued their partnership with the aristocracy and the nonecclesiastical elite.[8] They held to the encyclicals of 1864, *Quanta Cura* and *Syllabus Errorum*, and to the condemnation of political and religious liberalism expressed in these encyclicals.[9] Whereas liberals and nationalists were of the opinion that national loyalties and an international Catholic confession could not coexist without tension, the church stressed the common Catholic heritage of many European

4. P. Hertel, "Ich verspreche euch den Himmel" in *Geistlicher Anspruch gesellschaftliche Ziele und kirchliche Bedeutung des Opus Dei* (Düsseldorf, 1985), p. 78.
5. J. F. Pollard, *The Vatican and Italian Fascism, 1929–1932: A Study in Conflict* (Cambridge, 1985), p. 7.
6. Irving, *Christian Democratic Parties*, p. 2.
7. Pollard, *Vatican and Italian Fascism*, p. 47.
8. P. N. Siegel, *The Meek and the Militant: Religion and Power across the World* (London, 1986), p. 82.
9. T. Zwaan, "De katholieke overlevingsstrategie," *Intermediair*, 10 April 1987, pp. 57–61.

countries. The doctrine of the church converged with the interests of the Catholic aristocracy, who not only derived their historical status from the church but who, as a class based on kinship, were likewise threatened by modernism and liberalism. Starting in the late nineteenth century, both the church and important factions of the aristocracy began to consider European unity in terms of a citadel for Christian culture, and as a means to regain some of the power they had lost to modern nation-states and to the liberal bourgeoisie.

In the present century, too, the most persistent advocates of European unity are to be found among the aristocracy. After the First World War, Count Coudenhove Kalergi saw the aristocracy as the spiritual leader on the path to a Pan-European community, while the tragic Baron von Papen even believed the aspirations of the Nazis to be a vehicle for a united Christian Europe. When after the Second World War the idea of European unity obtained a foothold in the new democratic political parties, the apparently outmoded political ambitions of the aristocracy were offered new opportunities. Recently, these have been dramatized by the revival of monarchist sentiment among segments of East European society in the wake of the collapse of state socialism.[10]

On the other hand, the church gradually started to compete with and, to a certain degree, to reconcile itself with modernism. A turning point in Catholic policy in this respect was the encyclical *Rerum Novarum* in 1891, which combined Thomas Aquinas's doctrine of the right to property as natural law with the solution to the "social question," e.g., the poverty of the proletariat, within a corporative order. *Rerum Novarum* supported the already budding Catholic workers' movements, which were initiated by such lower clerics as Pieter Daens in Belgium, and which wanted to improve the living conditions of the working class as well as to combat socialist organizations which were fostering secularism among the workers.[11] In 1896, the church also started to compete with liberal capital,

10. R. Coudenhove Kalergi, *Pan Europa ABC* (Vienna, 1931), p. 26. Otto von Habsburg has said that he was asked to run for the presidency by the Liberal and Farmers' Party in the 1990 Hungarian elections. *Volkskrant* (Amsterdam), 30 December 1989.
11. L.P. Boon, *Pieter Daens of hoe in de negentiende eeuw de arbeiders van Aalst vochten tegen armoede en onrecht* (Amsterdam, 1971).

Ad van Wesel

when the priest Guiseppe Tovini established the Catholic Banco Ambrosiano in Milan.[12] Both tendencies, workers' organizations and capitalist competition, were united in Catholic Action, a network of banks, peasant cooperatives, industrial trade unions, cultural associations, and a Catholic press. According to Pope Pius XI, Catholic Action was "as an instrument nothing less than a Christian reconquest of a society corrupted and enslaved by the evils of the modern world."[13] In many Catholic countries Catholic Action provided the impetus for founding Christian democratic parties.

In the 1920s, the church was confronted with two anti-Christian ideologies which had conquered state power, communism and fascism. Due to its outspoken atheism, communism has traditionally been the natural enemy of the Vatican. The relationship between the church and fascism and Nazism has, on the contrary, been very ambivalent. Officially, the church was aloof towards fascism up to the Second World War, and remained neutral during the war itself. However, Pope Pius XII considered a German victory on the eastern front vital for Europe's future, just as his predecessor had regarded the defeat of the popular front governments in France and Spain in the 1930s of vital importance.[14] Although sharing its anticommunism, the Vatican's policies toward the Nazi and fascist governments between 1926 and 1944 were mainly directed at safeguarding the interests of the church.

After the Lateran Pacts with Mussolini in 1929, the Vatican concluded a concordat with Nazi Germany in 1933. The concordat was negotiated by Baron von Papen and the papal secretary of state, Cardinal Pacelli, who in 1939 was elected Pope Pius XII. Von Papen and the Vatican considered the concordat to be protection for Catholic institutions in Germany against the radical wing of the Nazi movement. To Hitler, the concordat served as a means of enhancing his international prestige. Although the Nazis regularly violated

12. R. Cornwell, *God's Banker: An Account of the Life and Death of Robert Calvi* (London, 1983), p. 27.
13. Plllard, *Vatican and Italian Fascism*, p. 5.
14. G. Lewy, *The Catholic Church and Nazi Germany* (New York, 1964), pp. 206, 250.

240

the spirit of the concordat, large segments of the German clergy remained faithful to the interests and the imperial ambitions of the fatherland, and Pope Pius XII himself began to condemn the Nazi regime only when the SS began to murder Polish priests on a large scale.[15]

In retrospect, it can be concluded that the Vatican was caught between the anticommunist sentiments it shared with the Nazis and fascists and the vehement anti-Catholicism of many Nazi leaders. On the national and local levels, this duality was illustrated by the fact that elements of the Catholic church could be found in the Resistance as well as in groups collaborating with the Nazis.

With the Second World War, the power of the United States became a factor in European politics, as well as for the Vatican. In 1937 Myron Taylor, a former director of U.S. Steel and a member of the Catholic order of the Knights of Malta, was appointed Roosevelt's personal representative to the Pope, since no official diplomatic relations existed between the White House and the Holy See due to opposition from American Protestants. After Hitler's defeat at Stalingrad, Pius XII had to give in to Taylor's pressure to permit Christian democracy to become the paramount political formation against communism in Italy.[16] After the war, Pius XII, who all along had believed in the usefulness of anticommunist right-wing movements, proved to be a faithful American ally in his support for the Christian Democratic party during elections in Italy, which he considered battles with communism. The death of the aristocratic Pope Pius XII heralded the eclipse of the elite orientation in Vatican policy.

In 1962 John XXIII, the "common man's Pope," summoned the Second Vatican Council to discuss renewal in the church in order to bring the church closer to the people. The council resulted in the extension of lay participation in religious work and in the admittance of mass celebration in the vernacular. On the initiative of Belgian Cardinal Suenens a movement of charismatic renewal was launched.[17] The

15. Ibid., p. 227.
16. Ibid., p. 239, M. Davis, *Prisoners of the American Dream* (London, 1986), p. 187.
17. S. Diamond, *Spiritual Warfare: The Politics of the Christian Right* (Boston, 1989), p. 124.

charismatic movement took shape in contacts between Catholic students and Pentecostals at universities in the United States in 1967.[18] The charismatic movement, like Pentecostalism, is a populist movement counteracting secularism and idealizing civil obedience.

In the political realm the Second Vatican Council paved the way for a dialogue with the Left and for a policy of reconciliation between eastern block countries and the Vatican. As for Latin America, the council provided ideological scope for progressive priests who were concerned with the causes of the growing poverty on that continent. Inspired by dependence theories, they developed a new concept of theology which rejected the idea of developmentalism and introduced, on the basis of class analysis and interpretations of biblical texts, the idea of liberation with theological as well as political connotations. In 1967 Pope Paul VI adopted aspects of their social and economic analysis in his encyclical *Popularum Progressio*, but he remained vague about possible political solutions.

Liberation theology was accepted by the Latin American Episcopal Conference in Medellín in 1968. The conference condemned communism in one breath with capitalism and endorsed the concept of the "church of the poor," despite a majority of conservative bishops. On ethical and moral issues, the Vatican stuck to its conservative course. The 1968 encyclical *Humanae Vitae*, which rejected birth control, aroused great controversy among Catholics.

The shift in policies by John XXIII and Paul VI from anti-communism toward rapprochement with the Left and Eastern Europe created dissension between the Vatican and the power elite in the West. In 1963 the Central Intelligence Agency (CIA) expressed its concern to the pope about gains made by the Left in Italian elections.[19] And in 1969, Nelson Rockefeller, in the report on his Latin American tour on behalf of the Nixon administration, even concluded that the Roman Catholic church in Latin America was no longer a reliable

18. M. B. McGuire, *Pentecostal Catholics: Power, Charisma, and Order in a Religious Movement* (Philadelphia, 1982), p. 5.
19. M. A. Lee, "Their Will Be Done," *Mother Jones*, July 1983, pp. 21–38.

ally of the United States and was vulnerable to subversive penetration.[20]

A Polish Pope Comes to Rome

The neoconservative political trend of the late 1970s converged with the election of Karol Wojtyła as pontiff in 1978. Wonjtyła's election was an important victory for those prelates who disdained the results of the Second Vatican Council, as it met many of the neoconservatives' demands, e.g., their call for the restoration of moral authority and of the position of the family. The return to the paradigms of conservatism by a segment of the capitalist bourgeoisie also paved the way for more offensive strategies by the Vatican, whereas in periods when classic liberalism or other nonconservative ideologies were hegemonic, the church was forced into defensive adaptations to secular trends.

Although the Vatican had never yielded to liberalism as far as morality was concerned, the rapprochment with the Left was at least a partial capitulation to modernism in politics. It had made the church an unreliable partner in politics, and secularization and the centrifugal forces unleashed by the Second Vatican Council jeopardized the Vatican's authority. To many conservatives Wojtyła must have been the ideal pope, given his anticommunist record and staunch opposition against liberal tendencies in the church. As archbishop of Krakow, Wojtyła opposed every deviation from official dogma. A supporter of Opus Dei, he considered Christianity a closed system which was not open to criticism. Moreover, Polish Catholics were reputed to be the most pious in the world, and the Polish episcopate had proved to be among the most conservative, going so far as to censure the translations of the documents of the Second Vatican Council.[21] Wojtyła himself had accused the Congregation of the Doctrine of Faith (CDF) of allowing theologians to deviate from the strict interpretations of the Revelation in the early 1970s.[22]

20. P. Lernoux, *Cry of the People* (New York, 1980), p. 59.
21. A. Krims, *Karol Wojtyła: Paus en Politicus*, trans. H. Lemmens (1982; reprint Haarlem, 1985), p. 34.
22. P. Hebblethwaite, *In the Vatican* (Oxford, 1986), p. 80.

The most important feature of Wojtyła's pontificate is without a doubt the fact that he has succeeded, to some extent, in the recentralization of church power. The reconstruction of the Vatican's centralism was, among other things, implemented by the appointment of Cardinal Ratzinger as head of the CDF. Ratzinger, who even opposes Opus Dei as a danger to central authority, leads the attack on theologians who deviate from the dogmas of the Vatican.[23] The pope has furthermore tried to reinforce moral orthodoxy with a media offensive and with his countless tours in which he combats individual responsibility by rekindling the attack on birth control and abortion. The tours also serve to counter secularization and to reclaim the position of the family. Wojtyła's firm backing of the conservative lay movements Opus Dei and *Communione e Liberazione*, and of the charismatic movement must be seen in the light of his attempt to restore the moral authority of the church.

The election of Wojtyła was also an important victory for those who resisted the rise of liberation theology. Three years after the denunciation of the Medellín Conference by American vice president Nelson Rockefeller as incompatible with American foreign policy interests, conservative bishops from Latin America and Western Europe started to campaign against liberation theology in the church. Among them were Opus Dei sympathizers Alfonso Lopez Trujillo, the bishop of Medellín; Cardinal Sebastiano Baggio, head of the Congregation of Bishops; and the Belgian Jesuit, Roger Vekemans, known for his connections with the CIA.[24] Wojtyła reinforced the position of conservatives within the rank of the church hierarchy and brought the Vatican's Latin American policy more in line with American interests. Ratzinger not only rejected the political implications of liberation theology, but forbade social analysis in theology altogether.[25] The reconciliation in policy between the Vatican and the White House was confirmed by the establishment of full diplomatic relations in January 1984. William Wilson, a staunch supporter

23. Hertel, "Ich verspreche," p. 87.
24. Krims, *Wojtyła*, p. 218.
25. Hebblethwaite, *In the Vatican*, p. 87.
26. Ibid., p. 101.

of the Nicaraguan Contras, became the first ambassador to the Holy See.[26]

In Europe, Vatican policies took a different course as well. In the Rome mayoral campaign in 1984, the Vatican, for the first time since the death of Pius XII, openly expressed its preference for the Christian Democratic candidate, Nicola Signorelle.[27] More important, however, was the pope's advocacy of European unity under a Christian banner, with the inclusion of Eastern Europe. Wojtyła considered the ideological and political division of Europe as unnatural. This logically implied renewed anticommunism and an end to the policy of peaceful coexistence between the communist regimes and the Vatican, because communist atheism is irreconcilable with the notion of Christian European unity.

In contrast to his predecessor's policy of trying to guarantee the survival of the church in Eastern Europe through silent diplomacy, Wojtyła used an offensive tactic aimed at the "liberation of Eastern Europe for Christianity" in which the unity and strength of the Polish church were considered vital as a support for the possible revival of other Catholic churches in the East, notably in Lithuania and the Ukraine.[28] Although recent developments in Eastern Europe may seem to indicate that the Vatican's tactic has been successful, it is more likely that the Vatican has reaped the windfall harvest of international political developments largely outside its reach.

With glasnost and the crisis of communism, the pope in recent years seems to have taken a position in his social doctrine equidistant from both capitalism and communism. In the encyclical *Sollicitudo Rei Sociales* in 1987 the pope scorned both because they lead to imperialism. Capitalism, moreover, leads to underdevelopment in the Third World and to overconsumption by some the pauperization of others in the center of the capitalist world.[29] But whereas Wojtyła has always condemned communism as an

27. Ibid., p. 22.
28. According to William Pfaff in the *International Herald Tribune*, 25 June 1983, quoted in Krims, *Wojtyła*, p. 69.
29. John Paul II, *Sollicitude Rei Sociales*, Dutch trans. in *Kerkelijke documentatie* 16, no. 3 (March 1988), p. 105.

unjust system, capitalist injustices are seen as excesses, thus leaving the principle of the right to private property and to economic initiative untouched. To Wojtyła, the capitalist system is not in itself wrong; rather, it is the attitude of man within that system that is to blame. The Catholic social doctrine as a moral doctrine and that integral part of the mission of the church which is evangelization are in the view of the pope the means of remedying these shortcomings.[30]

Christian Democracy and the Centers of Power

Since the Second World War, the Christian democratic parties make up the most homogeneous power bloc in Western Europe, that is, in the original six European Community members. Christian democrats have, since the war, been in government uninterruptedly in the Netherlands, Belgium, and Italy, while in West Germany, their reign has only been interrupted by the Brandt and Schmidt cabinets. France has not had a Christian democratic party since the liquidation of the *Mouvement Républicain* Populaire (MRP) in 1967. However, Christian democratic influences are strong among most of the right-of-center parties.

In Europe, Christian democracy has been almost completely dominated by Catholics. This has also been true in the Netherlands and West Germany, countries with largely Protestant populations. In 1973, although only 44 percent of the West German population was Catholic, 73 percent of the membership of the *Christlich-Democratische Union* (CDU) was.[31]

Christian democracy in Western Europe was originally based on the principles of *Rerum Novarum*, with its compromise between social justice and the right to property. After the Second World War, the concept of Christian democracy was to integrate rural producers into the modern economy and to reconcile liberal democracy and industrial society with traditional Christian values, based on class compromise instead of class struggle. The individual had to be integrated into the

30. Ibid., p. 125.
31. H. J. Veen, *Christlich-democratische und konservative Parteien in West-Europa* vol. 1 (Munich, 1983), p. 36.

"natural social structures": the community, the family, and the workshop.[32] Although Christian democracy predates the Second World War, it only claimed its place at the center of Western European power after the war, with a threefold agenda: the integration of West Germany into the economic and political system of Western Europe, the creation of a bulwark against communism, and the organization of political support for the Marshall Plan.

This agenda pertained in the first place to West Germany, where Christian democracy has its roots more in the *Wirtschaftswunder* than in the social doctrine of *Rerum Novarum*. After the war Adenauer's CDU was a promoter of the free market above all else. The Catholic state of Bavaria has a separate Christian democratic party, the very conservative *Christlich-Soziale Union* (CSU). The CSU considers Bavaria a Christian bulwark of European civilization, which must in time reincorporate the Christian regions of Eastern Europe, including those in the Soviet Union.[33] In the wake of the Second Vatican Council, Christian democracy in West Germany, as elsewhere in Europe, temporarily lost momentum.

The most hybrid Christian democratic party in Europe is Italy's *Democrazia Cristiana* (DC), which is made up of many *correnti*. The position of the DC is special because of the presence of the Vatican and of the largest communist party outside the former communist bloc, the *Partito Comunista Italiano* (PCI). That is why the CIA had a special interest in the DC and regularly sponsored it against the PCI in elections. During the pontificate of Pius XII, part of that aid to the DC and related Catholic organizations was furnished through the Vatican.[34]

The majority of the DC's postwar party elite was raised from the student movement of Catholic Action during the fascist regime. Among them were the present president, Cossiga, and a recent prime minister, Andreotti.[35] During the cold war of the 1950s, the integralist Catholic Action served

---

32. Irving, *Christian Democratic Parties*, pp. 30–31.
33. Ibid., p. 158.
34. G. P. Fogarty, *The Vatican and the American Hierarchy from 1870 to 1965* (Stuttgart, 1982), p. 335.
35. M. Clark, *Modern Italy, 1871–1982* (New York, 1984), p. 256.

as an important link between the Vatican and the CIA.[36] After the death of Pius XII, the influence of Catholic Action declined and within the DC antileftism gave way to the reformist policies of Aldo Moro. In the wake of the PCI's greatest victory ever (in the elections of 1976), the reformist *correnti* supporting Aldo Moro even accepted the proposal of the leader of the PCI, Berlinguer, for a "historic compromise," a proposal for cooperation between the PCI and the DC.[37]

In contrast to other Catholic European countries, France experienced institutionalized Christian democracy only from 1944 until 1967, during which period the MRP tried to reconcile the anticlerical tradition of the French Republic and the interests of the church.[38] Although the MRP played an important role in the European integration process during the cold war, its decline from 1958 onward, when it was ousted from the government, was inevitable because of the disjunction between the liberal reformism advocated by its leaders and the conservatism of the Catholic rank and file.[39] Since the dissolution of the MRP, Christian democracy has been a tendency among right-of-center parties in France.[40]

By the mid-1970s, Christian democracy had lost its dominance in the political spectrum and it began to reorient itself in a more conservative direction. This resulted in ruptures with the social democrats in the Netherlands and Belgium and in a break with the "historic compromise" in Italy. The crisis of the Keynesian welfare state, combined with an ideological crisis on the Left, helped Christian democrats regain their place in the European corridors of power in the 1980s.

Christian democratic policies in this period were marked by three main features. In the first place, the so-called recovery policies: a combination of privatization of public enterprise according to neoliberal prescriptions, pushing technological innovation and deflating the welfare state (in contrast to the Thatcherist demolition of the welfare state).

36. Lee, "Their Will Be Done," p. 23; M. Einaudi and F. Goguel, *Christian Democracy in Italy and France* (South Bend, Ind., 1952), p. 88.
37. Irving, Christian Democratic Parties, p. 98.
38. R. E. M. Irving, *Christian democracy in France* (London, 1973), p. 80.
39. Ibid., p. 82; W. Laqueur, *Europe since Hitler* (Harmondsworth, U.K., 1970), p. 55.
40. Irving, *Christian Democratic Parties*, p. 229.

These policies were accompanied by a shift in Christian democratic priorities from the interests of the traditional agricultural class, traditional independent entrepreneurs, and Christian labor unions, to the interests of large corporations and professional technocrats and managers who profit most from technological innovation and economic restructuring. Meanwhile, the independent farmer had lost part of his share in the food-producing process to large industrial corporations. The agricultural class had become less important in the Christian democratic electorate. For instance, Catholic and Christian democratic-dominated Bavaria had by the 1970s been transformed from an agricultural region into an industrial one.[41]

In the Netherlands, this shift in Christian democratic class interest and priorities can be illustrated by the fact that the Christian Democrats secured almost all cabinet posts dealing with the future economic and technological infrastructure in the 1989 coalition with the Social Democrats.[42] In post-Franco Spain, the Christian democratic UCD has incorporated segments of Opus Dei, known for its religious zeal and penchant for technocracy.[43] In France the Républicains Indépendents, led by Valéry Giscard d'Estaing, himself a Knight of Malta, has "brought together the most traditional Catholic (practicing) Parisian factions of the bourgeoisie with the closest links to the top levels of industry, banking, and commerce."[44]

The second feature of Christian democratic policy, at least in the first half of the 1980s, was that they were solid partners in the American global cold war policies in Western Europe, not only in the arms race with the Soviet Union but also in American strategy against the Left in Central America.

In the third place, the regained power of the Christian democrats and reshuffling of coalitions in many countries created new opportunities for specifically Catholic and neo-conservative policies. However, despite such slogans as "Ethical

41. Ibid., p. 155.
42. R. van Tulder, "PvdA heeft weinig invloed op modernisering economie," *Volkskrant*, 14 November 1989.
43. G. J. Hoek, "Opus Dei," *Vrij Nederland*, 11 September 1982.
44. J. Marceau, "France," in eds. T. Bottomore and R.J. Bry, *The Capitalist Class* (Hertfordshire, 1989), p. 52.

Revival," launched by Dutch prime minister Van Agt in 1980, the backlash against "libertinism" has up to now been mostly contained in pro-family economic measures or has been limited to concealing conservative measures under the cover of budget cuts and obstructing liberal legislation in the noneconomic realm. In line with Daniel Bell's "end of ideology," Christian democrats sell their policies as nonideological, which thereby excludes a crusade on moral issues.

In Europe, the most radical and reactionary measures to restore "public morality," however, were not taken by Christian democrats but by Margaret Thatcher in the United Kingdom, who restored television censorship and very nearly outlawed homosexuality by means of Clause 28. But Thatcher lacked nongovernmental instruments such as the Catholic church and Catholic education, lay organizations, and press to promote moral values, as well as Catholic "compassion."

The influence of Catholic lay movements can best be illustrated in Italy where conservatism in the public and private sphere is promoted by the ultraconservative lay organization Comunione e Liberazione – the successor of Catholic Action – which is very active in the universities.[45] One result of its influence is that, in spite of liberal abortion legislation in Italy, there are very few doctors prepared to carry out an abortion because of pressure it exerts.[46] When Prime Minister De Mita wanted to initiate a partial deconfessionalization of the DC, he came into conflict with Comunione e Liberazione, which contributed to his downfall as both prime minister and party leader.[47]

Christian Democracy and European Integration

The Second World War gave new prominence to the idea of European unity in American and European politics. To the Americans the Marshall Plan was to be the catalyst for European integration, with the Christian democrats the leading political force. American aid under the banner of the Marshall

45. Clark, *Modern Italy*, p. 395.
46. *Volkskrant*, 11 February 1989.
47. *Volkskrant*, 3 February 1989 and 30 August 1989.

Plan served several ends. During the war the Council on Foreign Relations and the State Department designed a scheme for a new postwar global order, in which the United States had to ally itself with an integrated West European economy in order to have free access to the raw materials of the British Empire and other colonies held by West European powers.[48] Secondly, Western Europe had to be politically and economically unified, including defeated Germany, to avoid major disturbances within the capitalist world system. To this end the Marshall Plan had to restore purchasing power in order to permit innovative production, while introducing American conditions of accumulation to Western Europe.[49] During the implementation of the Marshall Plan all the countries which would form the European Community in 1957 had governments dominated by or including Christian democrats.

The urge of deeper cooperation and continental unification also had European roots, such as Coudenhove-Kalergi's Pan-Europe Movement. In the late 1940s, European unity was prompted by the fear of another war. This resulted in the foundation of the European Movement, which was formed in 1948. The European Movement was an umbrella organization for several nongovernmental organizations which had a common goal: the erection of a barrier against communism, externally as well as internally. The communists were the only force in European politics not represented. The most powerful organization within the European Movement was the liberal European League for Economic Cooperation (ELEC), an elite group whose paramount aim, in addition to restricting communist influence, was to promote free trade and the free circulation of capital.[50]

The European Movement also incorporated groups resisting American influence in Western Europe. The noncommunist

48. L. H. Shoup and W. Minter, "Shaping a New World Order," in ed. H. Sklar, *Trilateralism: The Trilateral Commission and the Elite Planning for World Management* (Boston, 1980), pp. 135–56.

49. K. van der Pijl, *The Making of an Atlantic Ruling Class* (London, 1984), p. 14.

50. F. X. Rebattet, "The 'European Movement,' 1945–1950: A Study in National and International Non-governmental Organizations Working for European Unity," unpublished Manuscript (St. Antony's College, Oxford, 1962), p. 340.

Left envisaged a united Europe as a third force between communism and capitalism.[51] On the right, American influence was opposed by Catholic conservatives and "Carolingian" Europeans, who saw Europe as a Christian citadel besieged by communism.[52] They, too, wanted a united Europe to be a third force in the global division of power, not as an alternative to capitalism and communism, but as a means of maintaining the colonial empires.

The Christian democratic arms of the European Movement was the Nouvelles Equipes Internationales (NEI), renamed European Union of Christian Democrats in 1965. The NEI, which had the support of Pope Pius XII, aimed at a cultural and economic unification of Western Europe based on Christian ideals instead of individual materialism.[53] In the long run, the NEI hoped to integrate Central Europe into their concept of a Christian Europe, and therefore incorporated exile organizations from Central Europe.[54]

From 1953 onward the ideal of a united Europe weakened and gave way to the concept of an Atlantic partnership between North America and Western Europe, with NATO as the political and military pivot. The era of Atlanticism was marked by regular consultation and cooperation between the North Atlantic elites. The Bilderberg conferences, founded in response to growing anti-Americanism in Europe, contributed to the integration of Atlantic policies and as a forum for finding solutions to conflicts within the alliance.

In Western Europe, meanwhile, the idea of unification was eclipsed by the concept of functionalist integration, resulting in the 1957 Treaty of Rome, which established the European Economic Community (EEC).

At the beginning of the 1970s, Atlanticist policies were partly overtaken by a new dynamic toward European integration, stimulated by East-West detente; by the decline of American hegemony due to the military debacle in Vietnam and decreasing domestic productivity; and by economic recovery in Europe and the internationalization of European capital. In several phases, the European Community grew

51. Ibid., p. 460.
52. A. Sampson, *The New Europeans* (London, 1968), p. 4.
53. Rebattet, '*European Movement*,' p. 130.
54. Irving, *Christian Democratic Parties*, p. 244.

from six to twelve members and internal political integration was deepened by direct elections to the European Parliament. The new European dynamics are expected to lead to a Europe "without borders" in 1992, but, at present, European integration, in its official political manifestion, is no longer exclusively dominated by Catholic Christian democrats as it was at the time of the conclusion of the Treaty of Rome.

The Rise of the Conservative Tide

The change in the policies of the Vatican and Christian democratic parties and their revival as institutions of power since the late 1970s was accompanied by the breakdown of the postwar consensus on the Keynesian welfare state. This state had focused on state intervention in the market by means of countercyclical policies sustaining mass consumption, which were combined with high taxes on rentier incomes to foster industrial investment and activity. It relied on a productive class compromise that guaranteed social stability. The welfare state was originally conceived to ease the strain of economic necessity on human conduct; rather, it encouraged political activity and led to demands for greater freedom in the social and cultural fields.[55]

This enlarged space for cultural freedom, just like mass consumption itself, fostered the pursuit of personal happiness unconstrained by economic needs. This was expressed in the rise of the countercultures and subcultures of the 1960s. Political activities were marked by emancipatory demands by minorities on the state and by pressure on state institutions for greater popular participation. In a global perspective, political activism was directed against the American war in Vietnam and manifested itself in ideological support for liberation movements in the Third World. These political forces were associated with the New Left.

By the 1970s, the Keynesian welfare state was in a structural economic crisis, with declines in corporate profits and increasing middle-class resentment of the state's fiscal demands. There was also an ideological crisis within the consensus,

55. N. P. Barry, *The New Right* (Beckenham, U.K., 1987), p. 8.

since the Keynesian welfare state was seen by the Right as capitalism subsidizing its own destruction by stimulating cultural and political activities undermining the consensus on capitalism. The crisis engendered a search for other economic models and for new concepts of political and cultural hegemony which would sustain capitalist accumulation and technological development.

In the economic realm, the primacy of market incentives in place of state intervention was advocated. This school of thought was called neoliberalism. In varying degrees, neoliberal policies were pursued in most capitalist countries during the 1980s.

New concepts of political and cultural hegemony have not been developed as straightforwardly as the underlying economic concepts. In a free market system, opinion, ideologies, and policies which contribute to a hegemonic concept of control are expressed and exercised by a wide variety of institutions and opinion-making media. Besides, as the conservative American sociologist Daniel Bell has indicated, previous changes in culture are lasting and do not become outdated like technological and economic models.[56] Thus, a consensus may rest on a combination of hegemonic concepts which are contradictory in cultural and political matters, yet which reflect a single economic thrust.

One of the most important concepts of control which came forward in the 1970s was neoconservatism. Neoconservatism is in fact traditional conservatism pragmatically adjusted to a certain phase of capitalism and responding to certain contradictions within the capitalist system. Neoconservative ideology was formulated in various stages during the 1970s, in international elitist forums as well as by "independent" scholars and opinion leaders who, among other things, criticized both classical liberalism and the welfare state as leading to moral laxity and to overpoliticized societies.

The first concern of the West European and North American capitalist elites was political radicalism among students at the end of the 1960s. In the early 1970s the main point of

56. Bell, *Cultural Contradictions*, 12.

issue at Bilderberg conferences was "the future functioning of universities in our society."[57]

Neoconservatism took a more definite shape in the Trilateral Commission. The French political scientist Michel Crozier, coauthor of *The Crisis of Democracy*, saw radical students and intellectuals who challenged and delegitimated established authority as the main threats to democracy in Western Europe.[58] In Crozier's view, Western Europe's governability was hampered by a lack of civic responsibility and the breakdown of the "consensus of purpose," which had sustained democracy since the Second World War. Citizens were making too many claims on government, which had led to a bloated state. Society had become too involved in the decision-making process, which had led to an excess of democracy. This was due to the collapse of traditional institutions of social control, such as the church, marriage, and the traditional educational system.[59] Crozier therefore recommended a restoration of authority and order in Western Europe, without the complete dismantling of the welfare state.[60]

This orientation was strengthened by a current of opinion with roots in New Deal radicalism in the United States and which had henceforth evolved as a part of the common North Atlantic intellectual culture. This pertained, notably, to a group of opinion leaders from New England, of whom Irving Kristol and Daniel Bell are the most influential. Bell had played an important role in opinion-making in Western Europe. In the 1950s he had participated in the CIA-sponsored Congress for Cultural Freedom in Milan on "the end of ideology."[61]

---

57. P. Thompson, "Bilderberg and the West," in ed. H. Sklar, *Trilateralism*, 157–89. Founded in 1954, the Bilderbeg conferences are regular gatherings of representatives of powerful transnational and national corporations and institutions and serve as a "testing ground for new initiatives for Atlantic unity." Van der Pijl, *Atlantic Ruling Class*, p. 183.

58. In contrast to the Bilderberg conferences the Trilateral Commission reflected the common imperial interests of North America, Western Europe, and Japan. The Trilateral Commission's main objective was to come to some form of control of democracy within social democratic parameters. M.J. Crozier, S.P. Huntington, and J. Watanaki, *The Crisis of Democracy* (New York, 1975), p. 7.

59. Ibid., p. 25.

60. Ibid., p. 60.

61. Van der Pijl, *Atlantic Ruling Class*, p. 219.

Kristol argued that capitalism was in a crisis because secular libertarian capitalism had replaced the nineteenth-century religious bourgeois ethos of constraint. This had left capitalism helpless before any assault from the counterculture of the New Left, preaching the realization of the self.[62] Capitalist amoralism was illustrated by corporations which sponsored the adversaries of capitalism by publishing pornography and books which rejected the family.[63]

Like Kristol, Bell pleaded for normative capitalist behavior which was needed to underlay the economic superstructure. In *The Cultural Contradictions of Capitalism*, Bell observed a disjunction between the rational technoeconomic order and the irrational avant-garde that dominated the realms of culture and ideology.[64] As a consequence of the democratization of society, the art and philosophy of the avant-garde, stemming from the irrational romantics of the nineteenth century, had become the dominant cultural force in our society.[65] He argued that, because economic behavior was no longer guided by normative principles such as religion and the traditional value system of the family, mass consumption had generated a hedonist adversary culture that would lead to the destruction of civilization.[66]

In Western Europe, Christian democracy and the Catholic church became the major channels for applying neoconservative thought. Although in the economic realm Christian democratic policies have at times shifted back and forth between Keynesian and neoliberal policies, their social and cultural policies are conservative by nature. Like conservatism, Christian democracy opposes a liberalism seen as too permissive in matters of sexual conduct and artistic expression, and which ignores the importance of the family. Both

---

62. I. Kristol, *Two Cheers for Capitalism* (New York, 1978), pp. 62, 129.
63. Ibid., p. 61.
64. Bell, *Cultural Contradictions*, p. 26.
65. Irrationalism is a school of thought that rejects political action based on rational considerations because the springs of human action lay in regions outside human comprehension. Representative of this school are Baudelaire, Nietzsche, Carlyle, Schopenhauer, and Kierkegaard. I. Berlin, "Political Ideas in the Twentieth Century," In *Four Essays on Liberty* (Oxford, 1969), p. 13.
66. Bell, *Cultural Contradictions*, p. 72.

conservatives and Christian democrats consider the family the cornerstone of society. As Norman Barry has stated:[67]

> One important reason why conservatives should reject egalitarian economic policies is the effect they believe such measures have on the family. It is a fundamental conservative dogma that the autonomy and independence of this institution are essential for social stability. Naturally, the family is a source of inequality and to attempt to rectify this would be to destroy the institution. For a conservative, the family has value not merely because it is a natural phenomenon, but also because if it is undermined, it transforms an integrated society into a mere "collection" of anomic and alienated individuals without secure values. Furthermore, it is argued that easily available welfare encourages the breakup of the family and makes vast numbers of people dependent upon the state.

This explains the differing attitudes toward the welfare state of Christian democrats and social democrats. The welfare state of the 1960s and 1970s was dominated by social democratic forces and had to serve egalitarian ends. During the 1980s European Christian democrats, virtually unhindered by social democrats, reduced the welfare state to a mere system of social security, providing for essential needs only and on stricter conditions.

The conservative shift in capitalist thought at the expense of liberalism has provided room for a revival of the church's role as a conservative moral authority preaching constraint in social behavior. Moreover, the church has had a long history of propagating normative economic behavior. Conservative Catholic lay movements have also participated in the battle for conservative hegemony. They have encouraged their members to engage in the political, social, and cultural world for the reconquest of political and cultural space for Catholicism.[68] They thus contribute to the depoliticization of the nonelite layers of society.

In the United States neoconservatism included the notion of countering detente with the Soviet Union, combined with

67. Barry, *The New Right*, p. 90.
68. J. Seguy, "Introduction to the Modern in Religion," *Social Compass* 36, no. 1 (March 1989), pp. 3–12.

an ideological attack on liberation movements in the Third World, especially liberation theology and its liberal sympathizers in the United States, who had undermined the consensus on national security. These ideas were most powerfully expressed within the Committee on the Present Danger. Among the members of this committee were future-President Ronald Reagan and influential Catholic cold warriors. In contrast to the cold warriors of the New and religious Right, neoconservatives in the United States were much more concerned with a consensus on international politics among European political leaders and right-wing elements of the mainstream churches. We will point out below that the global cold war policies rekindled by the Americans have strengthened the conservative Catholic elite network in Western Europe. Furthermore, closer cooperation with the Vatican was indispensable in the conservative struggle with liberation theology.

Catholic Networks

Catholic power and influence are not confined to the Vatican or its official institutions or Christian Democracy, but is also exerted through a vast network of more or less secretive informal elite organizations. Secular political power is also often exerted through these Catholic organizations and institutions. Most prominent and exclusive are the Knights of Malta and Opus Dei, which link the Catholic church to the secular world of politics and corporate power. This Catholic network is held together through personal relationships and, to a certain extent, through the common interest and ideology that unite a heterogeneous collection of charity organizations, prelates, corporation managers, Christian democratic and conservative politicians, journalists, secret service agents, and lobbying groups. The Italian masonic lodge P2 has even been linked to the criminal manipulation of politics and financial dealings.

The Knights of Malta: Crusaders for All Seasons

The oldest organization of Catholic power and interest, apart from the church itself, is the Sovereign Military and Hospitable Order of St John of Jerusalem of Rhodes of Malta or, in short, the Knights of Malta. The political importance of the Knights of Malta lies not so much in their political agenda as in their membership. The Knights of Malta include ten thousand of the richest and most powerful Catholics throughout the world. The traditional purpose of the Knights of Malta is part of their official name: the military defense of Christianity and hospitable aid to the wounded and the needy.

The Knights of Malta have their roots in the defense of Christian Europe, dating back to the epoch of the Crusades, when successive popes urged Christians to defend Europe against Islam. To this end Pope Pascal II gave permission to establish independent knightly orders which would elect their own grand masters. The orders recruited their member from among the European aristocracy and then joined the Crusades. The most prominent orders were the Order of Saint John (the future Knights of Malta) and the warrior-monks of the Knights Templar. By 1312, the power of the Knights Templars had become a threat to Philip the Fair, who, with the aid of Pope Clement V, crushed the Knights after accusing them of heresy. Their extensive properties throughout the continent were taken over by the Order of Saint John. The Order of Saint John, which by then had become the single most important Christian knightly order, continued the Crusades against Islam until the seventeenth century. In the meantime, Sultan Suleiman had driven the Knights back to the island of Malta, where they established their headquarters until Napoleon invaded Malta and defeated the Knights in 1798. After thirty-six years of exile, the Knights of Malta finally established their headquarters in Rome, under the protection of the Roman Catholic church.

After the Napoleonic wars, the Knights of Malta had lost much of their power due to the rise of the bourgeoisie, although they included most of the European royal families like the Hohenzollerns, the Habsburgs and the Romanovs.[69]

69. D. Wemple, "Right-Wing Knights in Holy Armor," *The National Reporter*, Winter 1986, pp. 56–61.

Most of the time they were engaged in charity and ambulance services, which are still their official occupations.[70] During the twentieth century, however, the order reemerged as a factor in power politics, due to the incorporation of non-noble elites and the rise of communism, which incited a new crusading spirit. The Knights' vision of a Christian Europe besieged by atheist communism led to at least partial collaboration with and support for fascist regimes. Like the Vatican, the Knights of Malta supported Franco during the Spanish Civil War, and they awarded Franco the Bailiff Grand Cross as defender of the Catholic faith.[71] In Italy, several Knights of Malta, of whom prince Valerio Borghese was the most notorious, sided with fascism. Borghese, a commander under Mussolini, remained true to the fascist cause after the war.[72]

In 1948 Reinhard Gehlen, Hitler's intelligence chief on the eastern front, received the Knights of Malta's Gran Croci al Merito Con Placca, endowed with a preface by Pope Pius XII, for his contribution in the holy war against Marxism.[73] Knights of Malta were also involved in the organization of the flight of many war criminals to South America, including Klaus Barbie, a future recruit of the CIA.[74] In 1951, the renewed status of the Knights was confirmed by Italian president Alcide de Gaspari, who granted them territorial and diplomatic sovereignty at 68 Via Condotti in Rome.[75]

A second factor in the reemergence of the Knights of Malta in politics has been the incorporation of nonnoble Catholics. This especially concerned Catholic Americans of Irish descent, who entertained both utopian and nationalist feelings vis-à-vis their country of origin and held a grudge against British imperialism.[76] Although often owning large corporations in the United States, Irish-Americans continued to occupy a secondary position in the Protestant-dominated American es-

70. A. van Bosbeke, *Ridders van nu: Over occulte genootschappen en ridderorders in de 20ste eeuw* (Berchem, Belgium, 1987), p. 197.

71. F. Hervet, "The Order of Malta: The Knights of Darkness," *Third World* no. 2, 1986 (June–July), pp. 83–95.

72. S. Christie, *Stefano delle Chiaie: Portrait of a Black Terrorist* (London, 1984), p. 4.

73. Hervet, "Order of Malta," p. 88.

74. Krims, *Wojtyła*, p. 286.

75. R. Peyrefitte, *Chevaliers de Malta* (Paris, 1957), p. 148.

76. J. Holland, *The American Connection* (New York, 1987), p. 17.

5

5

5

tablishment.[77] While enhancing their grip on the American economy, Irish-Americans allied themselves with the Vatican. This alliance was initiated by Cardinal Pacelli and Nicholas Brady, at the time of his death the wealthiest man on earth.[78] In 1927 an American section of the Knights of Malta was founded, which is still dominated by Irish-American families such as the Graces, Buckleys, and Farrells.[79]

In 1936 Brady's wife Genevieve, a Dame of Malta, and Cardinal Pacelli took the initiative in American-Vatican relations, though only semiofficially, with Francis Cardinal Spellman acting as chief liaison between the White House and the Holy See, and with Myron Taylor as Roosevelt's personal representative to the Pope.[80] When in 1984 the United States and the Vatican established official diplomatic relations, Knight of Malta William Simon became the first American ambassador. He was succeeded by Frank Shakespeare, a fellow knight.[81]

During the Second World War, the basis was laid for cooperation between American secret services, the Knights of Malta, the Vatican, and other Catholic organizations in Europe. The American intelligence service, the Office of Strategic Services (OSS), was dominated by Catholics of Irish origin. The OSS was headed by William J. Donovan, a second-generation Irish Catholic whose mentor was Cardinal Spellman, himself an Irish-American.[82] In the meantime, Spellman had become Archbishop of New York and a Knight of Malta, and was involved in all sorts of international affairs until his 1967 death. Other Irish-Americans active in the OSS were William Casey and William Colby, both of whom would eventually become director of the OSS's postwar successor, the CIA.[83] In the 1980s the list of members of the Knights of Malta included CIA chief Casey and a former director, John McCone. William Colby is said to have rejected a membership out of humbleness.[84]

77. S. Birmingham, *Real Lace* (New York, 1973), pp. 156, 222.
78. Ibid., p. 190.
79. Hervet, "Order of Malta," p. 86.
80. Birmingham, *Real Lace*, p. 193.
81. *National Catholic Reporter*, 14 October 1983; *Jesus* (Italy), October 1988.
82. A. Cave Brown, *The Secret War Report of the OSS* (New York, 1976), p. 5.
83. A. Cave Brown, *The Last Hero: Wild Bill Donovan* (New York, 1982), pp. 5, 12.
84. Lee, "Their Will Be Done," p. 24.

During the war Christian democratic and Catholic exiles were involved in OSS policy formulation in Washington. Among them were the founding father of Italian Christian Democracy, Don Luigi Sturzo, and the future Italian minister of foreign affairs, Count Sforza.[85] In Italy cooperation between intelligence services and Catholic organizations continued after the war. In order to keep the strong Communist party out of government, a dense network of CIA agents, the Italian secret services, paramilitary organizations, and representatives of the extreme Right, the Knights of Malta, and the CD, was created. In the early years a vital role was played by Knights of Malta-decorated CIA agent James Angleton. Angleton already had had connections with fascist organizations when he studied in Italy before the war.[86] In 1945 he rescued Prince Valerio Borghese from the hands of the resistance at the request of the Knights. After the founding of the CIA in 1947, he began to incorporate paramilitary and neofascist elements into the network.

Elsewhere in Europe, Knights of Malta were also connected to cold war intelligence and propaganda activities. Radio Free Europe, founded to broadcast propaganda to Eastern Europe, was dominated by the CIA, Knights of Malta, and Russian exiles.[87] Another Knight of Malta ally, Reinhard Gehlen, founded the Bundesnachrichtendienst (the West German intelligence service) in West Germany with the support of the CIA, which depended on Gehlen's connections and information for their East European intelligence gathering during the cold war.

In recent decades the European section of the Knights of Malta seems to have adopted a low profile politically, with individual knights exerting influence via other organizations. This view may be deceptive, because the Knights of Malta remain the most exclusive elite network, rooted in the tradition of unifying Europe under a Christian banner. In this respect, the European nobility claiming a prominent role in the future of Europe and the Russian nobility preparing to

85. Cave Brown, *Secret War Report*, p. 98. Among these exiles was also Otto von Habsburg.
86. Christie, *Stefano delle Chiaie*, p. 12.
87. Arbeitskreis Nicaragua, *Propagandisten des Krieges Hintermanner der Contra* (Frankfurt, 1986), p. 14.

return after more than seventy years of exile may also reflect new ambitions on the part of the Maltese Knights and the church. Involvement of American Knights of Malta in politics has been more obvious, especially where the Left in the Third World has had to be defeated.[88]

Opus Dei: The Spartans of Catholicism

Opus Dei, or the Work of God, is the most ambitious Catholic lay organization. It is hard to tell to what extent Opus Dei has infiltrated European politics and society because members are strictly forbidden to disclose their membership to even their closest relatives. There is often a gray area between support from sympathizers and actual membership. Assumed members in the past have included former MRP leader Antoine Pinay and European Community architect Robert Schuman, but this is hearsay.[89] Sometimes politicians openly express their sympathy for Opus Dei, like Italian president Cossiga, who confessed to being "close to Opus Dei."[90]

Opus Dei shares its inclination for antileft crusading and its striving for European Christian unity with other conservative Catholic groups, but it differs from them in its rigid organization. Opus Dei is divided into a celibatarian nucleus of priests-*numerari* who command Opus Dei, *numerari* and associated members, and married members. They all have various religious duties. There is also a group of *cooperadores* who do not have such duties and who express their affinity for Opus Dei by means of financial support or by giving lectures.

The core of Opus Dei's ideology is the sanctification of daily work. It seeks to achieve the rule by faith of every aspect of everyday life, on the principle of the dualist separation between a supernatural spiritual life and a temporal life subjected to it.[91] Opus Dei's disdain for temporal life is

88. Knights of Malta were on the boards of directors of American companies which waged the economic war against the Allende government in Chile before the coup by Pinochet. In the 1980s the American Right was active in support of low-intensity-warfare projects. B. Wood, ed., *The New Humanitarians* (Alburquerque, 1986).
89. Hertel, "Ich verspreche," p. 50.
90. Hebblethwaite, *In the Vatican*, p. 23.

expressed in compelling its members to chastise themselves.[92] By educating people for key professions in business, finance, high-level management, and academia, Opus Dei seeks to disseminate its spiritual values in order to achieve a general mobilization of the laity.

Opus Dei was founded by Jose Maria Escriva de Balaguer in Spain in 1928 and has played a role in Spanish politics since the late 1940s, when it won the support of the "progressive" Catholic elite of Catalonia.[93] Opus Dei supported an authoritarian, Catholic, monarchist succession to the Franco regime, combatting both liberalism and the semiautarchic nationalism of the Falangists. During the reshuffling of the Franco government in 1957, members of Opus Dei replaced Falangists in cabinet posts dealing with economic and industrial policy. They were technical experts with university backgrounds, and they reorganized the state administration and economic policies on bases of technocratic authoritarianism and efficiency. Members of Opus Dei in the new cabinet included, among others, Navarro Rubio, the minister of finance, who urged more liberal economic policies, and Ullastres, the minister of commerce, who arranged a loan from Washington as part of a policy of opening the Spanish economy to the international market.[94] As early as the beginning of the 1960s, Opus Dei promoted Spain as a potential member of the EC.

By that time, Opus Dei had extended its influence outside Spain. Opus Dei was approved by the Vatican in 1946 and recognized as the first religious lay order in 1950. Its headquarters were transferred from Madrid to Rome, where Opus Dei began a worldwide penetration of banking, commerce, the media, universities, and the church itself. By the early 1970s Opus Dei had won substantial support among those clerics who disapproved of liberal and centrifugal tendencies in the church. Opus Dei won the support of such prominent prelates as Sebastiano Baggio and future popes Luciano and Wojtyla. John Paul I (Luciano), pope for one month, put the

91. Hertel, "Ich verspreche," pp. 12, 38.
92. *Volkskrant*, 17 January 1981.
93. S. G. Payne, *The Franco Regime, 1936–1975* (Madison, 1987), p. 438.
94. Ibid., p. 470.

prelature of Opus Dei on the agenda of the Vatican. In 1982 the Congregation of Bishops announced that Opus Dei had been appointed as "personal prelature" to the Pope.[95] The influence of Opus Dei, in the Vatican as well as among local bishops, has grown ever since. Sympathizers or members of Opus Dei in the Vatican include Congregation of the Doctrine of Faith counselors Hoffner and Lopez Trujillo, the new prefect of the Congregation of Bishops, Gantin, and the prefect of the Sacred Congregation of Causes of Saints, Palazzin, who is one of the most fervent advocates of the sanctification of Mgr. Escriva de Balaguer.[96]

Relations between the media and the Vatican are often conducted by lay members of Opus Dei. The best known of them is Navarro Valls, the director of the Vatican Press Office. Another important liaison between the Vatican and the public is the Italian television commentator Alberto Michelini, who is a member of both the European Parliament and Opus Dei.[97]

Local bishops and cardinals are increasingly becoming associated with Opus Dei, and in Latin America Opus Dei bishops are often appointed to curtail the influence of liberation theology.[98] Notwithstanding the social tone of his 1987 encyclical *Sollicitudo Rei Sociales*, John Paul II did not visit the slums of Lima during his visit to Peru in May 1988, as he did on the occassion of his first visit to Peru in 1985. The schedule of his second visit was arranged by Opus Dei. At the Peruvian episcopal gathering, which included seven bishops who are members of Opus Dei, the pope directly attacked the theologians of liberation.[99]

The influence of Opus Dei was not stopped by the Iron Curtain. Large amounts of money from the Vatican were transferred to Solidarity in Poland through Opus Dei.[100] The present archbishop of Kraków, Macharski, who claimed Auschwitz as a symbol of Catholic martyrdom, is a sympathizer

---

95. Hertel, "Ich verspreche," p. 132.
96. Hebblethwaite, *In the Vatican*, p. 111.
97. Ibid., p. 189.
98. *Time*, 16 January 1989.
99. C. Cadorette, "Towards a Contextual Interpretation of Papal Teaching: Reflections from a Peruvian Perspective", in Social Compass, vol. 36, no. 3, September 1989, pp. 285–94.
100. A. van Bosbeke, *Opus Dei in Belgie* (Berchem, Belgium, 1985), p. 102.

of Opus Dei.[101] The pope's enthusiasm for Opus Dei seems to have cooled of late due to scandals caused by its methods in recruiting children.[102]

One of the most prominent members of Opus Dei is Archduke Otto von Habsburg who, as the son of the last Austrian emperor, is also a Knight of Malta.[103] Von Habsburg has been a West German citizen since 1979, a prominent member of the European Parliament for the CSU, and one of the spiders in the web of conservative Catholic organizations. In line with the technocratic policy of fellow Opus Dei members in the cabinets of Franco, in 1969 he expressed his concern that Europe would miss the imminent technological revolution due to the European balkanization. Only a united Europe could keep up.[104]

This technocratic view of the world is characteristic of the Opus Dei elite. For example, one of the first countries where Opus Dei penetrated outside Spain was Chile. After the coup by Pinochet in 1973, Opus Dei provided the junta with civilian members and advisers whom it in turn had provided a technological and religious education.[105]

Opus Dei is probably the most extreme expression of neoconservatism, in which a stress on technological development and economic calculation is combined with authoritarian Catholicism. Because of Opus Dei's secrecy the exact parameters of its influence are hard to define. Moreover, Opus Dei makes use of satellite organizations whose connections with it are often carefully hidden. In Germany, for example, the Ruhr Institute for Research and Development is such a satellite.[106] Several key issues in the CDU's platform in the December 1990 elections converged with Opus Dei's points of view. After German reunification, stimulating technological progress and respect for the family, the police, and the army topped the agenda.

At the moment Opus Dei has about 80,000 members,

101. Hertel, "Ich verspreche," p. 142.
102. F. Bowers, "*Opus Dei* – Is the Pope Leaving It Isolated?" *Now*, August 1989, pp. 39–40.
103. Van Bosbeke, *Opus Dei*, p. 145.
104. *Weltwoche* (Germany), 12 September 1969.
105. F. Landis, "Opus Dei: Secret Order Vies for Power," *Covert Action* 18, 1983 (Winter), pp. 11–15.
106. Hertel, "Ich verspreche," p. 46.

including some two thousand priests in about ninety countries. Opus Dei is involved in the management of nearly five hundred universities and has relations with some seven hundred newspapers and magazines and fifty radio and television stations.[107] The University of Navarre in Pamplona, Spain, is owned by Opus Dei, and Opus Dei has contacts with Harvard University and the Instituto de Estudios Superiores de la Empresa in Barcelona, where Opus Dei trains students for activities in Latin America.[108] Opus Dei is affiliated with many banks, including Banco Popular Espanol, Continental Illinois, and the Inter-Alpha group which had included the Banco Ambrosiano.[109]

The Anti-Communist International

With the revival of the cold war in the 1970s, Catholic organizations in Western Europe linked up in a general movement against detente and for an acceleration of the arms race. These policies resulted in the removal of social democrats from government wherever it was possible and in the removal of reformist leaders in Christian democratic parties. In Italy Aldo Moro was executed by a faction of the Red Brigades in 1978. In the same year in the Netherlands, the centrist leader of the Christian Democrats, Aantjes, was removed after the disclosure of his collaboration with the Germans during the Second World War.

An increasingly dense network was created in support of the cold war, consisting of representatives of American conservative organizations, members of Opus Dei, Knights of Malta, Christian democrats, and conservative organizations urging a united Christian Europe. The activities of the groups and individuals in this network ranged from lobbying for conservative goals and financing counterpropaganda against peace movements to often fraudulent activities in politics and finance.

The most notorious branch of the network was founded in

107. R. Hasselerharm, "Opus Dei," in *De Tijd* (Amsterdam), 28 September 1984, p. 20.
108. Hertel, "Ich verspreche," p. 63.
109. Van Bosbeke, *Opus Dei*, p. 100.

Italy, where during the 1970s the masonic lodge Propaganda Due (P2) functioned as a state within the state. P2, led by Licio Gelli, was a network encompassing terrorist organizations, several Knights of Malta, representatives of all political parties with the exception of the PCI, chiefs of the secret services and, through the Banco Ambrosiano, administered by P2 members, even the Vatican's bank, the Instituto per Opere di Religione.[110] Although P2 had an international membership, it was a typical Italian phenomenon, with roots predating its reestablishment in 1971 by Gelli.[111] P2 had its roots in the country's Mafia tradition and could prosper because of Italy's rather weak state structure. But above all, P2 was the result of the paranoiac fear of communist participation in government on the part of the Catholic right, the secret services, and policymakers in Washington.

After the "opening to the Left" in the early 1960s, the Italian intelligence service unleashed a "strategy of tension," cofinanced by the CIA.[112] The strategy of tension, an elaboration of Angleton's postwar activities, consisted primarily of the execution of terrorist assaults under the cover of left-wing and anarchist groups, which would possibly pave the way for a coup d'état. Such a coup – the Salo Plan – had been planned in 1964 by the chief of the secret service, Giovanni di Lorenzo, and approved by President Antonio Segni. It would have culminated in the murder of Prime Minister Aldo Moro.[113] Fourteen years later, during a period of massive terrorism, "historic compromise" supporter Aldo Moro was executed by a faction of the Red Brigades which had been infiltrated by neofascist elements.

A central figure in the strategy of tension was Stefano delle Chiaie, who was to become the confidant of Gelli in the 1970s. Delle Chiaie and his commandos of the neofascist Avanguardia Nazionale (AN) infiltrated organizations under whose cover they carried out terrorist assaults or committed

---

110. The relationship between P2, Banco Ambrosiano, and the IOR is discussed in R. Cornwell, *God's Banker*, and D. Yallop, *In God's Name* (London, 1984).

111. Cornwell, *God's Banker*, p. 45.

112. J. Roth and B. Ender, *Dunkelmanner der Macht: Politische Geheimzirkel und organisiertes Verbrechen*, (Bornheim-Merten, Germany, 1984), p. 118.

113. Christie, *Stefano delle Chiaie*, p. 24.

political murders.[114] After the abortive coup by the AN and Prince Borghese in December 1970, Delle Chiaie and Borghese – "monitored by the Servizio Informazione Difesa" – fled to Spain, and from there Delle Chiaie went to Latin America. There he became involved in an even wider web of international terrorism, which included Pinochet's secret service and Klaus Barbie.[115]

Delle Chiaie's notoriety did not keep him from involvement in further terrorist attacks in Italy, the most sinister of which was the assault on the Bologna railway station in 1980 in which nearly a hundred people were killed. The public fury that this assault, which was probably ordered by Gelli, aroused, and the bankruptcy of Banco Ambrosiano, led to the downfall of P2.[116]

With the exception of Belgium, the strategy of tension has been limited to Italy as far as Western Europe is concerned.[117] A central role in the stimulating of less violent conservative action in Europe was played by the Cercle Violet, named after French lawyer Jean Violet. The Cercle Violet was a continuation of the Centre Europeen de Documentation et d'Information (CEDI), founded by Otto von Habsburg in 1949 in order to break the Franco regime's isolation and to advocate the liberation of Eastern Europe under the sign of the cross.[118]

During the second wave of cold war policies the Cercle Violet tried to influence elections in favor of right-wing parties through propaganda and agitation against detente. In June 1981, Cercle Violet members gathered in Zurich to discuss the possibilities of influencing the Bavarian elections in favor

114. Avanguardia Nazionale (AN) was financed by Carlo Pesenti, a member of P2 and Cercle Violet and a business partner of the IOR and Continental Bank. Ibid., p. 21.

115. M. Linklater, I. Hilton, and N. Ascherson, *The Fourth Reich: Klaus Barbie and the neofascist Connection* (London, 1984), p. 208.

116. Yallop, *In God's Name*, p. 107.

117. During 1983–1985 Belgium was terrorized by the so-called Nivelles Gang, which carried out a series of raids on supermarkets in which a great many people were killed and yet the loot was negligible. Several right-wing Christian Democrats, such as former prime minister Paul vanden Boeynants and Knight of Malta Benoit de Bonvoisim, and noble members of Opus Dei have been mentioned as possible invisible hands behind the Nivelles Gang. *Gazet van Antwerpen*, 7 November 1989; C. Groenenwegen, "Bananenrepubliek," *De Tijd*, 26 February 1988, pp. 17–20.

118. Arbeitskreis Nicaragua, *Propagandisten*, p. 59.

of Franz Joseph Strauss's CSU. Among those present were Strauss himself and the editor-in-chief of the *Neue Zuercher Zeitung*, Fred Luchinger.[119]

The Cercle Violet included a large variety of right-wing Christian democrats and high-ranking members of intelligence services, among whom were Otto von Habsburg; Alfredo Sanchez Bella and Frederico Munoz, both former ministers of the Franco regime and often mentioned as members of Opus Dei; Philippo Maria Pandolfi, a former Italian minister of finance and a member of P2;[120] the Belgian president of the World Anti-Communist League, Robert Close; and the former head of the French secret service and a Knight of Malta, Count Alexandre de Marenches, according to whom Reagan mistakenly thought we lived in a period of peace.[121] The United States was represented by Ed Feulner, president of the conservative think tank, the Heritage Foundation, William Colby, and Henry Kissinger.[122]

The Cercle Violet overlapped with other organizations of Catholic origin that combined cold war imperatives with the promotion of the unification of Europe, such as the Académie Européenne de Sciences Politiques (AESP), which prints on its letterhead the Carolingian cross, the symbol of a great and strong Europe.[123] The AESP includes many prominent leaders of the Catholic Right: Giulio Andreotti, Alberto Ullastres, and, until his death in 1984, Carlo Pesenti.[124] The AESP has a strong presence among prominent CSU members of the Pan-Europe Union: Otto von Habsburg, who is chair of both organizations, Alois Mertens, and the late Hans-Joachim Merkatz.

With the East-West conflict in Europe subsiding, it is unclear what role this network will play in the future. This is not a question for the Knights of Malta and Opus Dei, of course. The idea of a united Europe may have gained much more momentum, but it may turn out to be that the European elite

---

119. Roth and Ender, *Dunkelmanner*, p. 87.
120. Ibid., p. 86.
121. *Vrij Nederland*, 28 February 1987.
122. Van Bosbeke, *Opus Dei*, p. 147.
123. *Vrije Volk (Rotterdam)*, 12 January 1984.
124. Van Bosbeke, *Opus Dei*, p. 148.

was united on the cold war but will be divided on the role of a unified Germany. Fred Luchinger may have very well expressed the position of many European political leaders on German reunification when he said that they were opposed, but unable to speak against it.[125]

Epilogue

In the 1960s the Second Vatican Council sought a compromise between the church and modernism in the political realm, a compromise shattered with the pontificate of John Paul II. However, this did not imply a return to the precouncil period. In an attempt to regain power and authority the church broke out of its seclusion, stepping up evangelization with fashionable sales methods and a use of mass media. For instance, during the 1989 Tour of Italy the Vatican and Communione e Liberazione cosponsored two Italian cycling teams which wore jerseys with an antiabortion slogan and reading "God loves you."[126] In August 1989 the Catholic youth festival in Santiago de Compostela was graced with the presence of the pope. At the festival a half million juveniles from seventy-two countries pledged allegiance to the "pilgrimage to the millenium of chastity." A Catholic Belgian newspaper cheerfully called the festival, organized by Opus Dei, the Catholic Woodstock.[127]

The Roman Catholic church is also creating its own "electronic church." In 1989, Alberto Michelini launched Persona TV in Italy with the support of the Vatican. In Latin America, Communione e Liberazione and influential, rich charismatics launched the satellite project Lumen 2000, to counteract both American evangelicals and the influence of liberation theology.[128] Lumen 2000 is supported by Frank Shakespeare, the American ambassador to the Holy See, a Knight of Malta, and cochair of the Heritage Foundation.

125. From a television interview with Luchinger on ARD *Wochenspiegel*, 17 December 1989.
126. *Volkskrant*, 27 April 1989.
127. *Volkskrant*, 22 August. 1989.
128. W. Gijsbers, "Religieuze kruistocht per satelliet," *Bijeen* ('s Hertogenbosch), April 1989, pp. 4–7.

For the greater part of this century, cooperation between the liberal elite and the church in Western Europe had been mainly limited to the common defense against the Left in the political realm. But with the rise of neoconservatism, the church has gained prominence in the search for a conservative cultural hegemony, in which moral authority and depoliticization of the masses are the main objectives. In this process the "New Catholic Movements" have also had a role to play. The range of their influence, however, has not been widely treated above, because Opus Dei is too secret an organization to be subjected to a detailed analysis, Communione e Liberazione is primarily an Italian organization, and the charismatics are still on the margin of Catholic organization, although they may gain momentum in the struggle against liberation theology and as a counterweight to evangelicals in the Third World. As for the politically oriented elite organizations, they most likely will shift, or have shifted, their priorities from cold war endeavors to supporting, and influencing the nature of, European unification.

The convergence of interests between the church and conservative capitalist concepts is best reflected in the regained strength of Christian democratic parties in Europe. They serve as an intermediary between the restrictive welfare state and the principles of the market. Moreover, the conservative shift has provided a space for Christian democrats to pursue policies based on Christian morality, often concealed, but with more vigor and confidence than in the past. This concerns most notably policies on the position of the family and restrictions on social and cultural freedom, issues in which Christian democrats are archetypical conservatives.

· 8 ·

An American Pentecostal Mission to Poland in 1989

LAWRENCE JONES

Pentecostalism, the dramatic and highly emotional wing of American evangelicalism, has spread throughout the globe since the beginning of the twentieth century and is now a worldwide religious movement. The Pentecostal movement has always been characterized more by religious behavior than by doctrine or organizational structures. Speaking in tongues, laying on hands for healings, and lively worship meetings are its characteristic behaviors.

American Pentecostals tend to be apocalyptic in outlook. Ever since the 1906 Azusa Street revival in Los Angeles, shortly after the great earthquake that destroyed San Francisco, American Pentecostals have been anticipating the imminent end of the world.[1] From the early days of the movement, speaking in tongues (the most characteristic Pentecostal behavior) was considered to be a sign that Pentecostal believers were living in the last days.

After the Second World War, Europe, as well as the rest of the world, became active mission fields for American evangelicals, especially for Pentecostals. Their belief in the imminent Second Coming of Christ has motivated the heroic efforts of American evangelicals to evangelize the world. Because of their apocalyptic expectations American evangelicals have

---

1. F. Bartleman, "How Pentecost Came to Los Angeles: As It Was in the Beginning," in *Witness to Pentecost: The Life of Frank Bartleman* (New York, 1985). Bartleman, a participant and a leader in the early Pentecostal movement writes (p. 50): "I found the earthquake had opened many hearts. I was distributing especially my last tract, *The Last Call*. It seemed very appropriate after the earthquake."

planned especially aggressive missionary activity for the 1990s. The year 2000 has a special apocalyptic significance for some.

Many American evangelicals believe that the last days were signalled in 1948 with the formation of the state of Israel and by the Israeli capture of all of Jerusalem in 1967. They believe that the generation that witnessed these events is the "last generation" – the generation that will experience the apocalyptic events prophesied in some biblical texts. Many evangelical organizations have set special goals for the year 2000, and several have agreed to combine their resources to evangelize the world by that time. The idea that the 1990s may be the "last decade" of Christianity (before apocalyptic intervention), and a decade of unparalleled opportunity, has become increasingly popular among evangelicals in the United States.

YWAM

Youth With A Mission (YWAM) is one of many American evangelical organizations dedicated to "fulfilling the terms of the Great Commission" (Matt. 28:19) – that is, to evangelize the world, thought by believers to be a precondition for the Second Coming of Christ. YWAM (pronounced Y-WAM) was started in 1960 by an Assemblies of God pastor, Loren Cunningham, as a short-term missions program for youth. The youth would pay their own way and devote their full time for a couple of months or a year to missionary work, not to sightseeing.[2] By 1970 YWAM had forty full-time staff. The organization grew rapidly after 1980 and by 1987 had 5,945 full-time staff and 17,923 volunteers participating in short-term mission projects worldwide.[3] Besides specializing in short-term missions, the organization also developed schools to

2. L. Cunningham (with J. Rogers), *Is that Really You, Lord? The Story of Youth With A Mission* (Lincoln, Virginia, 1984), p. 38.

3. These numbers come from "Youth with a Mission International Operating Location Profile for 1987: Selected Summaries," compiled by Paul Filidis, Research & Information, YWAM International Operations Office, Amsterdam. According to this document there were 17,923 short-term volunteers in 1987 as well as 187,576 participants in one to fourteen–day YWAM events. YWAM recorded 62,576 "decisions for Christ" worldwide in 1987.

train its own leadership cadre (Discipleship Training Schools or DTSs) and a YWAM university in Hawaii.

This article is a case study of a YWAM short-term mission outreach (called a go-team in YWAM parlance, short for global opportunity team). In summer 1989 Youth With A Mission sent out a missionary team of twenty to evangelize Wrocław, a Polish city of some 576,000 souls. That same year the YWAM center in Amsterdam dispatched similar teams to Italy, France, Portugal, Northern Ireland, Hong Kong, and New Orleans.

YWAM had sent several teams previously to Poland and to other East Bloc countries, as well as to the USSR, but the 1989 Go-Team to Poland was the first YWAM group to go into a Soviet-bloc country with official permission to publicly perform street theater. YWAM had described itself somewhat deceptively as an "international theater company" (rather than a missionary organization) in its letter requesting exemption for team members from the obligatory currency exchange. Earlier YWAM teams to Eastern Europe had been smaller guerrilla operations – flying attempts at covert street evangelism and secret meetings in the homes of East Bloc charismatics and Pentecostals.

The "Go-Team"

The Go-Team to Poland first met on 10 June in Amsterdam, and after three days of training in a camp in a Dutch forest near Austerlitz, traveled by bus to Poland. In the Netherlands the team learned to perform a twenty-six-minute mime entitled "The Maze" which the team, after setting up camp in Poland, performed twice a day in public squares in the city of Wrocław. After busing back to Amsterdam, the Go-Team broke up on 1 July having accomplished its mission.

Of the twenty members of the team, six were full-time YWAM staff members who were the leaders of the team, and fourteen were volunteers (one of whom was also a full-time YWAMer though not one of the team's leaders). Most of the group (all of the YWAM staffers and several participants) had prior experience on a YWAM Go-Team. Egil, a 32-year-old Norwegian, had absolute authority over the other YWAM staff members and over the volunteer participants as team leader.

Excluding this observer, the group ranged in age from 18 to 32 with an average age of 24.8 years.

If they had not grown up in a "Christian home" (and sometimes even if they had), most members of the team had experienced religious conversions as teenagers or young adults. Most could recall the exact date of conversion and dated the "years they had been in Christ" from then on. Several had gone forward at a Pentecostal service to accept an altar call and "accepted Jesus into their hearts" publicly and very dramatically. Others had a more private but no less dramatic experience. The "youngest in Christ" on the team was "one year old." Most were led by friends or family members into their conversion experiences.

Testimonies, the stories believers tell of how they "came to Jesus," vary, but there are common themes and circumstances. Here are several testimonies told by team members:

Tim graduated from college as an engineer, then moved to California where he became bored with his low-level managerial job. He met a woman and dated her several times, but she told him one day that she had decided not to see him again because he was not a Christian. "She was a fanatic," he said. That started him thinking. Later another friend invited him to a Pentecostal church where he eventually answered an altar call. Tim was the "baby Christian" in the group having been a Pentecostal for only a year.

Rosie, a nurse, came from a Mexican Catholic background. She had been a devout Catholic charismatic for some seven years, a "believer in the church" as she put it. For a time she even considered becoming a nun. But after moving to another city she was introduced to a Pentecostal church by a boyfriend. At the time of the YWAM mission to Poland she was debating in her mind whether or not to devote herself to full-time medical missionary work.

Shaun also grew up Catholic. He began smoking marijuana in the sixth grade and began taking the hallucinogen LSD in seventh grade. His parents sent him to a Catholic private school after he became delinquent. That made him "clean up his act" but he still "partied." Shaun said he took a lot of acid, mushrooms, and the like, before he finally stopped taking hallucinogens at age 20. He used cocaine as well and often attended rock and roll concerts. He was introduced to a Pentecostal church by a friend and now works full-time as the church's janitor.

Peter, one of the YWAM team leaders, grew up as an Irish Catholic in Liverpool. At age 17 he was depressed, felt empty inside. He knelt down in an empty chapel and "gave his life to Jesus." Peter attended a seminary but became disillusioned and dropped out. He joined a Pentecostal group, again introduced by a friend, and became a full-time missionary with YWAM.

Natalie, age 20, grew up "colored" in a segregated township outside Cape Town, South Africa. When she was 13 her family emigrated to Melbourne, Australia. Her mother is a devout Catholic who attends mass every day. Her father, though, is not religious. Natalie became a leader in a Catholic youth group but became disillusioned with the Catholic church. A friend introduced her to a small but growing local Pentecostal church where she was baptized. The church's congregation paid her way to Poland.

One Church's Aggressive Missions Program

Seven of the volunteers for the go-team to Poland came from a large Pentecostal church in Fresno, California. This Foursquare Gospel church of about five thousand parishioners has a very active missions program which directly involves church members. In summer 1989 the church sent five teams outside the United States on YWAM-led short-term missions projects. Each of the 1989 teams had seven or eight members except for one team of twelve sent on a mission to evangelize Portland, Oregon. In 1989 the church sent teams to Poland, the Philippines, Kenya, and two teams to Amsterdam, all of them on YWAM missionary outreaches. The Fresno church also sends teams to Mexico each January, but these teams are not organized by YWAM. This model of intense participatory missionary activity had been adopted by a number of large Pentecostal churches in the United States.

The process of involving church members, training them, and raising their support was well organized and effective. The Fresno summer teams began their preparation and training in

November of the previous year. Raising money was a large part of the necessary preparations. Each team participant wrote ten letters asking for financial support. The effort was coordinated to ensure that no one person received more than two letters. The church also raised money with garage sales and a car wash. A local camera supply store provided gift coupons participants could sell, returning one out of every five dollars of sales for the church missions. The cost of sending one short-term missionary to Poland was $1,700.

The Fresno team sent to Poland had two leaders, a man and a woman. The woman was subordinate to the man and both were subordinate to the YWAM leadership during the course of the outreach. The Fresno teams prayed before the trip to be able to submit to the leadership. Their leaders in turn submitted to the YWAM leaders. After their short-term mission experiences, returning participants went through an organized "reentry" process within the church.

Training in the Netherlands

Two Go-Teams, one going to Poland and one going to Italy, trained and camped in a wooded campground in rural Holland, but each team met and trained separately to perform the same dramatic mime. Only after the training was completed did the two drama teams meet to perform their two identical mimes. Shortly after arriving on the site the teams met separately to share their testimonies – the life-histories told by Pentecostals which culminate in their "giving their lives to Jesus" and getting baptized by the Holy Spirit. The seven YWAM leaders gave theirs first. It required two evening sessions to hear the twenty stories. Besides telling and listening to each other's religious histories, the team joined together in "praise and worship" – an hour or more of singing, standing with upraised hands or in some other dramatic worship posture, "praying out" (praying aloud to the group), and clapping.

On the first morning of the training period the YWAM leader met with the team and talked about his own motivations and about the team's mission in Poland. The leader, Egil, a Norwegian, had read Brother Andrew's religious autobiography *God's Smuggler*[4] soon after his teenage encounter with Jesus. Brother Andrew's tales of smuggling Bibles and evangelical literature into communist countries had fascinated him. He felt he had a call to do the same thing.

Egil, a professional truck driver, worked five years with Underground Evangelism smuggling Bibles and evangelical literature into Eastern Europe from West Germany. He later became a YWAM staff member and led a small team of six people in two vans into Poland in 1983. At that time he made contact with members of Oasis, the Polish Catholic charismatic movement.

Since 1986 Egil had been thinking about sending a team to Poland to evangelize openly, with legal permits, but for that he needed an invitation from a Polish organization. He had wanted an invitation from a Catholic church, but that required permission from the bishops and the bishops were unlikely to invite a Pentecostal group to come and evangelize Catholic Poland. In 1983, however, Egil had met Frank, a Polish-American Pentecostal pastor with a small church in Wrocław. Pastor Frank provided the invitation and organized the necessary official permits for the team's public performances.

Team Prayer

Group prayer was a regular part of the team's program. Prayer and worship sessions usually began by singing several Pentecostal songs. Early on in the training period the leaders gathered the team together and encouraged them to pray out – "to let the Lord speak through you." During a praying-out session everyone sat or stood silently in a circle, eyes closed or half-closed, until someone prayed something out aloud. When none of the participants prayed out, one of the leaders did. A praying-out session might last fifteen to twenty minutes.

Egil urged the participants to "use the time for emotional outpouring." But the first attempt disappointed the leaders

4. Brother Andrew (with J. Sherrill and E. Sherrill), *God's Smuggler* (New York, 1967).

who were the only ones to pray out. After some twenty minutes they gave it up and started the group singing another song. Participants did, however, pray out in later sessions.

The prayer sessions (twice or more a day) were always dramatic events. Peter, a former seminarian, played guitar and usually led the singing. Other YWAM leaders modeled postures of praise and worship. Brigitt, an ex-Catholic from a Puerto Rican background, knelt through one song. Other leaders lifted their hands high in the traditional Pentecostal prayer posture. The YWAM staff told the participants that they should be "more spontaneous." Egil invited participants, if they needed help, to ask a member of the YWAM staff to pray with them individually. One participant immediately asked for intercessory prayer because he did not feel all the emotion that he thought he should.

Drama Team and Prayer Team

YWAM Go-Teams evangelize by performing street mimes. Casting for the drama began with a prayer session. Then came free movement to tape-recorded Christian music and breathing exercises ("Breathe like someone who's in a panic" – "like someone who's happy" – "who's in grief"). The two YWAM staff members directing the drama encouraged the participants to move and to emote, explaining absolutely nothing about the plot until after they had chosen their cast of nine.

The eleven members of the team not chosen for the cast became the "prayer-and-intercession team." They were to walk around the area, "engaging in spiritual warfare and taking authority in the name of Jesus." Besides praying, they were told to scout the audience for anyone "under conviction" – that is, anyone who looked like they were taking the drama seriously. The prayer-and-intercession team also helped "form a crowd" before performances if the group was having trouble attracting an audience. These two subteams trained separately after the casting was completed.

The Mime

The drama, a twenty-six-minute mime called "The Maze," was a biblical allegory. The players acted to a tape-recorded soundtrack that carefully cued all the actors' movements. Every gesture and motion was choreographed. The drama was easy to learn because the tape-recorded music dictated the timing. A large green tarpaulin painted with the "walls" of the maze contained the action. The drama, like all mimes, was acted with exaggerated emotion and without spoken words. YWAM teams perform these mimes around the world on their various outreaches. Ignorance of local languages is no handicap. The cast of nine learned the mime in three days of hard training. Three of the nine had already acted in an earlier production of "The Maze." Only one of the leaders acted in the mime, since they wanted as many non-YWAMers as possible to participate.

The Drama's Scenario

"The Maze" begins with nervous noise followed by explosive music. Adam and Eve run in panic onto the tarpaulin (painted like a maze) which confines the action. They push up against invisible walls which make up a maze in which, in their panic, they find themselves suddenly trapped.

The Carpenter (the Christ character) stands outside the maze miming the walls separating him from Adam and Eve. The Carpenter carries half of a torn golden cloth, representing (as do the walls) the broken relationship between God and humanity. Adam picks up the other half of the cloth. Six other players then enter the maze to a new musical theme. They represent social stereotypes: an intellectual (with a book), a businessman and his secretary, a "Disco Boy" (who just wants to have a good time), and an old man.

Adam and Eve show the torn cloth first to the intellectual and then to the others. No one knows what it means. Enticed by a Coca Cola offered by the waitress but lacking any money, Adam is forced to get a job. The secretary holds up a help-wanted sign written in Polish. Adam and the old man apply, and Adam gets the job. Rejected, the old man dies and is carried off the tarp.

Harried and overworked, Adam rejects an imploring Eve who gets in the way of his work. Eve in turn rejects Adam. She is led off to a corner by a sinister hooded character called Hopelessness. The audience is told beforehand that he represents the devil. After a disco scene Adam mimes an affair with the secretary. Led out by Hopelessness, a horrified Eve sees the two together and attempts to strangle the secretary. Adam pushes Eve away and she falls to the tarp. The other players circle her, pointing accusing fingers at the jealous Eve.

At this point the Carpenter enters the maze out of mimed concern for the tragedy inside it. He carries a crossbeam and mimes hammering. While he is working, the Disco Boy mugs the businessman. After the Carpenter reproaches him, the repentent Disco Boy gives back the money and helps the injured businessman to his feet. The players then circle the Carpenter miming the question "Who are you?"

The Carpenter offers them a way out of the maze and shows them his half of the torn cloth. The Disco Boy, the businessman, and Eve "get saved" and come over to the Carpenter. The others laugh at him. Hopelessness incites them to whip and crucify the Carpenter. After the Carpenter's death, Hopelessness removes his own hood to reveal a frightening skull mask. The saved characters, weeping, wrap the Carpenter's body in a winding sheet. But after dramatically rising from the dead, the Carpenter orders Hopelessness out of the maze. Adam, now repentent, embraces Eve. The Carpenter and Adam put together the torn golden cloth, representing a restored relationship between God and humanity. The Carpenter then triumphally "tears" a cloth barrier at the entrance to the maze and, with exaggerated joy, leads the saved players out.

A Swedish dancer working together with her husband, a YWAM manager, developed the drama. "The Maze" evolved over the course of a year before the summer 1989 Go-Teams learned the drama from YWAM instructors. On the last night of the training period both Go-Teams performed "The Maze" in costume. The next morning one team drove away in a bus to Italy, the other in a bus to Poland.

In Poland

A day after crossing the Polish border the YWAM team presented the drama in Wrocław, performing it a total of twenty times over the next twelve days. A local Pentecostal church worked closely with the YWAM team. At least one of the church's four translators attended each performance. (Only one team member could speak Polish.) Other members of the congregation often attended as well and stayed to talk with people in the audience. Before and after the drama, team members and local Pentecostals handed out tracts and "contact cards."

The team's work in Poland culminated with a "miracle crusade" conducted by a foreign evangelist, Christopher Alam. At every performance advertisements were posted and flyers about it given out claiming that at the Alam rally "The blind [will] see, the deaf hear, the lame walk." Church members fed the YWAM team, washed their costumes, and helped organize and manage Alam's "miracle crusade." The church had printed 100,000 tracts and had to arrange to have even more printed for their campaign.

Frank's Church

The local Pentecostal church had been registered with the government for only one year. The pastor, Frank, had studied at the Rhema Bible College in Tulsa, Oklahoma. He was an American citizen but his parents were Polish. After Bible college Frank felt a call to go to Poland. He moved there, married a Pole, relearned Polish, and started an American-style Pentecostal church in Wrocław. Frank received a modest monthly salary from the church that amounted to only some five American dollars. Most of his money, though, came from his family and supporters in the United States. Frank and his wife and children lived in a large and comfortable apartment and had an automobile (from outside the East Bloc), a color television set, and a video recorder, all rare symbols of wealth and status in Poland. The inflation rate of the Polish zloty to the dollar during the time of the 1989 outreach was 25 percent a week. Anyone, like Frank, with access to dollars had a considerable economic advantage.

Seven months before their evangelical campaign, Frank's church had split in two. More than half of the congregation left to follow a "false prophet," one of the men in the church who "had a gift for Bible study." According to Pastor Frank, the splinter group refused to recognize any eclessiastical authority. They had no pastors and no organized church but did meet sometimes for Bible study and prayer. Moreover, they believed that one was born again only after achieving a sinless and perfect life. Sometimes they preached against Frank's group and occasionally members of the splinter group showed up at the drama performances to say something against Frank's church. The schism had been quite bitter. Frank's church was left with only about one hundred members and badly needed a revival to replenish its membership.

The goal of the YWAM outreach was to double the size of the Pentecostal church, in effect restoring it to its former size. The YWAM team worked with Frank and his congregation to recruit new members into his church, though when questioned by two Poles in the audience, one of the YWAM leaders denied that the team was trying to recruit people into a denomination or sect.[5] The two Poles remained suspicious. The tracts the team distributed had the address, time of service, and travel directions to the movie theater where Frank's church met, printed inside.

Street Theater

The crowds varied from a low of only 65 to over 400. Adding all twenty performances together, some 5,000 people watched the drama. The average crowd size was about 250. For the most part people watched politely, arms folded, some smoking or talking with friends. Children laughed and made jokes. Most stayed to listen to the preaching after the drama. The YWAM team presented "The Maze" at fairs, markets, public squares, outside a Catholic church, and in a minimum-security prison.

5. When asked later about this contradiction, the leader explained that the team was working "with" but not "for" Frank's church and that the team would have distributed Catholic tracts if any Catholic church had invited them to do so.

The equipment was simple and mobile, easily packed into the storage compartments of the bus. There was the tarp which served as the stage, an electric generator, a sound system, costumes, and props. The loud music attracted crowds. The leaders introduced the YWAM team as an international drama team without a word about YWAM or Frank's church.

After each performance one of the leaders preached, amplified by the powerful sound system. The message was always the same: "Jesus wants to come and meet with you." Sometimes preachers referred to the stereotypical characters in the drama – "The businessman just wants to earn money. But that doesn't satisfy you." The speakers always personalized the message with their own testimonies, telling how they had come to "accept Jesus into their hearts." They spoke in English and a bilingual Polish Pentecostal translated, American and Pole each with microphone in hand.

The preaching always had two moments of climax. First, the point in the personal testimony when the speaker "accepted Jesus," the climax of the personal testimony. Sometimes speakers kneeled at this point. It was always a highly dramatic moment. The second climax came when the speaker invited everyone to "let Jesus come into your life." After the invitation, the preachers asked those who wanted to accept Jesus to raise their hands and then asked the ones who had raised their hands to come forward onto the tarp to be prayed with. It was a typical Pentecostal altar call.

Many came forward, much to the surprise of the YWAM staff, which was used to the indifference or opposition they often encountered in Western Europe and the United States. When about forty people came forward after the first performance one experienced YWAMer said, "That's as many as we've received the whole time on other outreaches." After the first day of the outreach one of the leaders, who had toured South Africa with a YWAM team, remarked, "I think we'll see people healed here. It's that kind of atmosphere. It's like Africa."

Prayer and Healing

Six of the participants reported "leading someone to the Lord" on the first day of the outreach. The leaders taught the team, by modeling and by instruction, how to lead people to the Lord. First, it was necessary to know whom to approach: "Normally I don't like to discuss with people. It's not worth it to argue with someone who's not open. Just go to the one that's open." The encounters went something like this: "Hello, how did you like the drama?... Have you accepted Jesus?... Would you like to?... Would you mind if I prayed with you?"

The YWAM leaders taught the team how to pray for healing with individuals in the audience after performances. "Be prepared to be spontaneous," urged the leaders. They taught a five-step formula for praying with someone: (1) the prayer request, the interview that asks "What's the problem?"; (2) the diagnosis of the person's greatest need; (3) prayer selection ("Sometimes the words just jump out of your mouth");[6] (4) "feedback," asking "Do you feel anything?" "Is God touching you?"; (5) "post-prayer direction," giving the person prayed for some guidance for the future. The YWAM leaders used a "healing model" developed by John Wimber, a popular Pentecostal healer based in Southern California.[7]

Many people in the audience enjoyed being prayed for, and the team members were happy to pray with them. These encounters were often highly emotional personal dramas. Individuals told of loneliness and confusion, sickness or an accident, and family problems. After each performance, a leader paired with one or two participants (working together with a translator from the Pentecostal church) prayed with receptive individuals in the crowd. This little group huddled around the person to be prayed for. The YWAM leaders directed and manipulated these little scenes. They encouraged team members to take an active part in these encounters and urged them to aggressively "lead people to Christ."

Healing was a constant prayer concern and was always very dramatic. YWAM leaders encouraged team members to pray with individual Poles for physical healing. A puffy-eyed, "spaced-out" old woman claimed that the burning in her

---

6. In cases of demonic possession the participants were urged to "grab one of the team leaders."

7. John Wimber is the author of several books. See, for example, Wimber (with K. Springer), *Power Evangelism* (San Francisco, 1986).

eyes went away after a pair from the YWAM team laid hands on her and prayed. Healing reports were much talked about. The stories were told over and over again. One of the leaders said, "There's no reason why we can't see the blind see, the deaf hear," and later expanded that, saying, "There's no reason we can't do more than Jesus did." The leaders created expectations of miraculous results and consequently the group experienced "miracles."

A case of a young woman in her early twenties with a liver condition, "healed" by a pair from the team, became the chief "miracle" of the outreach. She later joined the local Pentecostal church, happy to be the focus of attention. Because of what was diagnosed as a liver condition she had been on a restricted diet for eight years. One of the YWAM leaders and a participant prayed with her. One placed her hands on the woman's abdomen. The woman reported a warm sensation and "something moving in [her] liver." Natalie, the team participant who "laid on hands" also reported a feeling of warmth in her hands.

Several days after this dramatic encounter the young woman returned and said, "I went home the day you guys prayed for me and I ate all the foods I wasn't supposed to eat. No problem." This became the "proof" that the woman was cured, at least for the ten days or so that the YWAM team remained in Poland. She told her story during Sunday service at the Pentecostal church and was warmly applauded. Frank, the pastor, annointed Natalie, the team member who laid her hands on the girl. Natalie was visibly moved by the ritual. The enthusiastic Sunday service lasted more than three hours.

Sometimes the leaders also prayed for the healing of members of the YWAM team who were suffering from some minor illness or discomfort. The people playing leading roles in the drama (the Carpenter, Adam, Eve) were especially singled out to be prayed over. A dizzy feeling or an oncoming cold, if one of the leading actors had it, might cripple a performance. However, when one participant became so violently ill that she cried and moaned, the YWAM leaders did not attempt to heal her by prayer but rushed her off to a physician instead.

Lawrence Jones

Demons: The Dualistic Worldview

Demons, according to the YWAM leaders, caused the illnesses
that members of the group were able to heal in these prayer
encounters. "Demons" lurked behind almost anything or
anyone that got in the way, and were first mentioned during
the training period in Holland. A YWAM leader had detected
occult oppression at the training center. "Maybe some kids
have been playing with the Ouija board or something," he
explained. One afternoon YWAM staff members systematically prayed together in a group once in every room of the
center to "spiritually purify" the place. It seems that the night
before several people had had trouble sleeping in the crowded
barracks-like building.

When an encounter with someone in the audience went
wrong it was often attributed to demonic influences. One
individual disrupted the sermon after a performance, shouting (in Polish), "It's not that simple." Team members felt that
they were "under attack by the enemy." The leaders diagnosed the interruption as demonic. Egil explained, "That's
typical for street meetings. That's a dangerous moment for
the devil."

One afternoon when the YWAM team arrived in their bus
at the site of the performance, another theater group had
already gathered a crowd by beating drums and holding up
signs to advertise their own play about the Jewish philoso-
pher Martin Buber. The Buber group left the area before the
YWAM team could set up their props and equipment and did
nothing to interfere with the YWAM team's use of the space,
but the YWAM leaders immediately interpreted the Buber
group's drum beating as a demonic attack against them. The
Buber people had obviously used the temporary fame of the
YWAM performances (featured on a local television news
program) in order to advertise their own drama.

Solidarity, the Polish opposition movement, had also used
the YWAM dramas as an opportunity to scatter anti-Jaruzelski
flyers over crowds from a window of a nearby tall building.
Ironically, with their drumming, the Buber group had probably helped gather an even larger crowd for the YWAM drama.
But YWAM leaders were certain that they were being attacked
and responded with "spiritual warfare." They assembled the

team together for a loud prayer and singing session to "take authority" over the square where the drama team would perform and to "drive out the rival spirit."

Team Dynamics

The outreach had two purposes, both to work with the local Pentecostal church in a campaign to double its membership, but also to change the go-team participant, to transform his or her life and also, incidentally, to recruit them for YWAM Discipleship Training Schools and for a possible career as a full-time YWAM staff member. Graduation from a DTS was a prerequisite for becoming a YWAM staff member. The team leaders focused their attention on several likely candidates for recruitment and recommended that they attend a DTS.

Everything was done in a group and normally no one was left alone. The team traveled together on a bus and camped together in tents. The six YWAM leaders, three men and three women, controlled and scheduled everything for the participants. Egil told the team members not to go alone into the city ("It's not that we don't trust you, it's just for safety"). One YWAM leader told the team that hermits cannot be effective Christians. Solitude, as well as unsupervised contact with Poles, was discouraged.

The team leaders met separately, often in the bus after the participants had been dismissed. The two leaders of the Fresno group were invited to attend the staff meetings as observers. Egil, as overall team leader, could make all important group decisions autocratically, though he often consulted the other YWAM leaders in a staff meeting. The others submitted to his leadership. The structure of YWAM has always been paternalistic, with one man in charge. However, YWAM has become a large and complex international organization. Larger YWAM centers have recently been governed by three leaders, each of whom is in charge of an important operation. This troika controls the center and makes all important decisions.

Participants in the go-team willingly submitted to the leaders. Some even asked the team leader if they could go to the toilet, take a shower, and so on. Though they were young adults, they behaved like obedient children and willingly became dependent on the leaders for most decisions. The Fresno team had even prayed during their training period in California to be able to submit to the leadership. Consequently, the leaders easily manipulated their charges. Freedom was considered somewhat dangerous. After talking (unsuccessfully) with two Polish-American brothers who wore heavy-metal T-shirts, one YWAM staff member sighed, "Lord, why do we have to have free choice?"

Though the group was almost always together, some activities were segregated by sex. The female leaders, for example, were assigned the task of organizing the kitchen. The ten women slept in tents on one side of the campsite, the ten men on the other. Most of the preaching after performances was done by the male leaders. The men preached seventeen out of twenty times, the women only three times. The three male leaders worked mainly with the seven male participants, the three female leaders with the seven female participants. The female leaders were subordinate to the male leaders. Everyone submitted to the team leader (a man) who himself preached most often after performances of the mime (nine out of twenty times).

Emotions

While emotions appeared to have free play in group worship – people emoted visibly, assuming dramatic prayer postures – they were all actually carefully controlled. Prayer was carefully managed. Once the leaders instructed tired team members to "put on their worship faces" just before an early morning praise-and-worship session at the home of the local Pentecostal pastor. The YWAM leaders were extremely suspicious of felt (inner) emotion (as opposed to the displayed emotions for the sake of evangelism or during praise-and-worship sessions).

As one explained, "The greatest thing that can kill our expectations is our emotions. Our feelings have absolutely nothing to do with what God is able to do through us." The leaders encouraged participants to discipline their minds and emotions, especially during street performances. The participants had their own problems with emotions, not feeling the

way they thought they should. Negative emotions and critical thoughts had to be suppressed and the leaders labelled
them satanic. The YWAM leaders told participants that "the
enemy [Satan] comes against us through our emotions."

One leader remarked, "You learn a lot more from experience than from facts." This odd statement reveals something
about the Pentecostal mentality. Experience is worth more
than facts and is also somehow disassociated from facts. One
can have "experiences" which have no factual basis.

The drama of praise and worship was more important than
how participants actually felt. Whether or not a healing had
a factual basis was not really important so long as the people
involved believed in it and acted it out, preferably in public.
Participants in the dramatic world of the YWAM team, even
if they did not initially do so, began to "feel" the powerful
emotions implied by the exaggerated gestures and postures of
public Pentecostal prayer.

All the team's public presentations were highly orchestrated,
even the personal stories the participants told in public. In
preparation for Sunday service at the Pentecostal church the
leaders instructed team members how to give their own testimonies to the congregation ("Keep it personal and short"):
tell about life before conversion, "how you became a Christian," and how life has consequently changed – the typical
Pentecostal testimony.

Before meeting with a group of Catholic charismatics the
YWAM leaders warned participants about telling about any
apocalyptic feelings and convictions (though typical of
American Pentecostals) that might have played a role in their
own conversion experiences. That sort of story, if told, might
have caused controversy and alienated the Polish Catholics.

Often the small, more intimate prayer sessions between a
leader and one or two participants focused on some emotional problem. Such prayer encounters were always inher-
ently dramatic, with sweeping gestures and sometimes weeping. Emotions publicly displayed during prayer or preaching
were always encouraged, but those private feelings (of doubt,
for example) had to be repressed or exorcised. The opposition
between private emotions and the emotions displayed during
prayer had its counterpart in the dualistic demonology
YWAMers invoked to explain opposition and to castigate

private emotions. The leaders had defined these public displays as "evangelism." And, in fact, Polish audiences were often very moved by the mime, the preaching afterwards, and the public prayers.

To an outside observer, everything seemed to be spontaneous and deeply emotional, but that was a carefully staged illusion. ("Be prepared to be spontaneous," as one leader said.) How to give a moving personal testimony and how to behave in the dramatic and noisy prayer meetings had been learned by imitation and rehearsed and staged (e.g., "Put on your worship faces"). The behavior preceded and defined the experience. When "charisma" (in the sense of such spiritual gifts as speaking in tongues, and the like) is more acted out than felt it becomes easy to imitate. Spirituality becomes a matter of behavior (praying out, dramatic prayer gestures, and so on). This is one way charisma can be tamed, routinized, and readily reproduced on an individual level.

Opposition

Though the YWAM team had surprising success in Poland, there was still some resistance. Some Poles took them for Jehovah's Witnesses. A man spoke against the group at one performance. Afterwards a woman ran onto the "stage" (the tarp) and placed a few holy cards on a box that was one of the props. A Catholic priest told one crowd not to listen but to go home (most stayed for the performance and sermon). When a member of the local Pentecostal church passing out tracts after one performance handed one to a nun, she looked at it skeptically, asked a few questions, returned the tract, and walked away. A man came onto the tarp during the sermon after one performance and released four or five ducklings. Members of the Pentecostal church took him and his box of ducklings aside and talked with him about his personal relationship with Jesus. A woman handed the man a tract and finally took his name and address for future contact.

Attitude Toward Catholics

Because nearly half the YWAM team were former Catholics

who had converted to a Pentecostal church and the team was attempting to evangelize Polish Catholics, one of the leaders remarked that it was "really neat because of [their] Catholic background – God desires to bring that completeness." Team leaders considered Catholics to be incomplete Christians who lacked a personal relationship with Jesus. The YWAM leaders instructed participants to find out, when talking with Catholics, if they were "trying to earn their salvation."

The YWAMers refered to Catholics (as well as to noncharismatic Protestants) as "religious." Frank, the local Pentecostal pastor, told his flock that it was time for Poland to be harvested: "Religious people are difficult to win for the Lord because they don't know who they are serving. For religious people it is more difficult to enter the kingdom of God." "Religion" and "religious people" were frequently targeted in postperformance sermons. One YWAM preacher told the crowd, "You know what religion is? It's trying to reach out to God. We do good things and we think that will do it. It doesn't matter how many good things we do. God is not impressed. . . . He did not die to make people religious."[8]

But the leaders were eager to cultivate allies in Oasis, the Catholic charismatic movement in Poland. The team performed twice at the invitation of Oasis groups, once outside a Catholic church and once in a courtyard of a high-rise development. One YWAM preacher, the former seminarian, told his testimony of having encountered God in a lonely chapel but left out of the story (which he had told to the team in Holland) the part about his having left the Catholic church in favor of a Pentecostal group.

The Revival Rally

The YWAM outreach culminated with a large rally attended by between 1,500 and 2,000 people. Christopher Alam, a

---

8. Floyd McClung, the YWAM executive director of international operations, expressed a similar attitude in one of his essays in *Nine Worlds to Win: Missions and Evangelism in the 1990's* (p. 39, see following note): "God does not need more 'do-gooders' in the world but he does want more people from all nations going to all nations, who love him and who proclaim the good news in word and deed."

Pakistani evangelist based in Sweden (but with strong connections with U.S. evangelicals), led the meeting. A band and singing group called Miracle Music played electronic instruments and sang. Alam preached in English, and Frank's wife translated. Nearly the entire congregation of Frank's church attended. Most of the people in the crowd had some prior involvement with Oasis. Alam conducted a typical Pentecostal healing meeting.

From the outset Alam easily manipulated the crowd. "Let's all stand up together," he ordered, "and I want everyone here to lift up both hands to God." But what seems manipulative to an observer is happily accepted by Pentecostal believers as an opportunity to participate. Alam had the crowd chanting "Jesus, Jesus, Jesus" in unison. "Please put your hands down," he commanded.

"How many people here are deaf in one or both ears?" he asked. Many raised their hands. Alam asked them to come forward and form a line in front of the stage. The ushers, as well as members of the Pentecostal church and the YWAM team, came forward at Alam's request to stand in front of each person to be healed. Alam chanted again "Jesus, Jesus, Jesus" and told the ushers to close their eyes, stick their finger in the deaf ears of the people who had come forward to be healed, and to "pray after me. . . ."

"Ushers, pray louder," commanded Alam. They repeated a prayer after him. Alam then told them to open their eyes and to say with a loud voice, "You deaf devils, I command you now. Leave the people now in Jesus' name. Leave these people right now and don't come back. And I command you, ears. Be open now in the name of Jesus. It is done. Take your fingers out. How many believe it is done?" Alam "tested" the healing by having the ushers put their fingers in the good ears and snap their fingers or whisper. Alam asked the people who thought they had been healed to raise their hands. He counted thirty-five "whose ears have been healed."

Using repetition and simple language, Alam invited the crowd to "become clean and nice" and to "smell like Jesus." He described Jesus as a fountain where all are cleaned and healed. Alam began to tell his own testimony. He had met Jesus thirteen years before and his life was "completely changed." He drifted off, however, into a tale of ministerial triumph in Africa: "I tell you I saw six thousand come running to the front to give their hearts to Jesus." He next told the crowd to bow their heads, close their eyes, and pray.

At the climactic moment when Alam asked people to stand up if they wanted to be saved, nearly the entire crowd got to its feet. Alam asked them to come to the stage, and perhaps a thousand or more surged forward, blocking all the aisles. Alam told the people standing to close their eyes and to lift their hands up toward God "as a sign of surrender." Then he led them in prayer:

> Say after me: Oh Lord Jesus, I come into your presence in the power of the precious blood. I give my life sin to you. I give my life to you and I receive your life. Wash me and make me clean. Jesus, come into my heart. From this day onwards you are my Lord. You are everything to me and you are first in my life. Thank you, Jesus, that you have heard me now. I belong to you now. Thank you, Jesus. Thank you for saving me. Alleluia. Everybody shout alleluia.

After the prayer Alam said, "Put your hands down. Talk to two or three people standing around you and shout, 'I am saved, alleluia.'" Frank and his wife took the microphone and ordered the ushers to distribute contact cards to the crowd. The meeting had completed the first of its two episodes, each with its own climactic moment. The first culminated in Alam's altar call, the second culminated in another mass healing, this one celebrated by singing in tongues and confirming testimonies.

"Now," said Alam, "I want only the sick people to come to the front. Everybody else go back to your seats." Alam instructed the sick where to place their hands (finger in ear, hand on eye, and the like) They stood before the stage and did what Alam told them. There were several hundred. Alam told them to be quiet and to close their eyes. "While I'm praying I want you to imagine Jesus and I want you to reach out and touch him. . . . He's taking away the tumors right now. Tumors and growths are disappearing right now. I curse every tumor and cancer right now in Jesus' name." Alam kneeled center stage and commanded the demons to come out. Then he rose dramatically and ran about the stage shouting, "In Jesus' name it is done. Everybody lift up both hands to God . . . and say thank you for healing me. I receive your touch."

Alam began singing in tongues, and then the singing group joined in. Everyone in the crowd held their hands in the air. Alam's shouts of "Thank you, Jesus!" and "Alleluia!" punctuated the lilting tune of tongues singing. Then Alam ordered the sick to check themselves for a healing. ("I want you to do something you couldn't do before. Leave your crutches, sticks or whatever. . . . Take it by faith.") Alam asked "the healed" to raise their hands and began to count: "Twenty, forty, I don't know. I can't count this many people." (He later said that there were 175.) He called them to the stage to testify to their healings. Many did. After being screened by Frank's assistant pastor, a translator, and a member of Alam's staff, several were allowed, one by one, to step up to the microphone. They said they had felt something leave them during Alam's prayer or that they did not feel the pain anymore.

The two-and-a-half hour really ended with enthusiastic music and clapping and Alam dancing in triumph on the stage. Alam told the crowd as they left, "I want you to keep on coming back. Tell your friends about what Jesus is doing. Tell them, 'I saw miracles with my own eyes.'"

The End of the Outreach

The YWAM outreach ended much the same way as the Alam rally. The leaders instructed the participants how to tell the folks back home in the congregation about their YWAM experiences ("Don't push it on them [the pastors]. Be wise about that."). The team sang, prayed out, and spent time in a group "evaluation." After a day spent breaking camp and packing, the team got on the bus for the long ride back to Amsterdam. The 1989 outreach to Poland was an enormous success and YWAM planned another for 1990. By presenting the street mime the team had "formed crowds" (twenty of them totaling altogether some five thousand people), helped form an audience for Christopher Alam's crusade, and, consequently, contributed to the re-formation of the local Pentecostal church which several months earlier had been halved by schism.

As Eastern Europe opens its borders, aggressive American-style evangelicals will rush in and likely experience similar success, at least temporarily. Polish Catholics, as yet, have little experience with American evangelicals. The Catholic hierarchy may become increasingly critical of them, especially if they succeed in converting many Catholics. Catholic charismatics, like the members of Oasis, are the most likely to be attracted to Pentecostalism. In the United States 50 percent or more of some Pentecostal congregations are ex-Catholics, many of whom converted from the Catholic charismatic movement. The Foursquare church in Fresno which sent its team to Poland was approximately 50 percent ex-Catholic.

Before glasnost, YWAM and other evangelical organizations like Open Doors concentrated on smuggling Bibles and other literature into East Bloc countries as well as on publicizing real and alleged communist atrocities against evangelical Christians. In the late 1980s YWAM leaders decided on a more aggressive strategy for evangelizing the "communist world." The opening in the East Bloc has given them new opportunities. YWAM claimed to have recently established discipleship programs inside the Soviet Union and has planned one thousand such programs throughout the Soviet bloc for the 1990s.[9]

The YWAM outreach was designed not only to evangelize Poland, but also to provide a highly structured and transformative experience for the participants (one, though, of a peculiar sort, since inner emotions and feelings were demonized and rejected). How one felt (tired, embarrassed, or bored) was not central to the experience. The experience itself was defined, manipulated, and finally interpreted by the leaders. Individual feelings were interpreted as disruptive (satanic) influences, not as part and parcel of the experience itself but somehow outside it. Feelings, at best, became suspect and, at worst, were demonized.

9. F. McClung, Jr., and K. Moala (with G. Benge), *Nine Worlds to Win: Missions and Evangelism in the 1990's* (Amsterdam, 1988), p. 90.

Conclusions

A network of American evangelical organizations, including Youth with a Mission, have targeted Eastern Europe and the Soviet Union for an aggressive evangelization campaign in the 1990s. Everything depends on whether or not the East Bloc becomes more open. Many new opportunities for American evangelists appeared in the revolutionary year of 1989. In 1989 Pat Robertson's Christian Broadcasting Network distributed its animated biblical series (*Superbook* and *Flying House*) for broadcast in the Soviet Union. Pat Robertson plans an extension of his Regents University (formerly CBN University) to Poland to teach business, communications, and theology. In 1989 Richard Roberts, the son of Oral Roberts, held an evangelization meeting in the Soviet Union. Roberts was invited to Estonia by the National Jazz Society and, though billed as a jazz singer, sang Christian songs, preached, invited his audience to accept Jesus, and laid hands on the sick.[10] The Argentine evangelist Luis Palau held open-air evangelistic meetings in Riga, Leningrad, Kishinev, and Moscow in September 1989.[11] The YWAM go-team to Poland represents only the beginning of an aggressive American evangelical outreach in Eastern Europe and the Soviet Union, provided glasnost continues.

Unpopular official atheism and communism have little or no claim to cultural hegemony in Eastern Europe. In Poland only the Catholic church can be realistically described as exercising cultural leadership. Could American-style Pentecostalism eventually challenge the cultural hegemony of the Catholic church in Poland? It seems impossible. How could Frank's church of some one hundred members hope to rival the overflowing Catholic churches of Wroclaw? In 1989 evangelicals were only 0.2 percent of the Polish population (0.5 percent including members of Oasis).[12] However, in other parts of the world Pentecostalism has spread rapidly in Catho-

10. "Richard Roberts Live in the USSR," *Charisma and Christian Life*, August 1989, p. 27.
11. T.C. Much, "Under the Eye of the Big, Red Machine," *Christianity Today*, 15 December 1989, pp. 21–25.
12. These are YWAM figures from the orientation package given to participants in the 1989 YWAM go-team to Poland.

lic countries, to the point that evangelicals comprise 30 to 40 percent of the population and the evangelical worldview has became a part of popular culture. Guatemala and Brazil are examples of this process.

Eastern Europe and the Soviet Union are new frontiers for evangelicals. The 1990s will be a period of frenzied evangelical missionary work. Believing that the end is near, they will exploit every opportunity to carry their version of the Gospel to all the parts of the world. Because the money, broadcasting and publications come mostly from the United States, American cultural forms will dominate, and sometimes American evangelicals actively collaborate with United States foreign policy goals and with U.S. intelligence operations.[13]

Since the end of the Second World War American popular culture has spread around the world. American cultural forms have dominated such instruments of popular culture as broadcasting and mass marketing. National Religious Broadcasters, the trade organization of American television evangelists, already controls more than 80 percent of religious broadcasting worldwide.[14] American popular Evangelicalism, like jazz and rock and roll, spreads at the level of popular culture. Evangelical organizations are far more aggressive in their use of the technologies and forms of popular culture (preeminently television and radio, but also street theater, popular songs, comic books, and the like) than any other contemporary religious groups. American Evangelicalism is gradually becoming an important element in an evolving worldwide popular culture. What that ultimately will mean is impossible to predict.

Even though American evangelicals control religious mass media, the evangelical movement has no unifying organizational structure. Local evangelical movements and local churches in different countries around the world will develop their own ways of thinking and acting. The schismatic group that broke away from Frank's church in Wroclaw is one example of the evangelical tendency toward fragmentation

13. See S. Diamond, *Spiritual Warfare: The Politics of the Christian Right* (Boston, 1989).

14. B. Armstrong, ed., *The Directory of Religious Broadcasting 1989*, (Morristown, N.J., 1989), p. 8.

and schism. Despite American cultural hegemony, there will be many new varieties added to the seemingly endless varieties of Christianity.

Pentecostalism is one kind of popular American religious culture that has proved readily exportable. The content, and worldview, of this Pentecostalism is a simple-minded dualism – demons and the Holy Spirit, the devil and God, and demonized inner feelings and sanctioned emotional displays for the sake of evangelism. Right-wing American evangelicals also make it a political dualism by demonizing communism, socialism, political and religious liberalism, and humanism.

Evangelical apocalyptic theory is loaded with political content, and consequently, the leaders of the YWAM go-team to Poland warned participants not to talk about apocalyptic beliefs when they gave public testimonies. On the one hand the apocalyptic (and political) aspects of the movement can be deemphasized if they create difficulties with public relations. On the other hand apocalypse and politics can be emphatically reemphasized in order to motivate rallies of uncritical fellow believers to ever more heroic feats of evangelism.

Adapting to an Uncertain Future

If American-style Pentecostalism contends for cultural hegemony in Poland, its chief rival will be the Catholic church and not the Communist party. American Evangelicalism has a long tradition of anti-Catholicism to draw on. The dualism inherent in the American Pentecostalism exported to Poland might easily take on a strongly anti-Catholic content.

There were signs in 1989 that Polish Pentecostals could become increasingly anti-Catholic. Several members of Frank's congregation had in their possession pamphlets and tracts (in Polish) from Chick Publications, a fundamentalist organization based in California that produces tracts, comic books, and other literature, much of which is decidedly anti-Catholic. Chick comics portray the Catholic church as the Whore of Babylon and as the apostate church of the anti-Christ. One member of Frank's church distributed Chick tracts but no one distributed anticommunist literature.

American evangelicals have been doctrinaire anticommunists since 1917. Are they flexible enough to adapt to a post–cold war world? Their anticommunism is often incorporated into their apocalyptic ideas. Evangelical apocalyptic theorists commonly identify the Soviet Union with Gog and Magog, the prophesied invaders of Israel in the last days. This notion dates to the Crimean War.[15]

A still older Christian apocalyptic tradition identifies the Turks with Gog and Magog and could be called on in the future to demonize Islam rather than Russia. It is possible, provided that the East Bloc continues to open up, that communism and anticommunism will, in time, become increasingly irrelevant. American groups evangelizing Eastern Europe and the Soviet Union may find themselves competing for cultural hegemony with Catholicism in countries like Poland and with Islam (demonized as Gog and Magog) in some parts of the Soviet Union. However, any such speculation on the future requires too many ifs.

15. D. Wilson, *Armageddon Now! The Premillenarian Response to Russia and Israel Since 1917* (Grand Rapids, Mich. 1977), p. 24 ff.

· 9 ·

Apocalyptic Responses to the War with Iraq

LAWRENCE JONES

T he war against Iraq sparked a revival of apocalyptic expectations among American evangelicals. One evangelical company marketed sweatshirts that read: "Get Ready for
the Big One – Jesus is Coming." The war seemed like another
confirmation of evangelical expectations of the imminent end
of the world.

Even before Iraq invaded Kuwait in August 1990 many
American evangelicals were convinced that the decade of the
1990s was a "decade of destiny" or "the last decade" (before
the Second Coming of Christ). The turn of the century exerts
a special fascination. There have been several apocalyptic
revivals since the Second World War, the first after the founding of the state of Israel in 1948. The 6-Day War of 1967 was
the occasion for another wave of apocalyptic enthusiasm, as
was the fortieth anniversary of the creation of modern Israel
in 1988. The Iraqi war in 1991 has occasioned another end-
of-the-world revival among American evangelicals.

Apocalyptic tracts and images incorporating Iraq and Saddam Hussein were prominently on display at the 1991 National Religious Broadcasters (NRB) convention in Washington, held 25–30 January, less than two weeks after the
American attack on Iraq. More than two hundred evangelical
organizations were represented at the annual convention, the
trade show of religious broadcasting, with new products and
services displayed on the floor of the huge exhibition hall.

The convention was a showcase for new works on biblical
prophecy focusing on Iraq and the war. Apocalyptic writers
with books in print were also revising their old works to

incorporate the new war. Many broadcasters were convinced that the war was the prelude to Armageddon. Some thought the "tribulation period" had already begun, while others expected imminent rapture. Others cautiously avoided speculation. Many wore plastic American flag lapel pins, and stickers that read "Support Our Troops," both of which were distributed free by the exhibitors. One couple, dressed in desert camouflage, sold copies of the ninety-first Psalm also bound in desert camouflage with the title, *The Ultimate Shield*.[1]

Apocalyptic writers came to the convention to sign autographs and promote their books. For them Iraq was the equivalent of biblical Babylon, not the Babylon of history but the Babylon of Daniel and the Apocalypse – a cipher in their end-of-the-world calculus. At the convention the following titles were on display: *I Predict the World in 1991*; *Armageddon, Oil, and the Middle East*; *Toward a New World Order: The Countdown to Armageddon*; *The Mid-East Wars – Who Will Win?*; *Storm in the Desert: Prophetic Significance of the Crisis in the Gulf*; and *Islam, Israel, and the Last Days*. Most of this rash of apocalyptic literature focused on the war with Iraq-Babylon.

Saddam Hussein had conveniently identified himself with Nebuchadnezzar and his propaganda neatly coincided with the American evangelical habit of "understanding" current events within the framework of biblical prophecy. As the new Nebuchadnezzar, Saddam played a role in evangelical expectations for the last days.

Iraq was quickly incorporated into the apocalyptic scenario. The Americans turned the Saddam-Nebuchadnezzar equation on its head and used it as anti-Iraqi propaganda shortly after Iraq invaded Kuwait in August 1990. Iraq became Babylon and the new focus of evil (at least for the duration of the war) for American evangelicals. Dyer wrote in his 1991 book *The Rise of Babylon*:

> God declares that he will destroy Babylon when he "will punish the world for its evil, the wicked for their sins" (Isaiah 13:11). From shortly after the time of the flood, Babylon has symbolized humanity's rebellion against God. When God destroys Babylon, he will destroy all of the evil in the world.[2]

1. *Psalm 91: The Ultimate Shield*, (Mt. Juliet, Tenn., 1990).
2. C.H. Dyer, *The Rise of Babylon: Signs of the End Times*, (Wheaton, Ill., 1991), p. 165.

This kind of imagery and language was broadcast widely over the evangelical media empires. Member organizations of the National Religious Broadcasters controlled 90 percent of all religious broadcasting in the United States, and some 80 percent of religious broadcasting worldwide.[3] Within a few months, evil Iraq-Babylon became a part of American and, perhaps, also worldwide popular culture.

Although the apocalyptic writers readily identified Iraq with Babylon, the United States was not so easy to place in their biblical schemes. The absence of any explicit reference to the United States in Isaiah or Daniel or any of the other prophetic books has long troubled nationalistic American evangelicals. Some have tried in various ways to read the United States into Scripture. For example, Pat Robertson found a possible reference to the United States in Ezekiel 38:13 in the mention of traders of Tarshish in his book *The Secret Kingdom*.[4]

The United States, "strangely absent" from prophecy, was a disturbing problem for the author of *The Rise of Babylon*: "But the United States is a major world power – how could it *not* play a major role in the last days?"[5] All the apocalyptic writers assumed, of course, that the last days coincided with contemporary times. The Bible and the news could be read together. Dyer listed four possible explanations for this "strange absence":

1. The rapture: the United States will become a "second-class international power overnight when God removes Christians from the earth."
2. Secularization, moral decline, or lack of support for Israel will make the United States "a second-class society."
3. A nuclear war will destroy the United States.
4. A military defeat (or "anything short of victory" in the American-Iraqi war) will "weaken our national resolve and increase our isolationist tendencies" and "force us to abdicate our role as a world power."

3. M. Stevens, ed., *The Directory of Religious Broadcasting*, (Morristown, N.J., 1990), p. 9.
4. P. Robertson (with B. Slosser), *The Secret Kingdom: A Promise of Hope and Freedo:n in a World of Turmoil* (Nashville, 1982), p. 214.
5. The preceding quotations come from Dyer, *Rise of Babylon*, p. 166.

This apocalyptic calculus of "possibilities" acknowledged the decline of the United States as a world power just as it offered the most unrealistic escapist hope, a "rapture," to magically remove "over 28 million" American believers from the most unpleasant earthly realities.

The apocalyptic imagery was very dramatic. More specifically, it was cinematic. The end of the world unrolled like a Hollywood film spectacular. In *The Rise of Babylon* there are such section headings as "Two Starring Roles in the Final Drama" and "The Roman Beast and His Leading Lady."

One chapter was entitled "The Scene is Set." God was imagined as a cosmic stage manager and director:

> We should expect God to begin arranging the stage for the final act of his drama. The stage may yet be empty of actors, but if all the props are in place and the house lights begin to dim, you can be sure the final act is soon to begin.[6]

The most direct film analogy was to popular westerns. At one point the writer compared God (perhaps confused with the United States) to a cowboy gunslinger:

> It is almost as though he "calls her out" for a final duel. But this time, the conflict between God and Babylon ends decisively. The city of Babylon will be destroyed, and the city of Jerusalem will be restored in an everlasting covenant of forgiveness.[7]

At least in theory, the script for this cosmic drama was the Bible, but the popular scenarios mixed biblical references with newspaper accounts of contemporary events. The structure of this odd mixture was a nineteenth-century theory of biblical prophecy,[8] but a deeper emotional structure lies beneath. There are undercurrents of fear and hope and a complex of psychological projections just beneath the surface.

Some earlier versions of evangelical apocalyptic had identified the United States as the Babylon of Revelations.

---

6. Ibid., p. 207.
7. Ibid., p. 182.
8. E.R. Sandeen, *The Roots of Fundamentalism: British and American Millenarianism*, 1800–1930 (Chicago, 1970). T.P. Weber, *Living in the Shadow of the Second Coming* (New York, 1979).

The author of *The Persian Gulf Crisis and the Final Fall of Babylon* cited another apocalyptic tome called *Is the U.S.A. in Prophecy?* The writer of that book had argued that the United States was (or could become) the mysterious Babylon of end-of-the-world prophecy. Moral deline in America is a common theme in evangelical apocalyptic and is often considered a sign of the end time. Iraq as Babylon became, among other things, a projection of America as Babylon: an evil (but cloaked) mirror of American identity, corrupt and casually brutal.

This sort of psychological projection during the war took other than religious forms. The Iraqis, for example, were demonized for threatening to wage chemical and biological warfare. Within a month after the war began, however, some Americans had begun to advocate a nuclear war against the Iraqi army. Americans bought gas masks and shunned air travel for fear of terrorists. It was Iraqi cities being bombed, however, not American ones. War violence was portrayed as a video game (though the viewer was told explicitly that "this is not a video game"). The "game" of war was easily incorporated into the cosmic drama of the evangelical end-time scenarios. It was thereby "explained" and "justified."

Evangelical apocalyptic literature after the Second World War casually disregarded the world. The earth was portrayed as disposable and its destruction imminent. The apocalyptic writers seemed to relish the wars and environmental catastrophes that they cited as signs of the times. Such a hostile attitude toward the world had political consequences. This hostility was usually focused on one or two, or even a full list of, special enemies. Communism, as a vast international (and supernatural) conspiracy, has served as the chief enemy of God in the apocalyptic conflict since the end of the Second World War.

The apocalyptic scenario has often included a nuclear war, triggered by a crisis in the Middle East. Nuclear war was the mechanism for resolving the conflict (between the believer and the world) at the heart of this apocalyptic drama. It was also a possible mechanism for fulfilling the prophecies of world destruction in the Apocalypse of John. Looked at in this way evangelical apocalyptic could be understood as a religious response to nuclear weapons. As in the title of Jerry

Falwell's 1983 tape set and pamphlet, *Nuclear War and the Second Coming of Christ*, the two had become, as Falwell wrote, "intimately intertwined."[9]

For believers, though, the terrifying cloud of nuclear destruction had a silver lining. It heralded the Second Coming of Christ and the millennial kingdom. Belief in the rapture becomes a magical escape from nuclear war. Popular dispensationalism retained its nineteenth-century structure but took on a new and different emotional content after the Second World War.

Let a simple model provide a psychological picture of the mentality behind the apocalyptic visin. Imagine the world – everything and everyone outside of the self – as just a screen upon which the self – a kind of movie projector in the center of a round theater – projects images of itself. The screen – or the reality beneath the projections and behind the screen – has a life of its own under the overlaying images. It moves and distorts the projections and requires new projections to cover it over. The self at the center of this world of self-projections is frightened by the unpredictable and uncontrollable "motion" of the world. The "drama" is a contest between the self at the center of this solipsistic theater and the outside world always threatening to erupt from beneath an organizing overlay of projected images. More than anything this self wants suddenly to disappear from its imprisoning hall of mirrors.

A better analogy, perhaps, is to a person driving a car and seeing the world through the windows of the vehicle as it rushes past. The driver races to leave a threatening world behind, but the fleeting images are themselves threatening. The world is everywhere. Only a crash resolves the painful dichotomy.

Indeed, a common image evoked by American evangelicals to describe the rapture is the car crash. A raptured believer, behind the steering wheel, suddenly disappears and the driverless car spins out of control. A postcard sold in evangelical book shops shows a highway littered with crashing cars abandoned by raptured occupants.

9. J. Falwell, *Nuclear War and the Second Coming of Christ* (Lynchburg, Va. 1983), introduction.

American popular culture in the late twentieth century has been shaped largely by television and the automobile. The view through the windshield of a car or through the screen of a television set defines (and limits) the perspective of the self. The dualism of the apocalyptic mentality is resolved in the crash. At the culmination of the apocalyptic drama both the self and the world disappear. The self disappears in a magical rapture. The world, though, is destroyed. The cosmic car crashes. The world, so threatening before, is shattered and remade into the millennial kingdom where the self will rule and reign with Jesus. The troubling and unpredictable world would then be firmly under control.

The postcard published by the Bible Believers' Evangelical Association of Sherman, Texas, combines the imagery of car crashes with the disguised geometry of a nuclear explosion. Jesus appears high over the city in a bright light. Cars crash on the highways below. An airplane crashes into a building. Little white "souls" dart up to meet Jesus in the air. If nuclear war and the Second Coming of Christ have become intimately intertwined in the evangelical imagination, then the image of Jesus high above the car crashes in the postcard might be read as a nuclear bomb detonating high above a city. As in the title of a popular song of 1950, "Jesus Hits Like An Atom Bomb."[10]

Evangelical apocalyptic embraces nuclear weapons as a source of salvation. At the same time any feelings of guilt or remorse at American use of nuclear weapons has been projected onto the enemy (the Japanese Empire, communism, and, in 1991, Babylon) as evil intent. Demonization of the enemy justifies the construction of huge nuclear arsenals. Huge arsenals make war seem inevitable, and the looming threat of war counts as yet another sign of the end time.

In the early 1990s apocalyptic literature, while still wary of the Soviet Union, singled out Islam and Europe as the new great enemies of God in the last days. The Gulf war focused evangelical attention on Islam and the Arab nations. Evangelicals also saw the emergence of Europe as a political and

---

10. Lowell Blanchard with the Valley Trio, "Jesus Hits Like An Atom Bomb," recorded ca. April 1950.

economic union as the birth of "the revived Roman Empire" of the Antichrist.

These beliefs and the obsessions they inspired injected an element of irrationality into American politics. Judging from the apocalyptic literature inspired by the Gulf war, evangelical believers will tend to oppose Arab nationalism, and the new Europe as well, and these prejudices may ultimately become expressed in American foreign policy. Earlier demonization of the Soviet Union and of communism as an apocalyptic conspiracy predisposed evangelicals to favor a hard line against the USSR, an expensive arms race, and ready attacks on any revolutionary movement around the world that could be fitted into communist conspiracy theory. Old fears of communism will not disappear soon but will continue to be featured in evangelical apocalyptic visions, but Islam and Europe have become the more threatening specters of the apocalyptic imagination.

Prophecy prepared believers for an extremely violent war between the United States and Iraq. A video called *Saddam Hussein, the Persian Gulf, and the End Times*, produced in fall 1990 before the war began, predicted chemical and nuclear warfare and the final destruction of Iraq:

> Because of chemical weapons and maybe nuclear warfare the city of Babylon could be desolate forever.

The video was an illustrated lecture. Bible verses about Babylon were cited as well as many news clips about Saddam Hussein and Iraq. Both the Bible and the news served as authorities and confirmation for growing apocalyptic expectation. The lecturer, a mechanical engineer named Dr. Rob Lindsted, said he believed that the Bible predicted the destruction of Babylon, by which he meant the annihilation of Iraq. The rather dull but bloody-minded presentation ended with the promise of rapture and a final altar call to anyone who had not yet "received Christ" during this "great time of excitement."

American evangelicals quickly became the chief religious apologists for the war against Iraq. Other Christian churches, Catholic and Protestant, refused to justify and support the war. Televangelist Pat Robertson, on the other hand, had already called for airstrikes against Iraq in August 1990. Good relations with evangelical leaders, like Robertson, were cultivated by Presidents Reagan and Bush. Robertson visited the White House to consult President Bush several times after the Iraqi invasion of Kuwait. Billy Graham stayed the night at the White House on the day of the attack against Iraq. Evangelicals later were the first to call for the use of nuclear weapons against Iraq. Representative Dan Burton, a conservative Republican from Indiana and a graduate of the Cincinnati Bible Seminary, urged that tactical nuclear weapons be used to destroy the Iraqi army in Kuwait. Cal Thomas, a conservative journalist who used to work for Jerry Falwell and the Moral Majority, echoed the congressman's call for nuclear war in print and on television talk shows.

Apocalyptic-minded evangelicals could easily and glibly explain and rationalize the war and even urge that it become a nuclear conflict. If Iraq were Babylon, the evil enemy of God, then nuclear war could be justified. God would destroy Babylon. That was predicted in the Bible. For the apocalyptic mind, at least subconsciously, God and the United States became identified, just as Iraq and Babylon had. God–United States would destroy Babylon-Iraq, and possibly do it with chemical, biological, and nuclear weapons. The identity of Iraq and Babylon was explicitly acknowledged, but the identity of God as the United States was only murkily hinted at. Somehow, in the heady mixture of the Bible and the news, the utter destruction of Iraq seemed not only likely but desirable because it could be construed as a fulfillment of prophecy and a godly act.

Notes on Contributors

Sara Diamond is the author of *Spiritual Warfare: The Politics of the Christian Right* (Boston, 1989). Her work as an investigative journalist has appeared in numerous periodicals such as *NACLA Report on the Americas* and *The Guardian* (New York), and in programs produced for Pacifica Radio. She has has taught journalism at the University of California, Santa Cruz. She received her B.A. in Spanish from the University of California, Irvine, and her M.A. in sociology from the University of California, Berkeley, where she is currently pursuing her doctorate.

Paul J. Gifford is the author of *The Religious Right in Southern Africa* (Harare, University of Zimbabwe Publications and Baobab Books, 1988; London, Pluto Press, 1991). He was born in New Zealand and taught religious studies at the University of Zimbabwe. He has published in *The Journal of Religion in Africa*, in *Religion*, and in *The Journal of Theology for Southern Africa*. His research on Christianity in Africa extends to West Africa. He is presently affiliated with the Department of Theology and Religious Studies of the University of Leeds and with the Ecumenical Documentation and Information Centre for Eastern and Southern Africa (ECIDESAC) in Harare.

Alexander Hulsman received his M.A. from the Department of International Relations of the University of Amsterdam. He is presently conducting research on the changing status of Gypsies in Europe.

Lawrence Jones received his Ph.D. in religious studies from Columbia University in 1988. He has taught at Union Theological Seminary and at La Guardia Community College. He has published on both early and contemporary Christianity. His articles have appeared in *The Journal of American Culture*, *Transformation*, *Old Westbury Review*, and other publications. His recent field research has focused on American evangelical missions in South Africa and in several European countries, about which he is presently writing a book.

Jeffrey M. Marishane was a student leader at Mamelodi High School in Pretoria. As an organizer of the June 1976 youth revolts he was forced to flee South Africa into exile. He received his M.A. in history and the history of US foreign policy from the University of Havana. Since 1983 he has been Senior Research Officer in the ANC Research Department in Lusaka and a regular contributor to *Sechaba*. In 1989–1990 he was a fellow of the Dr. Govan Mbeki Fund at the University of Amsterdam. He recently published *Prayer, Profit and Power: The American Religious Right and Foreign Policy* (University of Amsterdam, 1990). He is presently doing research on South African right-wing organizations and other aspects of the South African situation.

Notes on Contributors

Jan P. Nederveen Pieterse is the author of *White on Black: Images of Africa and Blacks in Western Popular Culture* (Amsterdam, 1990; New Haven and London, 1992) and *Empire and Emancipation: Power and Liberation on a World Scale* (New York, 1989; London, 1990). The latter received the 1990 J.C. Ruigrok Award of the Netherlands Society of the Sciences. His articles have appeared in *International Sociology, Development and Change, Race & Class, The Journal of Ethnic Studies, Alternatives, Crime and Social Justice, The Journal of Malaysian Studies, Sociologische Gids, The Unesco Courier*, and other journals. These include articles on Israel's role in Third World countries, e.g. *Exporting West Bank Expertise: Israel's Role in the Third World* (Amsterdam, 1984). He edited a special issue of *Development and Change* on "Rethinking Emancipation" (1992). He received his Ph.D. from the University of Nijmegen. He has taught sociology and international relations at the University of Amsterdam, the University of Cape Coast, Ghana, and the State University of New York, Binghamton. He is presently Senior Lecturer at the Institute of Social Studies in The Hague.

Ad van Wesel received his M.A. from the Department of International Relations of the University of Amsterdam. He has published articles on the Contadora initiative, on evangelical missions in Guatemala, and on the politics and history of Mexico.

Index

Index

Botswana, 73
Brady, Nicholas, 261
Brazil, 8, 27, 35, 177, 299
Bright, Bill, 44, 124, 129, 133, 188
British colonial authorities, 61
British Israelite Movement, 209, 212
Broederbond, 64
Brother Andrew, 278
Brown, S.E.D., 64
Buchman, Rev. Frank, 5
Buchmanism, 30
Bundy, Edgar, 65
Bush, George, 34, 311
Businessmen Bishops Conference of the Philippines, 182
Buthelezi, Chief Gatsha, 85, 93, 108

Cain, Edward, 101
Calero, Adolfo, 34, 51
Campus Crusade for Christ, 37, 44, 89, 124, 129, 188
Cape Verde Islands, 117
capital, 9
capitalism, 21, 206, 245
Carter, Jimmy, 220
administration, 77
Carter, J.J., 130
Carter Report, 130
Casey, William, 261
Catholic Action, 153, 171, 238, 240, 247–48, 250
Catholic Church, 8, 235. *See also* Roman Catholic Church
Catholicism, 169
Center for Policy Studies, 106
Center of Research and Communication, 182
Central America, 100, 148, 185, 249
Central Europe, 252
Centre Européen de Documentation et d'Information (CEDI), 269
Cercle Violet, 269
Cerullo, Maurice, 129
Chamorro, Edgar, 53
Chamorro, Violeta, 33
charismatics, 219
movement, 38, 242
organizations, 8
in Poland, 291

wing of the evangelical movement, 40
Chiaie, Stefano delle, 268
Chiang, Kai-shek, 5, 161
Chicane, Rev. Frank, 13
Chile, 14, 27, 65, 266
China, 14, 159
Christ for all Nations (CFAN), 84, 127
Christian Anti-Communism Crusade, 51, 67
Christian Broadcasting Network (CBN), 28, 35, 37, 180, 225, 298
"Operation Blessing," 28
Christian Democracy, 26, 172, 190, 237, 241, 246–53, 256, 267
Christian Democratic parties, 31, 153, 172, 181–82, 258
Christian Emergency Relief Teams (CERT), 50
Christian Institute of Southern Africa, 69, 104
Christian League of Southern Africa (CLSA), 102–3
Christian Marching Church of Central Africa, 136
Christian Mission International, 102
Christian Nationalism, 63
Christian New Right, 179
Christian Retreat, 29
Christian Socialism, 170, 172, 182
Christian Zionism, 191, 208, 211, 215, 231, ch. 6
Christlich-Democratische Union (CDU), 246
Christlich-Soziale Union (CSU), 247, 266, 270
Church League of America, 65, 69
church and state, 3, 4, 156, 238
CIA, 27, 29, 43, 53, 60, 110, 126, 163, 165, 183, 187, 242, 244, 247, 255, 260, 262, 268
civil society, 11, 148, 189
Clark Amendment Act, 78
Cline Ray, 67
Close, Robert, 270
Club de l'Horloge, 23
Cohn, Norman, 195–96
Colby, William, 261, 270
cold war, 30
Cole, Ed Louis, 129, 133
Coleridge, Samuel Taylor, 208

Index

Index

Forum World Features, 67
France, 22, 237, 246, 248
Franciscans, 149, 153
Franco, 172, 260
Frankfurt, 128
Freedom Association, 106
Frontline Fellowship, 116
Full Gospel Businessmen's
  Fellowship International
  (FGBMFI), 37, 55, 125, 186
fundamentalism, 7, 217, 228

Gehlen, Reinhard, 260, 262
Gelli, Licio, 268
Giscard d'Estaing, Valéry, 249
Goetsch, Andy, 89
Gospel Outreach, 29
Gospel Crusade, Inc., 49, 225
Graham, Billy, 1, 6–7, 40, 43, 46,
  129, 219, 311
Gramsci, Antonio, 10–11, 26, 148
"Gramscism of the Right," 2, 29,
  76–77
  of the American Right, 28
Grange, Louis le, 86
GRECE (Groupement de recherche
  et d'étude pour la civilisation
  Européene), 22
Grenada, 72
Guatemala, 14, 28, 45, 299
Gulf war, 22, 309

Habsburg, Archduke Otto von, 266,
  270
Hadad, Maj. Saad, 225
Hagin, Kenneth, 127–28
Hammond, Peter Christopher, 117,
  141
Hearst, William Randolph, 1, 68
Hechler, Rev. William H., 211
hegemony, 2, 4, 9–11, 21, 166,
  189, 193, 236, 300
  American, 159, 166
  counter-hegemonic, 230
  hegemonic, 230
  U.S., 10, 21, 147
Heritage Foundation, 44, 270–71
Herzl, Theodor, 211, 216
High Adventure Ministries, 225
Hinduism, 79
Hobsbawm, Eric, 12
Honduras, 34, 35, 50, 73, 225
Hussein, Saddam, 304, 310

Idahosa, Benson, 84
IMF (International Monetary Fund),
  138
India, 14
Indonesia, 14
Inkatha, 78, 85, 93
Inspirational Network (formerly
  PTL), 35
Institute of Economic Affairs (IEA),
  106
Institute of Religion and
  Democracy (IRD), 16, 46, 83
Instituto per Opere di Religione,
  268
integralism, 237
Inter-church Anti-Communist
  Action Committee, 63–64, 69
International Christian Embassy in
  Jerusalem (ICEJ), 224
Iran-contra affair, 50, 225
Iraq, 303
Irenaeus, 195, 226
Irish-Americans, 260
Irving, Reed, 67
Isaiah, book of, 305
Islam, 79, 301, 309
Israel, 191, 303, 305
Italy, 11, 237–38, 246, 248

Japanese fascism, 160
Jehova's Witnesses, 229
Jerusalem, 3, 192, 197, 210
Jesuits, 149, 153–54, 171–72, 175,
  177, 181, 188
Jesus Christ for Peace in South
  Africa, 89, 97
Jewish Zionism, 211
Judaism, 79

Kennedy, John F., 69
  administration, 60
King, Martin Luther, Jr., 98
"kingdom" theology, 16, 39
Kirkpatrick, Jeane, 74
Kissinger, Henry, 270
Knights of Malta (Sovereign
  Military Order of Malta), 8, 29,
  34, 115, 186, 241, 249, 258–63,
  267, 270
Knights Templar, 259
Koornhof, Dr. Piet, 64
Korea, 13
Kristol, Irving, 255–56
Kuwait, 303

Index

Index

Index

Swaziland, 73

Taiwan, 13, 67
Tawney, R.H., 9
Taylor, Myron, 241, 261
Tear Fund, 51
Temple Mount Foundation, 223
Thatcher, Margaret, 106, 250
Third Century Publications, 44
torture, 92
Tradition, Family and Property (TFP), 8, 65
transnational corporations, 176, 180
Trans World Missions, 52
Treaty of Rome, 252
Treurnicht, Dr. Andries P., 64
Trilateral Commission, 255
Trinity Broadcasting Network, 35
Trujillo, Alfono Lopez, 244
Tuchman, Barbara, 199, 210, 212
Tutu, Archbishop Desmond, 87, 104, 113, 135

Ukraine, 245
UNITA, 73, 90, 110
United Christian Action (UCA), 101–3
United Christian Conciliation Party (UCCP), 108–11
United Churches of Christ, 159
United Democratic Front (UDF), 109
United Methodist Church, 122
universalism, 232
urbanization, 12
U.S. Agency for International Development (USAID), 126
U.S. Center for World Missions (USCWM), 41
U.S. Council for World Freedom (USCWF), 65
U.S. hegemony. See also American hegemony, 10, 21, 147
utopia, 230

Vale, Prof. Colin, 110
Vatican, 5, 101
Vekemans, Roger, 244
Venezuela, 17
Verbo Church, 45
Verwoerd, Hendrik, 69

Victores, Gen. Oscar Humberto Mejía, 34
Vietnam, 29, 171
Viguerie, Richard, 44, 219
Viljoen, Dr. Gerrit, 94
Villegas, Bernardo, 177, 182
Violet, Jean, 269
Voice of America, 73, 163, 175
Von Hayek economists, 23
Vorster, Dr. Jacobus D., 63, 69
Vorster, John B., 63

Waghelstein, Col. John, 71
Wallerstein, Immanuel, 222
Weber, Max, 9, 206
welfare state, 237, 253
West Germany, 246, 266
Weyrich, Paul, 44
Whitney, Courtney, 160
Wilson, William, 244
Winter, Ralph, 41
Wojtyla, Karol, 243, 264
World Anti-Communist League (WACL), 64, 65, 110, 184, 270
World Bank, 174, 176–77
World Christian Anti-Communist Crusade, 184
World Council of Churches (WCC), 8, 41, 46, 66, 102, 137, 159
World Relief, 52
World Vision, 55, 97, 126
Wutawanashe, Andrew, 132
Wycliffe Bible Translators/Summer Institute of Linguistics (WBT/SIL), 42, 89

Youth with a Mission (YWAM), 39, 42, 50, 89, 124, 274

Zaire, 73
Zimbabwe, 121, 124
Zimbabwe Christian Council, 123
Zion, 192, ch. 6
Zion churches,
    in Africa, 4, 217
    in United States, 216
Zion Christian Church (ZCC), 88, 93
Zion City, 217